I0729521

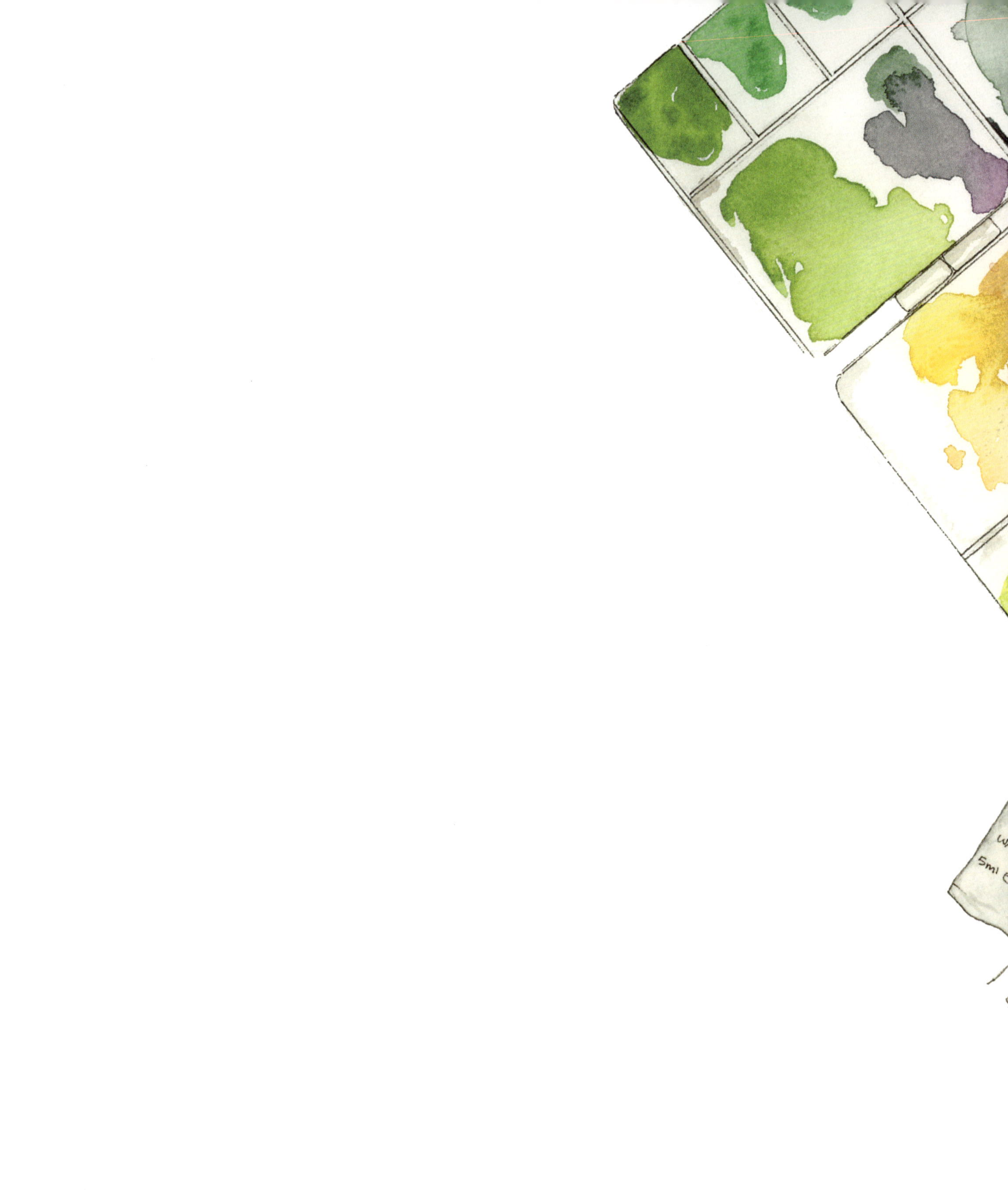

Wa
5ml e

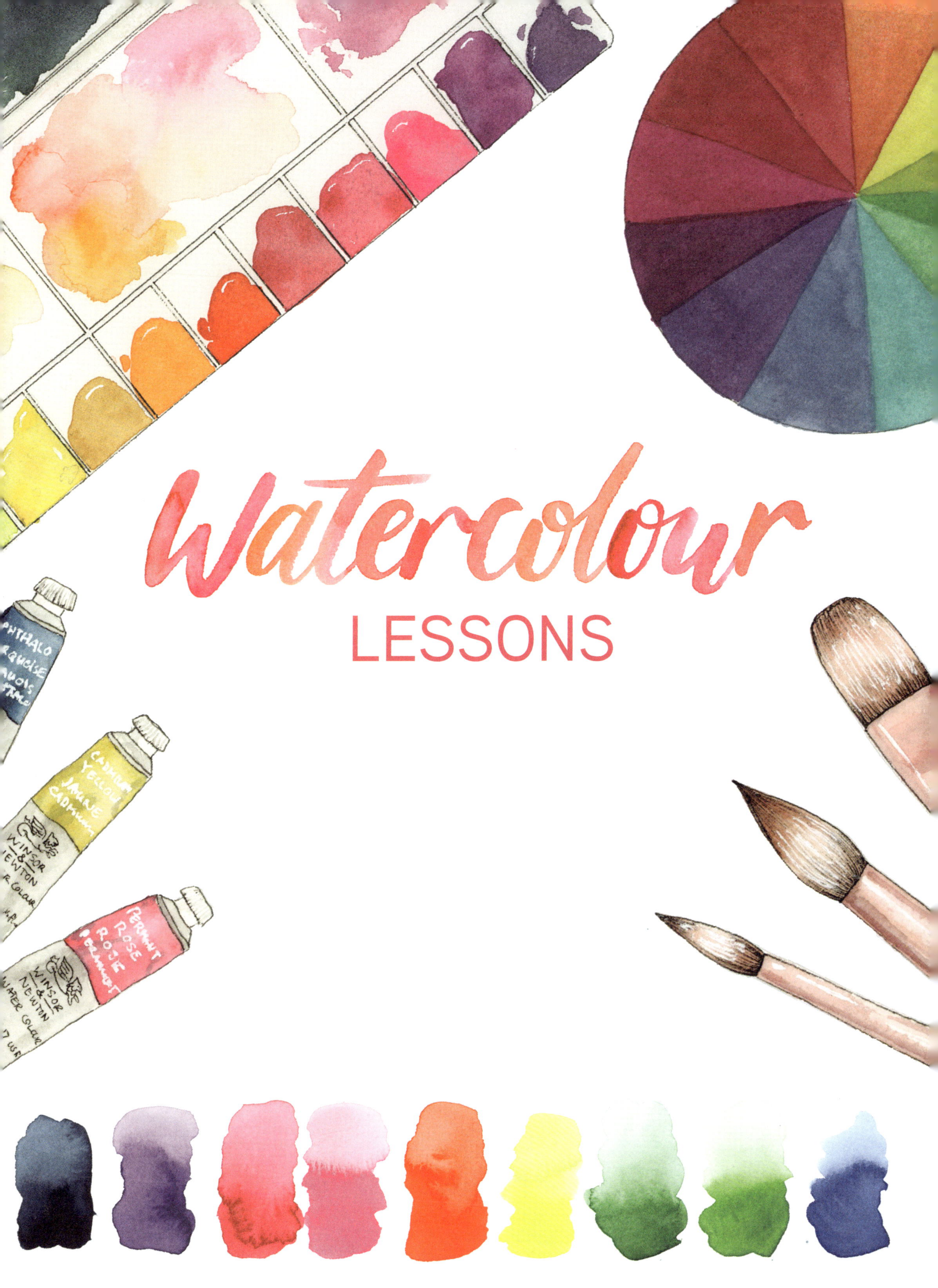

Watercolour
LESSONS

Watercolour LESSONS

How to Paint and Unwind in 20 Tutorials

emma lefebvre

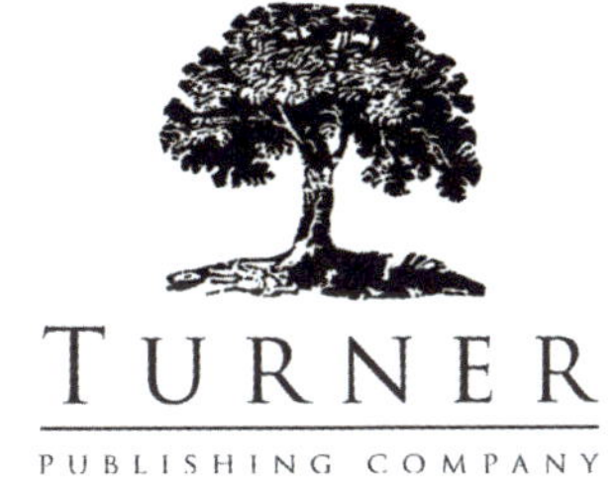

TURNER
PUBLISHING COMPANY

TURNER PUBLISHING COMPANY
Nashville, Tennessee
www.turnerpublishing.com

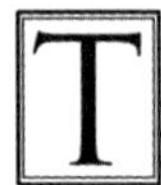

Watercolour Lessons: How to Paint and Unwind in 20 Tutorials
Copyright © 2022, 2025 by Emma Lefebvre.

Cover Design & Art Direction: Morgane Leoni
Cover Illustration: Emma Lefebvre
Interior Illustrations: Emma Lefebvre
Layout & Design: Katia Mena

Library of Congress Cataloging-in-Publication number: 2022940958
ISBN: (PB) 978-1-68481-007-9 | (HC) 978-1-68481-251-6 | (ebook) 978-1-68481-008-6
BISAC category code ART029000, ART / Techniques / Watercolor Painting

Printed in the United States of America

To my husband Matthew—without your support and encouragement, none of this would have been possible. You saw something in me that I couldn't, and showed me that my dreams didn't have to remain dreams, but could become a reality. Thank you from the bottom of my heart for being the most incredible partner in life.

Thank you to my mother, who always made sure I had art supplies as a child and encouraged my love for being a creative.

And lastly, to my boys Noah and Myles. Thank you for inspiring me to be the best version of myself that I can be. You are my motivation for everything. I want to become an example to you both that, with hard work and perseverance, you can do anything. I am so excited to see the incredible things you do in your life. I love you more than you will ever know.

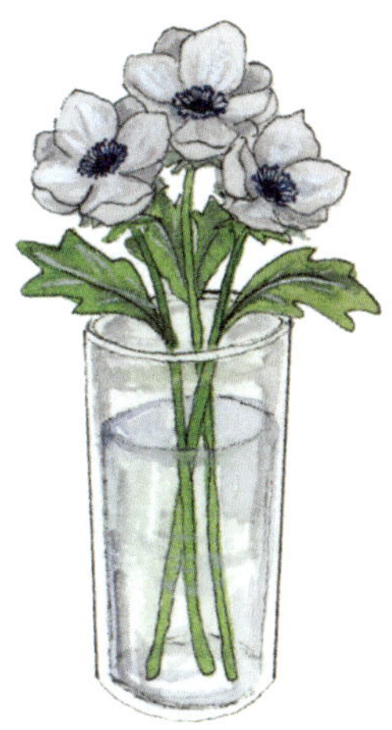

Contents

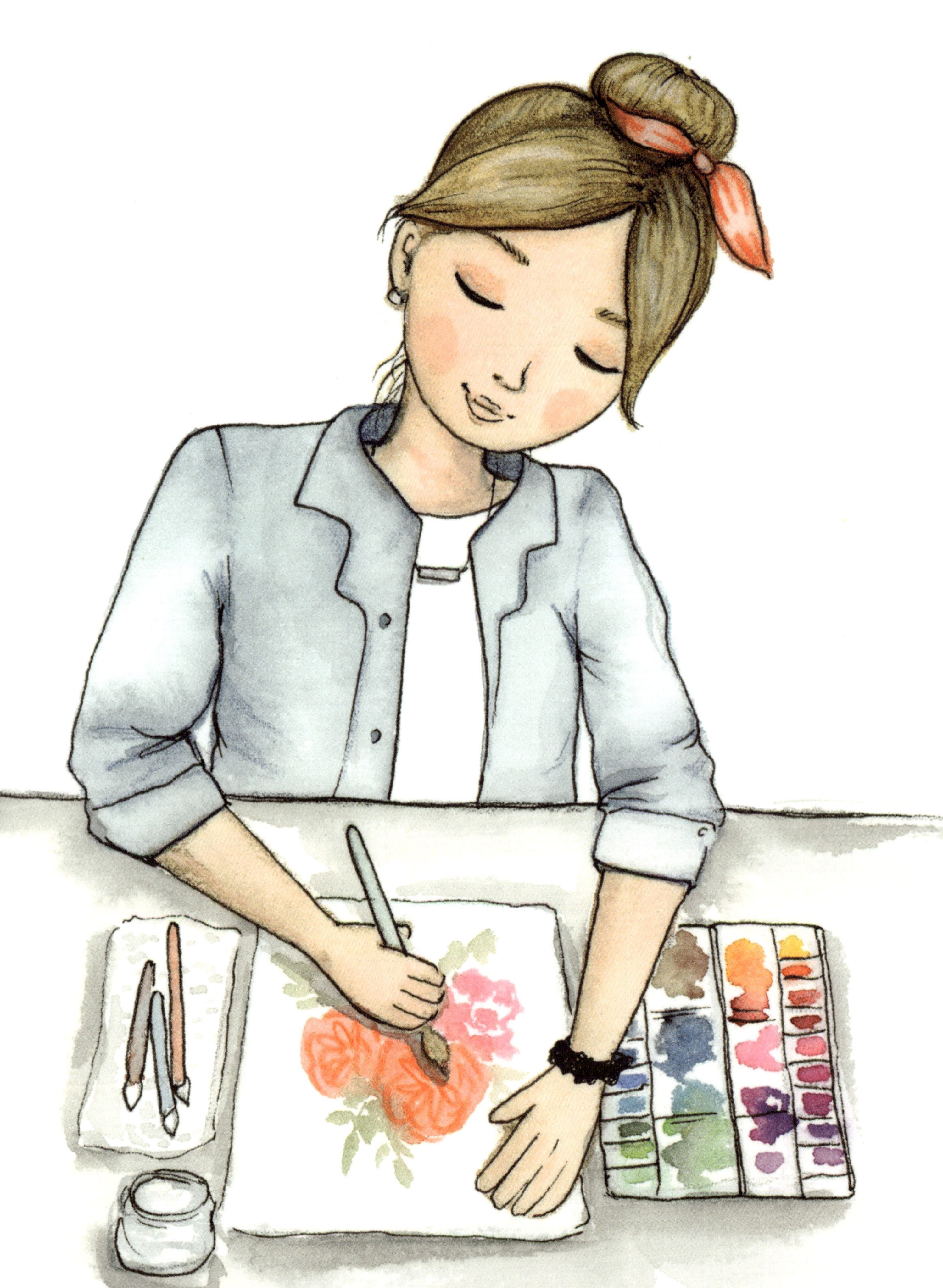

Introduction

Art has been a part of my life for as long as I can remember. When I was young, I was fascinated with the illustrations in books. I would imagine—and create—my own cover pages for books I hoped to write and illustrate one day. In math class, I doodled in my notebooks when I should have been concentrating on the equations being presented. I don't condone not paying attention in school, but the need to be creative had my constant attention.

In my adult life, I lost my passion and interest in art for a long time. It wasn't until I was struggling with my mental health that I rediscovered my love of art and began to be creative again. I decided to get my butt out of the house and walk to the closest art store. I had forgotten the joy and calmness that browsing through an art store can bring. That day, I went home with the cheapest watercolour palette and paper I could find, made a cup of tea, threw on my favourite Billie Holiday album, and began to paint. An immediate rush of peace and happiness came over me. When Monday rolled around, I had to go to work, but I remember counting down the hours until I could go home and paint again.

I began to browse Instagram for ideas. There I found an incredible community of artists who were encouraging and inspiring. Soon, I built up enough courage to post my own work, so I created a public art page. I found an incredible watercolour floral artist who was teaching a workshop in my city and decided to attend. Attending that workshop gave me the confidence to create, and eventually teach, floral watercolour painting myself. My days of coming home from work to paint and chat with fellow artists in my off time turned into months and years of painting and teaching.

In 2017, I decided to film my first art tutorial on watercolour florals for YouTube. I had previously taught art to kindergarten children, so I knew there was a simple way to teach watercolour lessons that would encourage others to try.

More than a year later, the views on my simple watercolour video started to rise. With growing interest, I decided to create more videos. I discovered that, not only did I have a passion for painting with watercolour, but I also actually loved teaching it. Since then, I went from a small community of around a hundred Instagram followers to around 60,000 today. I currently have more than 350,000 subscribers on my YouTube channel. My subscribers are people I love and support, and they support me in return. My community is full of people of varying ages, from countries all around the world, and from different cultural backgrounds, but we all have one thing in common—our love for art.

I want to start by saying that, in this watercolour book, you're not going to find complicated language about the technical side of watercolour. It's not me, and it's not how I approach art. While there are a lot of important technical things you need to know when painting with watercolour, I want to make it as simple as possible to get started. The most important thing is to be creative.

There is a lot of information in this book, but it will be simple to follow. I've included small painting projects to go along with each technique presented in the lessons, so you can paint and create while making your way through the practical information. This book is easy, humorous, and fun. After all, that's what making art should be about. I want you to have an open mind while navigating through this book. So, leave your expectation of perfection at the door, because you'll have no need for it here. You might not get things "right" the first time. Everything takes practice. But I guarantee that with every attempt, you will learn something new! So, take a breath, grab your favourite tea or coffee…or heck, even a nice glass of wine, and let's get started!

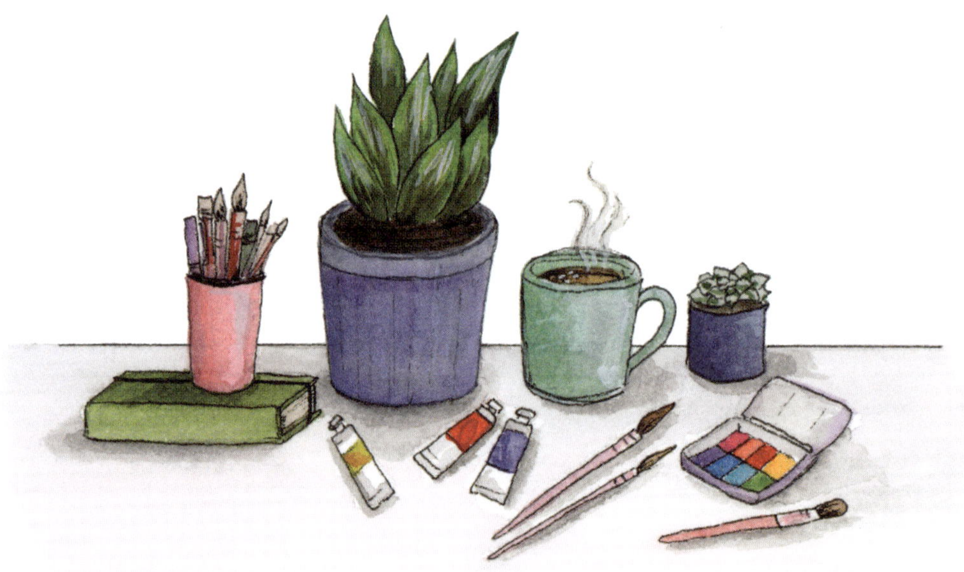

let's get Started

PART I

TECHNIQUES

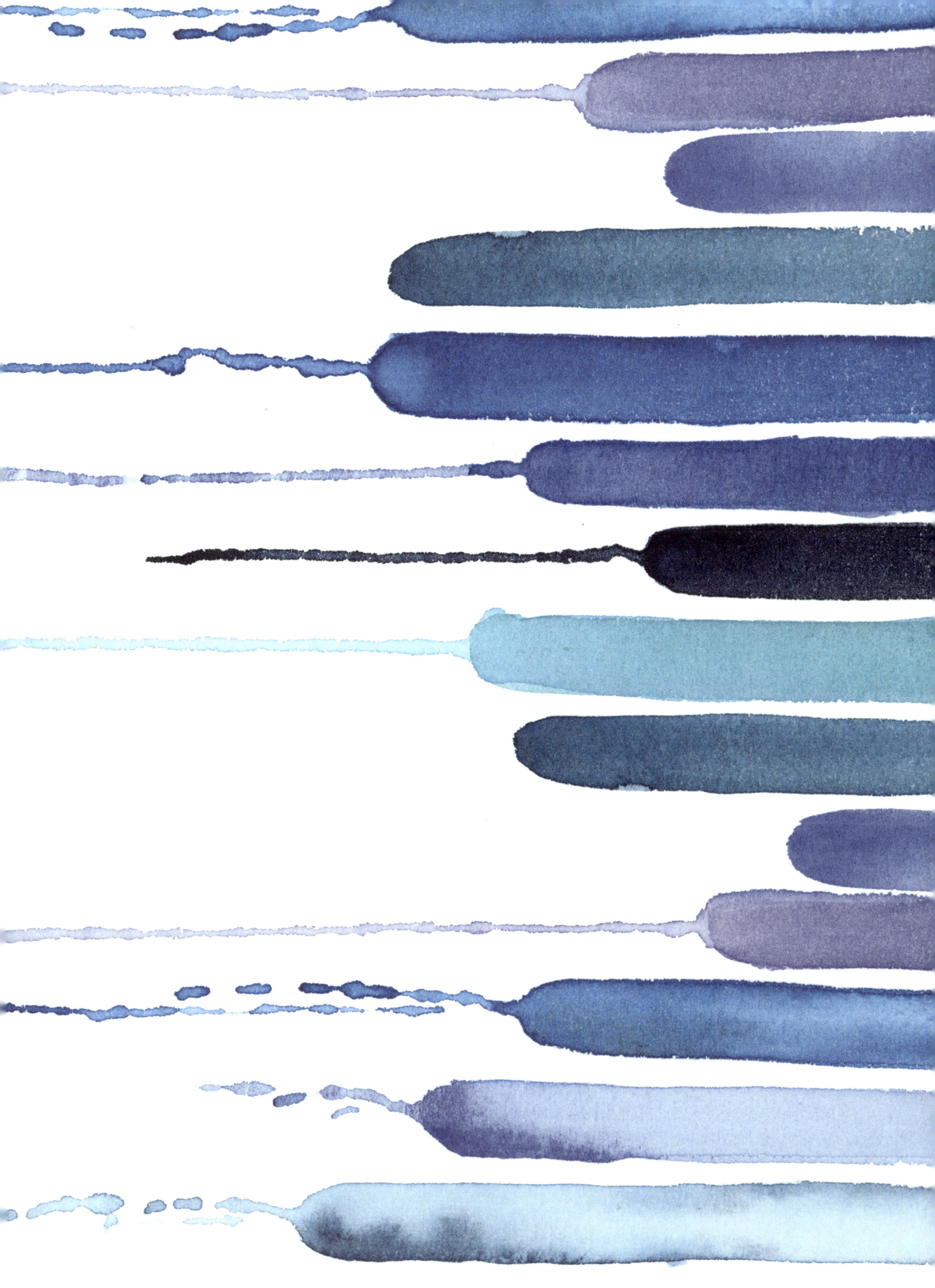

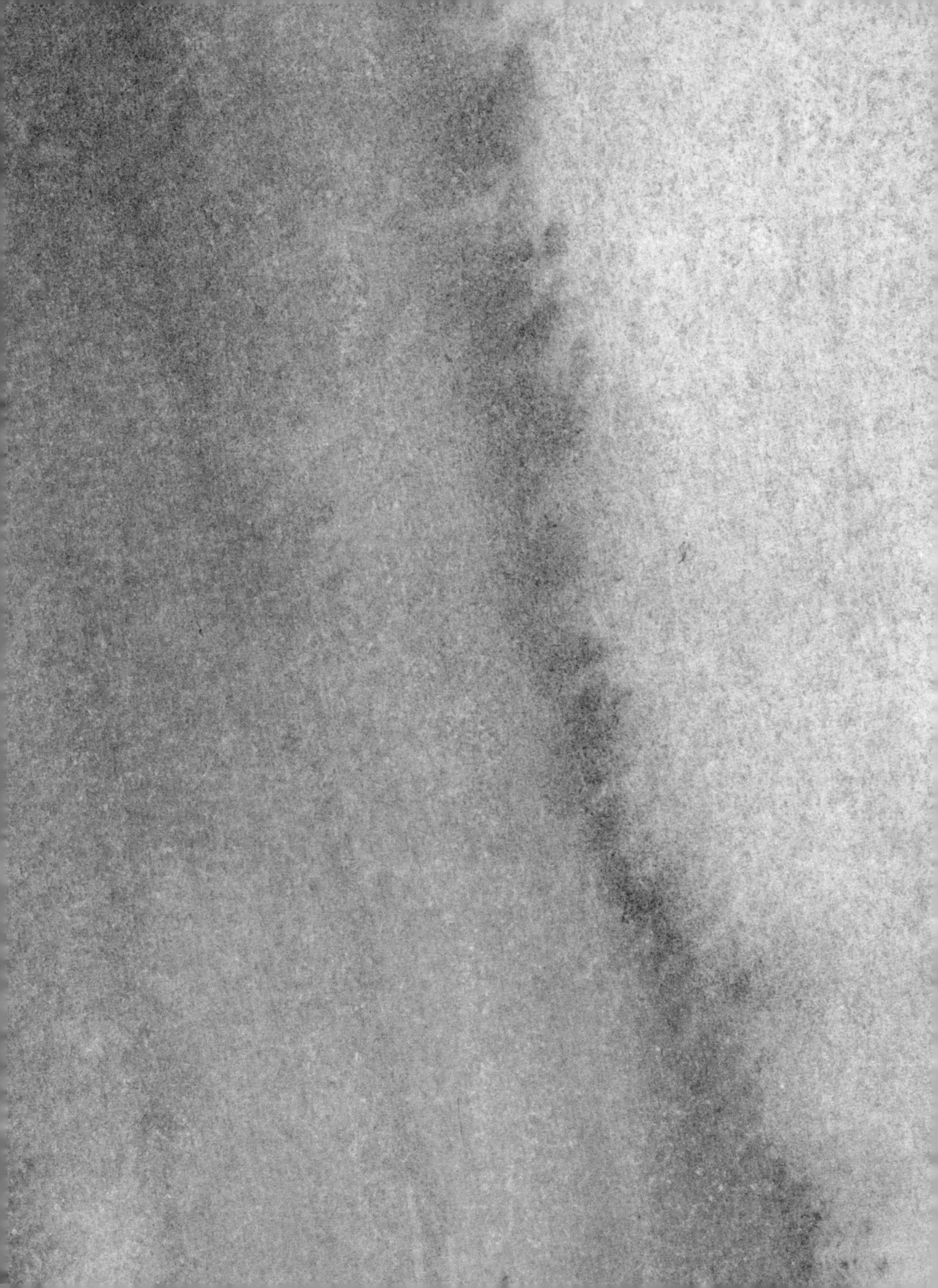

SUPPLY GUIDE

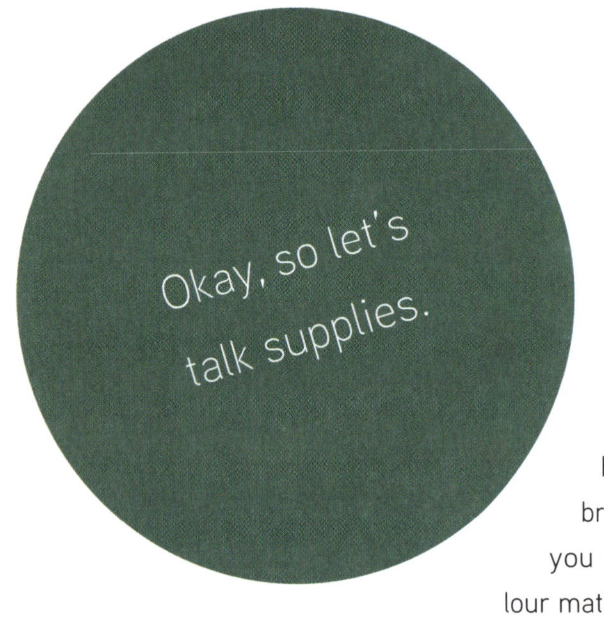

Art supplies are probably one of my favourite things. I've always enjoyed walking into an art store to pick out some new supplies. But it can also be a daunting task, with all the different types and brands to choose from. In this section, I'm here to help you know what to look for when picking out watercolour materials.

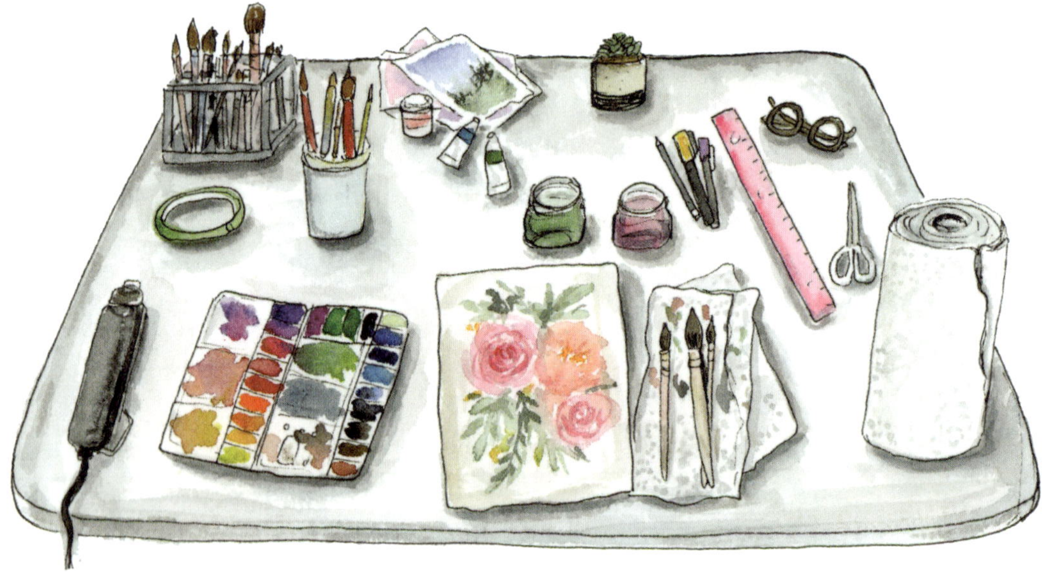

First, work with what is in your budget. While there are definite benefits to buying high-quality materials, I personally don't believe it's a necessity when starting out. When I first picked up a brush again, I was using the cheapest of the cheap materials! It wasn't until months later, when my love for watercolour grew, that I decided it was time to upgrade. So, while I go through different materials and brand suggestions, please do what works best for you and your wallet!

paint

Watercolours come in a few different forms. There are pans, tubes, and concentrated liquids.

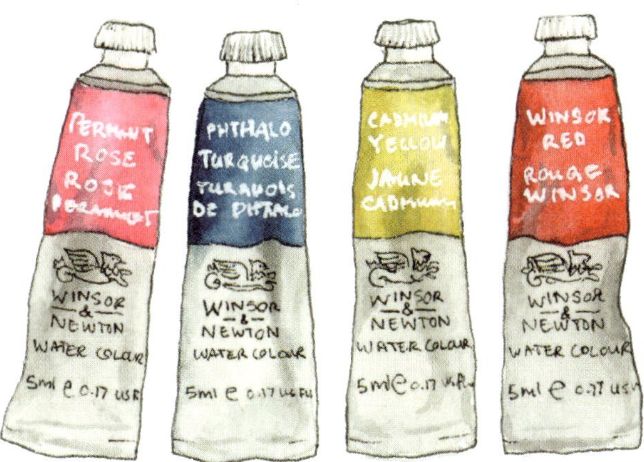

First, let's talk about tubes. Watercolour tube paints come in small tubes, ranging in size from 5 to 37 ml. The consistency of tube paints can kind of resemble that of toothpaste, or even a slightly softer liquid. They come in a variety of colours and brands, ranging from student grade to professional grade watercolours. You can buy tubes individually or in sets.

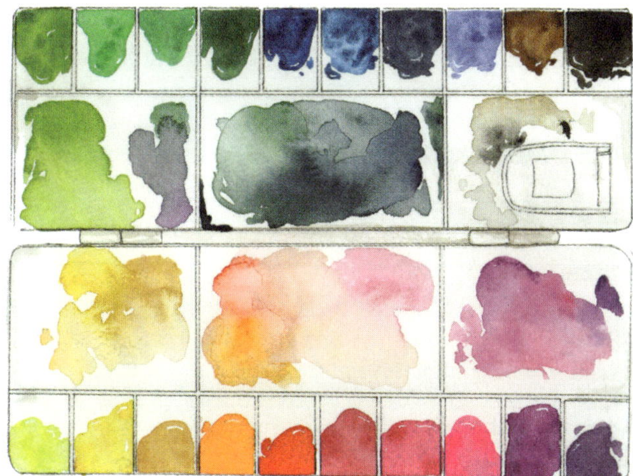

To use tube paints, you need to buy a palette. A cheap plastic palette from the dollar store will do the trick, or even a dinner plate will work. Personally, I love to use my ten-dollar plastic foldable palette I purchased online. It makes it easy to travel with my paints.

There are two ways you can use tube paints. The first is to use it fresh out of the tube. Squeeze a small amount of paint onto your palette and pick up some of the pigment with a wet brush. The more paint you have on your brush, the more pigmented the colour will be, and the more water you mix with it, the lighter the colour will be. The downside to using paint straight out of the tube is that you tend to use more paint than you need. And you can end up wasting paint. I find this especially true for beginners. The second way to use tube paint is to squeeze a good amount of paint into one of the wells in your palette and let it dry overnight. Once the paint is completely dry, take your wet paint brush and create a small puddle in your paint. You then swish it around to reactivate it. The more you swish your brush around, the more pigment you will pick up. I find that the second method helps paint last much longer.

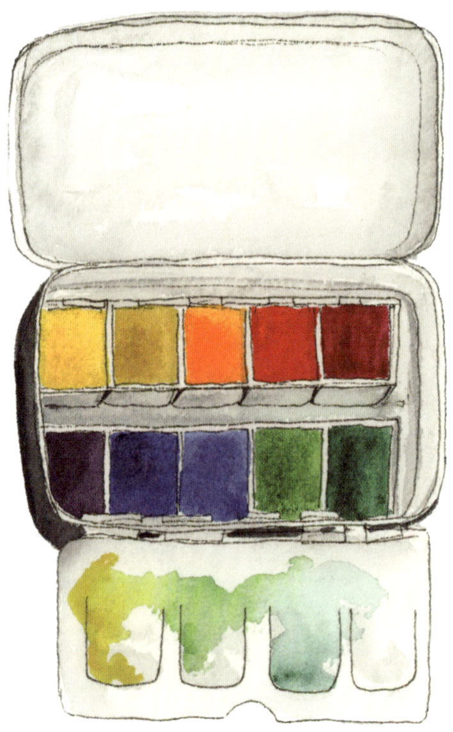

Pan sets are a great option as well. Watercolour pan sets are premade palettes with small rectangular blocks of hardened watercolours that you reactivate with water. Pan sets are much like the tube paints after letting them harden in your palette. They come in sets of different sizes, ranging from eight to forty-five colours, and in half pans or full pans. The benefits of getting a pan set are that you will already have a palette (no need to purchase one separately), their portability makes them great for travel, and they provide a variety of colours. A pan set is a great tool for beginners. To use them, take your wet brush and swish it around in the dried watercolour to reactivate it.

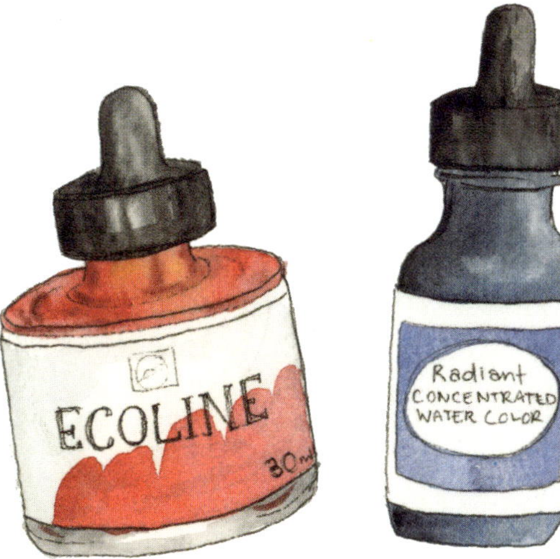

The last type of watercolour paint I am going to talk about is liquid watercolour. This form is something I have only dabbled in a few times. Liquid watercolours such as Ecoline and Dr. Ph Martin's Hydrus watercolours are an actual liquid that comes in a small bottle with a dropper-type applicator. They are very pigmented watercolours, and almost resemble a dye or stain. To use them, squeeze the watercolour into a palette using the dropper applicator (you will need to purchase a palette separately) and use your wet brush to start picking up pigment to begin painting. The more concentrated pigment you have on your brush, the more vibrant it will be, and the more water you mix with it, the lighter the pigment will become.

The downside to liquid watercolours is that they may not be as lightfast, meaning that they maintain their colour vibrancy in natural light, as traditional high-quality watercolours. They can also be quite expensive. They can be fun to work with down the line, but I don't recommend them for beginners.

One of the major benefits of using watercolour is that, even after your paints have dried, you can reactivate them easily just by adding water. However, I have found that liquid watercolours don't perform as well once dried in a palette. They perform best straight out of the bottle.

So, what type of watercolour should you use? It is completely up to you. I started with five colours of Winsor & Newton Cotman tubes, which are student-grade watercolours. I also bought a foldable plastic palette. This way I could start cheaply. I learned how to colour-mix with a limited palette, a great skill that has come in handy as I have progressed. Over time I was able to build up my collection of colours and arrange my palette in a way that best suited my preferences.

I personally prefer individual paints over pan sets, because I like to pick out the individual colours that are in my palette. I also like the ease of being able to find tubes in any art store when I need a refill. I personally have never seen pan refills in a store, although you may be able to find them online. Most often, you have to buy a whole new pan set. Don't get me wrong, though, using a pan set is a great and easy way to start painting with watercolours. Having a ready-to-go palette set up with colours can relieve the stress of choosing colours if you aren't sure what to get.

I have now upgraded to professional watercolours, but I will always be an advocate for using budget-friendly supplies. Do what works best for you!

brushes

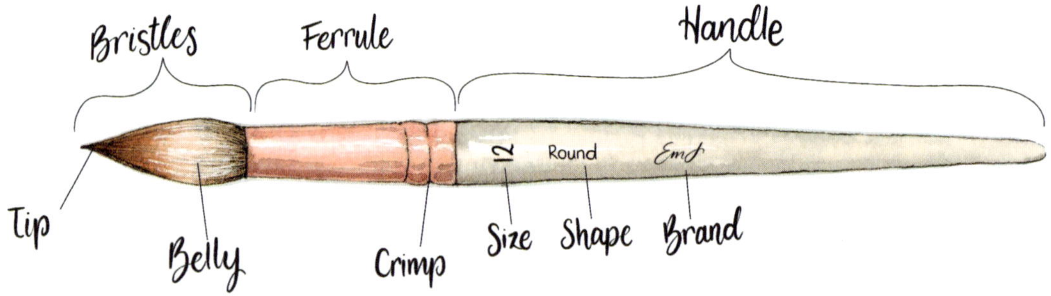

Now, let's talk brushes. Watercolour brushes come in all different shapes, sizes, bristle types, materials, and brands. Different brush shapes are used to create different shapes and lines. Here are some examples of different types of brush shapes.

The choices can be a bit overwhelming if you're not sure what to look for. I suggest starting with a round brush. I like using round brushes, because they are the most versatile when it comes to creating different type of lines, curves, and shapes. Now that you know you need a round brush, what other brushes do you need? I believe that brushes are a personal thing, and every artist has their own brush preferences. For myself, I have three criteria I go by when looking for the right brush:

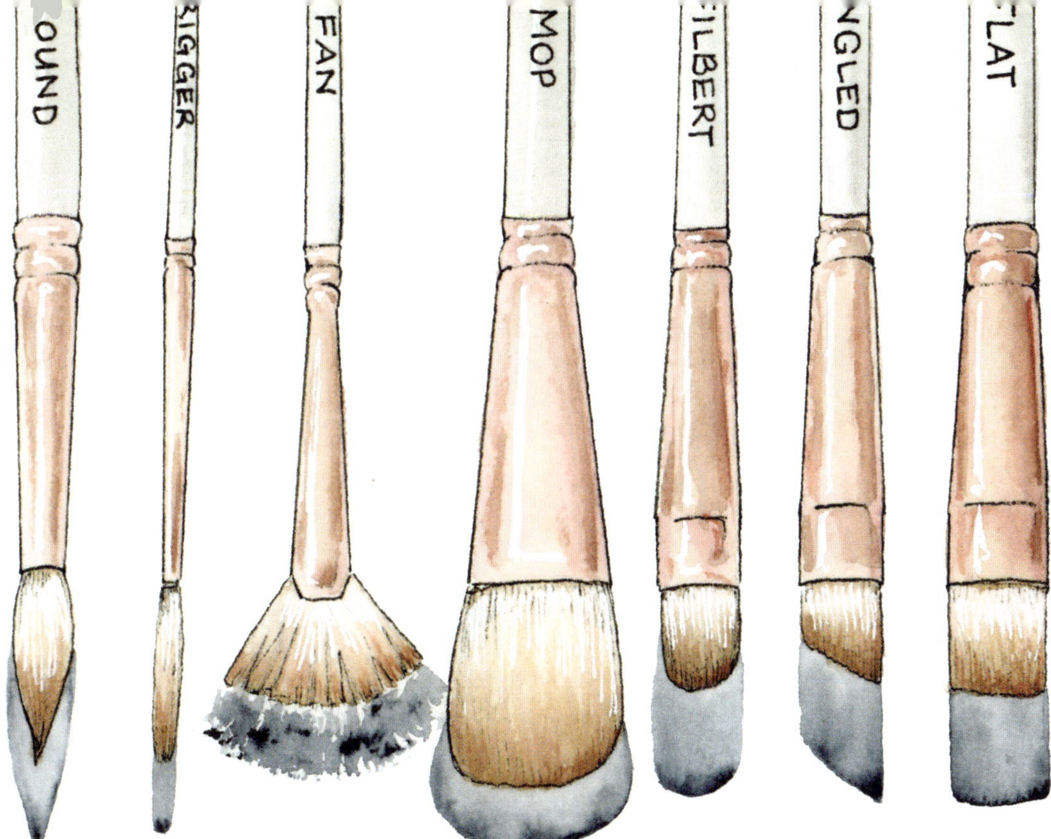

1. **The Point:** A sharp point is most important when creating lines, from thin to thick. To get most out of a brush, it has to have a very sharp point.
2. **The Snap:** I really like a stiff, snappy brush. You can test this by running your fingers over the bristles to get a sense of how well they snap back into place.
3. **Hair Type:** I like synthetic hair, as opposed to animal hair, for animal-friendly reasons. And, in my opinion, synthetic bristles perform better while also being more affordable.

Now that you know what to look for, let's learn about sizes. I have four sizes that I use most often: numbers 12, 6, and 2 round brushes, and some sort of wash brush for large background areas. With these brushes, I can paint larger pieces as well as smaller pieces with detail.

HOW TO KNOW WHAT SIZE BRUSH TO USE

The bigger the brush, the more water and paint it will hold. If you are painting a large surface area, such as a landscape background, it is best to use a bigger brush. If you are painting small detail, use a smaller brush. If you're unsure, try a size 6 and see what happens. With those brushes, I can paint anything, and so can you! Always purchase what's best for you and your own brush preference.

paper

In watercolour, the paper is one of the most important supplies. Painting on good-quality paper can make all the difference in your work. Because watercolour is a very wet medium, you need to use paper that will withstand a lot of water. Watercolour paper is thicker and more absorbent than regular paper. For decent watercolour paper, you don't want anything under 140 pounds, or 300 GSM. The weight of the paper refers to the thickness and is usually written on the front of the pad.

Watercolour paper also comes in different textures, or tooths. A paper's "tooth" describes the feel or texture of the paper's surface. The toothier a paper is, the rougher it feels.

COLD-PRESSED, HOT-PRESSED, AND ROUGH

Hot-pressed paper has a smooth surface, while cold-pressed has a toothier texture, which helps it absorb the paint and water well. My recommendation is to always use cold-pressed paper. The material that the paper is made of is crucial as well. Some lower-quality watercolour papers are made of cellulose, while most good-quality paper is made of cotton. The quality of the paper will make a huge difference in your paintings. The catch is that the good-quality paper can be more expensive. So, when starting out, find a watercolour paper that is 140 pounds, or 300 GSM, and practice using it until you are ready to upgrade to higher-quality paper. When you do, the difference will be astounding. I like to think the difference is comparable to painting on plastic versus cotton material. When you paint on plastic, the water just sits on top. Plastic isn't a porous material, so colour or water does not sink in. That is how some of the cheaper watercolour papers react. A cotton paper reacts like a piece of clothing. The watercolour sinks right in and becomes one with the material. The paper also stays wet longer and thus provides optimal results for watercolour painting. I advocate for using cotton watercolour paper, because I don't want new painters to get discouraged when their paintings

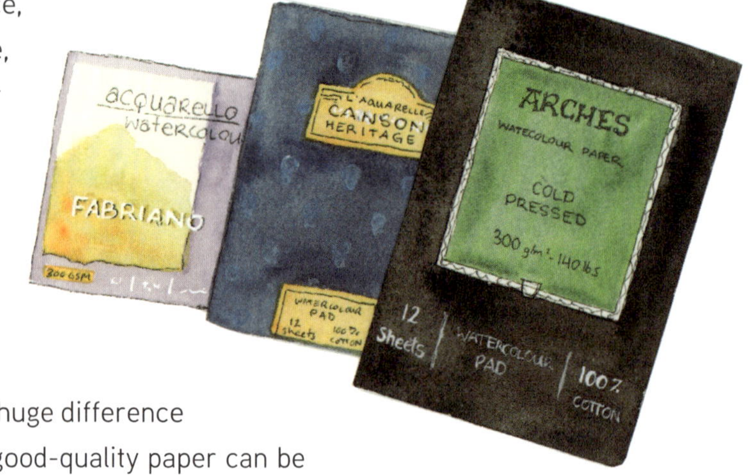

do not look as wonderful as they had hoped. Usually, their skill level isn't the problem; it's the paper quality. So, if you're feeling frustrated, give some cotton paper a go!

My all-time favourite cotton paper is Arches Cold Pressed. I buy them in pads, not blocks, because blocks are twice the price. I cut them up into quarters. This way, I'm able to practice on smaller sheets. Some other great 100 percent cotton paper options are Canson Heritage Watercolour Paper and Fabriano.

extras

Now that I have covered the three main supplies you need to paint, what else do you need? Well, with watercolour painting, water is a must. I recommend having two jars or cups of water on hand to work with. Some artists use one jar to rinse their dirty paint brushes and the other to pick up clean water, while some use one jar to clean their brush of cool colours and the other to clean their brush of warm colours. Either way you use them, get yourself two jars of water.

You will also need some paper towels to dry off your brushes, and for some blotting techniques.

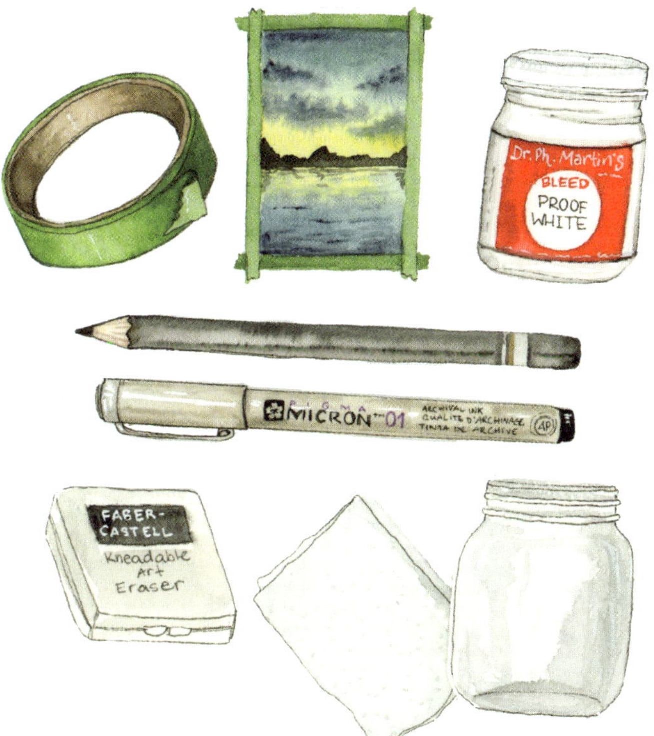

Cheap painters' tape from the dollar store is also something I use often.

For example, if I am doing a landscape painting using lots of water, taping the paper down prevents the paper from warping, prevents pooling, and creates a nice border.

Other materials I keep handy are a pencil, kneaded eraser, and black ink pen. I love using Pigma Micron pens for outlining and fine black details.

There are times where I like to add white highlights to my paintings. Because watercolour is a transparent medium, it's hard to get a white watercolour paint to cover darker areas, so for white highlights, my go-to paint is Dr. Ph Martin's Bleedproof White ink. Some other great options are white gel pens or white gouache.

caring for your supplies

Now that you have everything you need, here are a few tips on caring for your supplies.

Firstly, if you are using tube watercolour paints, make sure that the tube's cap is screwed on tight when you're not using it. You don't want the paint to dry in the tube. It is possible to reactivate with water once it's dry, but it's not ideal. Also, once your paints are in your palette, cover it when you're not using it, so it won't get dusty. I use a foldable palette since it makes it easy to cover my paints.

Secondly, never leave your brushes in your water jar. Has it happened to me? Of course! Did I learn from my mistake? Yes! Leaving your brush in water for too long can do a couple of things to it. First, it can misshape the tip of your bristles. And it is hard to get the bristles back into their original pointed tip form. Second, leaving your brush in water can loosen the glue that holds the ferrule to the handle and the bristles to the ferrule. This can cause the bristles to fall out, or the handle to detach from the brush. When you are done painting with your brush, lay it flat on your paper towel. Do not leave it in water, or even in a cup holder with the handle side down. That could trap leftover water in the ferrule. Ideally, if you could have your brush suspended, bristle side down, that would be great, but it's not imperative. Letting it dry flat on a paper towel will do the trick. If you take care of your brushes, they will last for years!

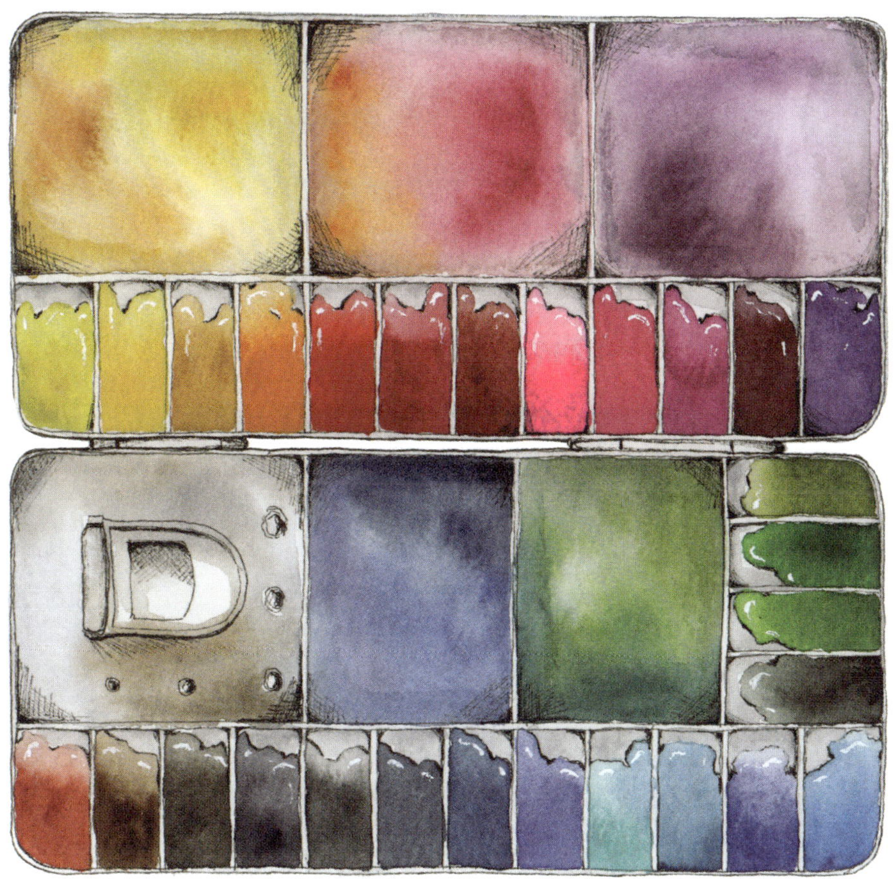

WHAT'S IN MY PALETTE?

I get a lot of people asking me what exact colours I use in my palette. In my videos, I use my twenty-eight well palette that holds twenty-eight Winsor & Newton professional colours. I can tell you right now that you DO NOT need that many colours! A lot of the paints that I use have been gifted to me or purchased over the years. Because painting is my career, I have invested a lot in my palette. However, I will say that even I don't use all the colours in it. But for curiosity's sake, I will list the colours I have, and maybe a shade or two that you really love will be a good investment for you!

Winsor Violet, Perylene Violet, Quinacridone Magenta, Permanent Rose, Opera Rose, Perylene Maroon, Alizarin Crimson, Winsor Red, Cadmium Orange, Yellow Ochre, Cadmium Yellow, Lemon Yellow, Olive Green, Hooker's Green, Sap Green, Perylene Green, Winsor Blue (Green Shade), French Ultramarine, Phthalo Turquoise, Cobalt Turquoise Light, Cobalt Blue, Indigo, Payne's Gray, Lamp Black, Neutral Tint, Sepia, Burnt Umber, and Brown Madder

THE BASICS OF USING YOUR SUPPLIES

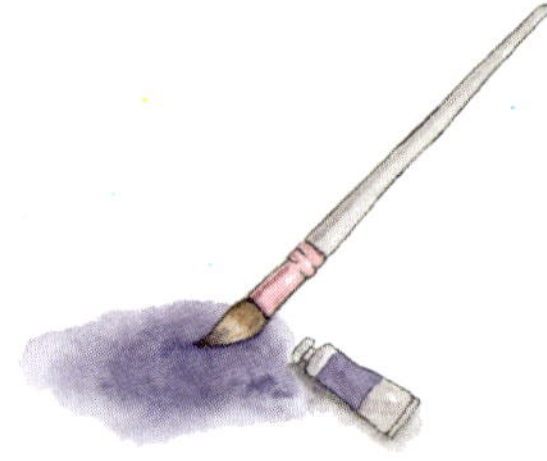

I know I touched on how to use each type of paint in the supply guide, but there are a lot of questions I get regarding the specifics of exactly how to paint with watercolour. The two most frequently asked questions I get from beginners are "How do I load my brush?" and "What is the proper water-to-paint ratio?" So, let's start from the very beginning.

You always want to start with a wet brush. Watercolour is activated by water and will only move smoothly across your paper when wet. I think beginners may try to use watercolours as they would use acrylics, but the two types of paint are very different. With acrylic, you take a glob of paint from the jar and slap it on your canvas. With watercolour, it's not quite the same. You want to work with the qualities that make watercolour unique. Water will make the paint dance and glide across your page, which is truly the magic of this medium.

So, you have a wet brush—now what? I like to activate my paints by using a small spray bottle filled with water and spraying all the paints in my palette. You can also take your wet brush and add drops of water to each colour you would like to use. There should be a little puddle in your colours. This goes for using a pan set, or watercolour tube colours dried in your palette, as well. Again, as a beginner, I wouldn't recommend using fresh paint straight from the tubes, because you will most likely end up using way more paint than you need.

Now that your brush and paints are wet, you can choose the colour you want to use. Once you have the colour picked, swish your brush around in the colour a few times. This will allow you to pick up pigment. Test it out on your paper. If the colour comes out bright and saturated, that means you have more paint on your brush than water. If your paint comes out light in colour, you have more water on your brush than paint. If the paint doesn't seem to glide across your paper at all, you do not have enough water on your brush and will need to add more. The question I get about the proper paint-to-water ratio is a tricky one because, with watercolour, it is constantly changing, and different ratios are used to create different values of light and dark. I will cover this more deeply in the section on water control. But for now, the key is this: If you want a lighter value of colour, add more water. If you want a more saturated, brighter value of colour, add more paint. Also, keep in mind that, the bigger the brush you are using, the more water it holds. For the technique exercises and examples in this chapter, I will be using a size 12 round brush.

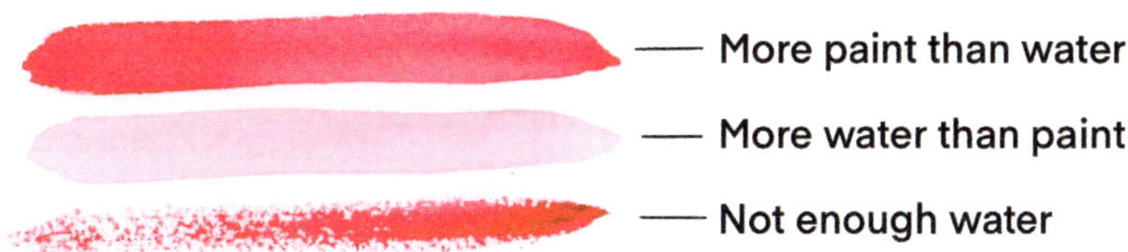

What about mixing colours, especially if you only have a limited palette? To mix colours, you will need to bring pigment over to a separate section of your palette. These are called mixing wells. Grab some pigment on your brush and bring it over to a mixing well and swish it around. Then wash off your brush, grab another colour, and bring it to the same mixing well, then swish your brush around to mix them together. Keep adding different amounts of the paint to achieve the colour mixture you are going for.

basic strokes

THIN AND THICK LINES

So now that you have a better idea of how to use water to activate the paints, I'm going to demonstrate some of the basic strokes you'll need to begin.

Get out a piece of watercolour paper (don't use the high-quality stuff for practice) and start painting! Begin with these three basic strokes. They will help your hand gain the muscle memory you need. Eventually, the basic strokes will become second nature, and you'll be able to paint without thinking about it.

Start by creating thick and thin lines. To paint lines of different thickness, you'll have to play around with pressure. Don't feel like you must be too delicate with your brush. I see lots of beginners use a sketching motion with their hand when they first start to paint, as if they are hesitant to paint on the paper. You don't need to do that. Instead, my advice is, really go for it. Just dig in and paint lines. Thin lines, medium lines, and thick lines. The difference, if you are using the same brush, is only in the amount of pressure you are exerting.

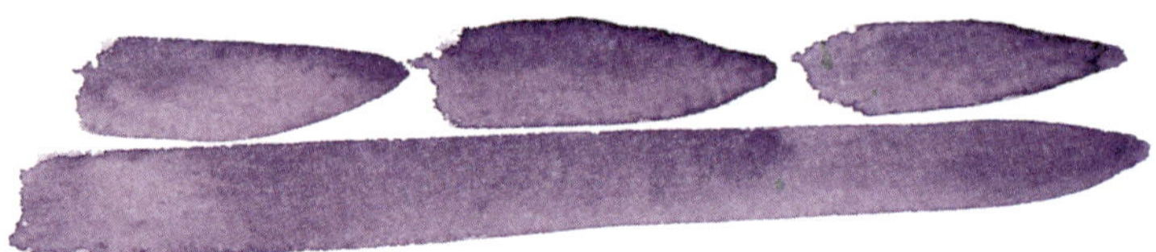

To create thick lines, use heavy pressure. Push your brush all the way down to the belly, or the middle, of the bristles (but not to the edge of the ferrule). With practice strokes, there is no such thing as a mistake. Take full advantage of the practice and get a feel for what your brush can do!

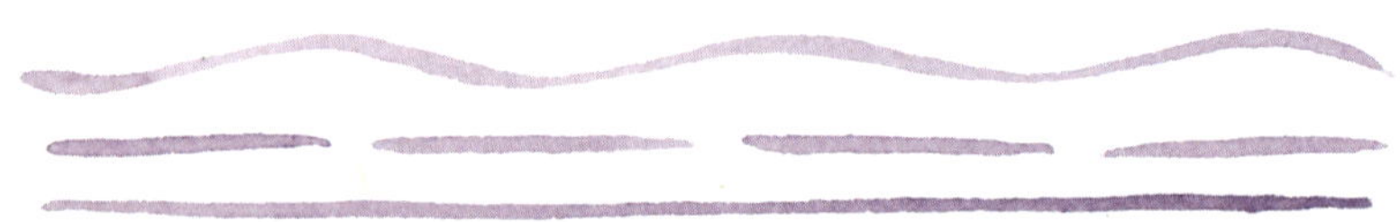

To create thin, delicate lines, use light pressure with the tip of your brush. Play around by creating different shapes and lines to get used to this feeling and adjusting pressure.

Let's create a fun abstract piece by using both basic pressure strokes. Try to incorporate different shapes, lengths of lines, and movement. Most importantly, have fun.

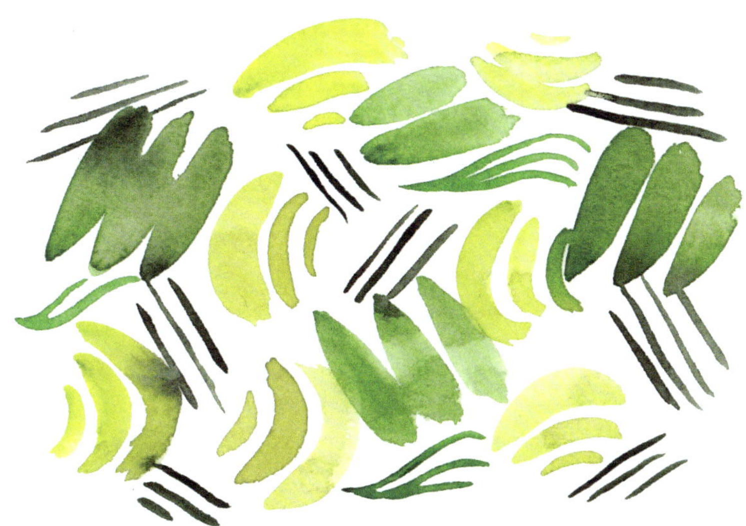

For our next stroke, practice going from thin to thick lines by alternating from light to heavy pressure. This will be an important skill in a lot of our floral work.

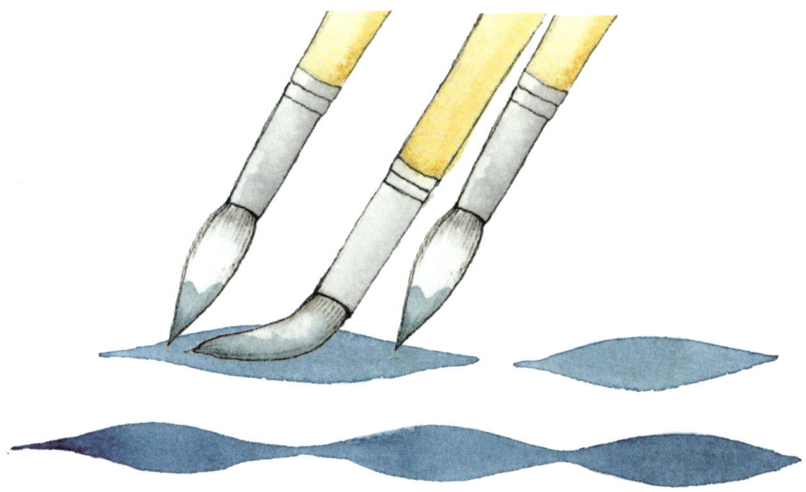

To create thin to thick lines, you are going to start by pressing down the tip of your brush, applying light pressure. Next, we gradually move to heavier pressure by pushing down to the belly of the brush. Then, in the same stroke, come back up to light pressure with the tip of your brush. You'll hear me referring to this technique as "light pressure, heavy pressure, light pressure."

C-CURVES AND S-CURVES

Now that you have mastered those, let's work on our next strokes. These strokes I like to call C-curves and S-curves. I use them most frequently in my loose floral work. For this exercise, we are going to practice creating leaf shapes. They are created by combining our pressure strokes together and curving our brush to give our stroke movement in the shape of either a C or an S.

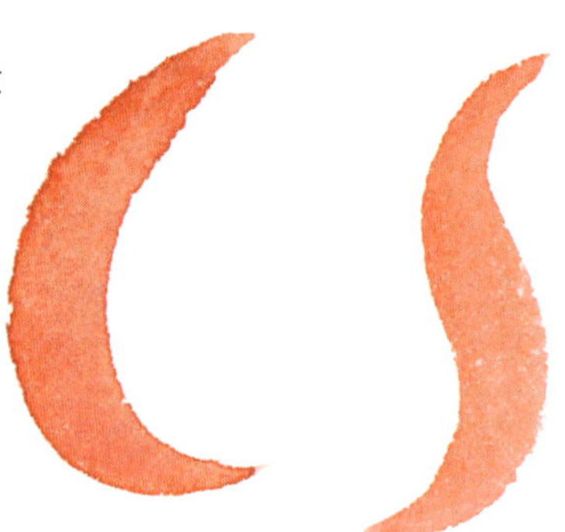

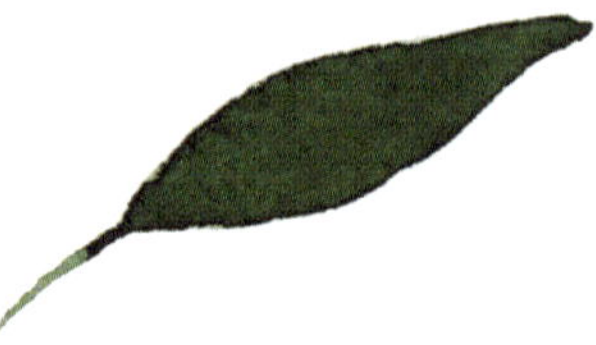

You can use that one stroke to create a thinner leaf.

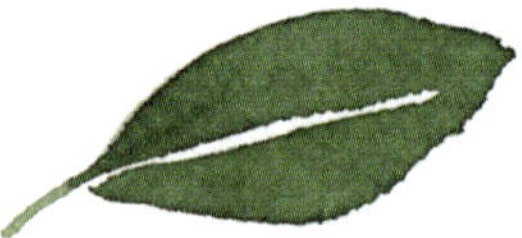

You can connect the stroke to another one, creating two sides of a leaf, to make it thicker.

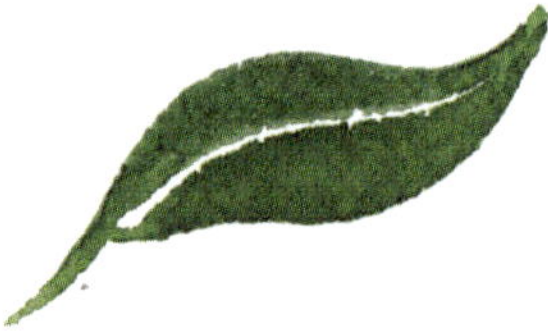

You can curve the stroke in the shape of an S to create movement.

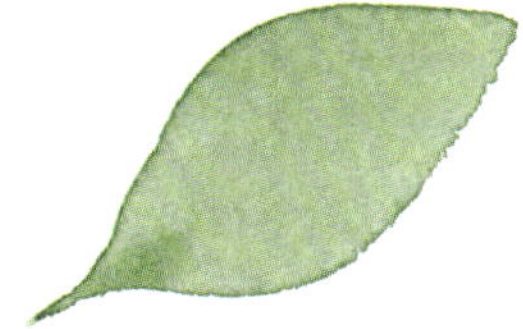

You can use a bigger or smaller brush to create different sizes of leaves.

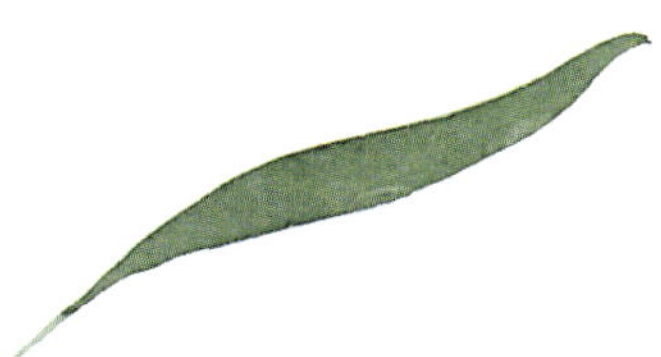

By increasing the time spent on the heavy pressure, you can create longer leaves.

DABBING

The next stroke I want you to practice is called dabbing, which is doing quick up and down (dabbing) motions with the tip of your brush to make gentle spots of colour on the paper.

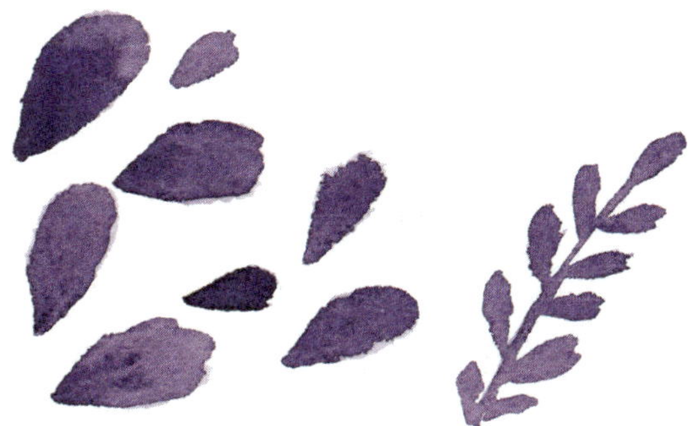

Try alternating between lighter pressure and heavier pressure to create different sizes and shapes. How big can you make them? How small can they be? See if you can create tiny raindrop shapes. Play around! With this stroke, I love to create small buds and lavender sprigs and many other details in my florals.

holding the brush

I am frequently asked about the correct way to hold the brush. My answer is, hold it however is comfortable to you! I suggest you play around with different angles to see what feels right. A more vertical ninety-degree hold may give you better control for thin detail lines. A flatter forty-five-degree angle may give you better opportunity to get right down to the belly of the brush for heavy pressure strokes. See what works best for you!

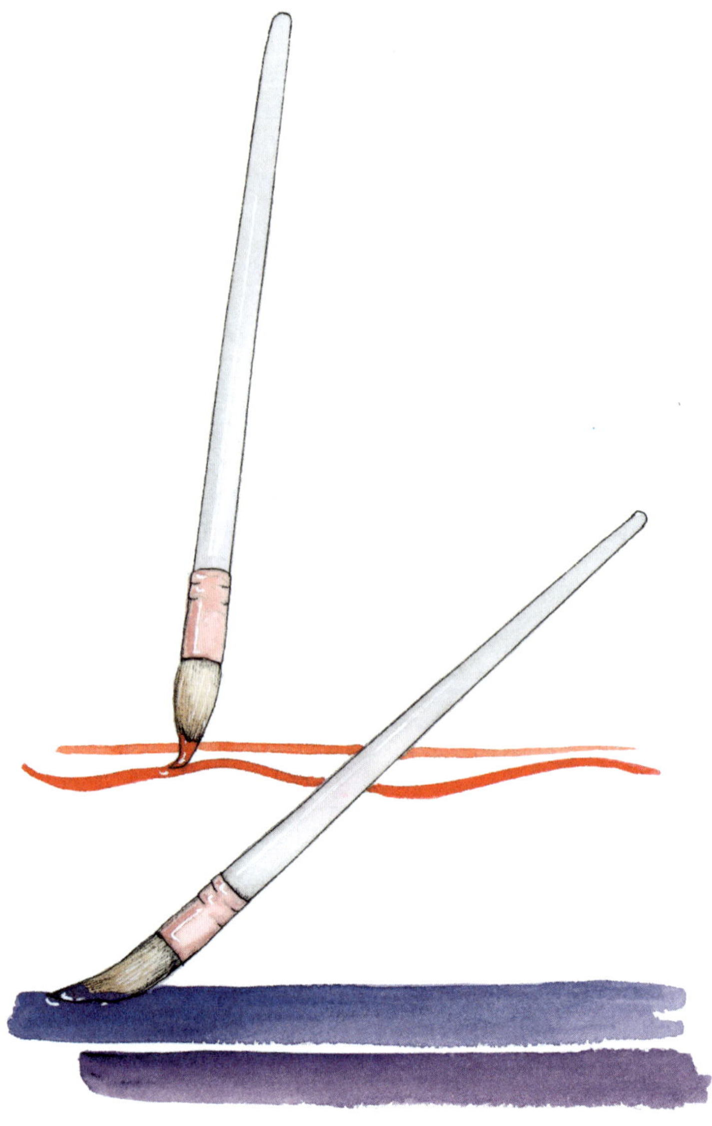

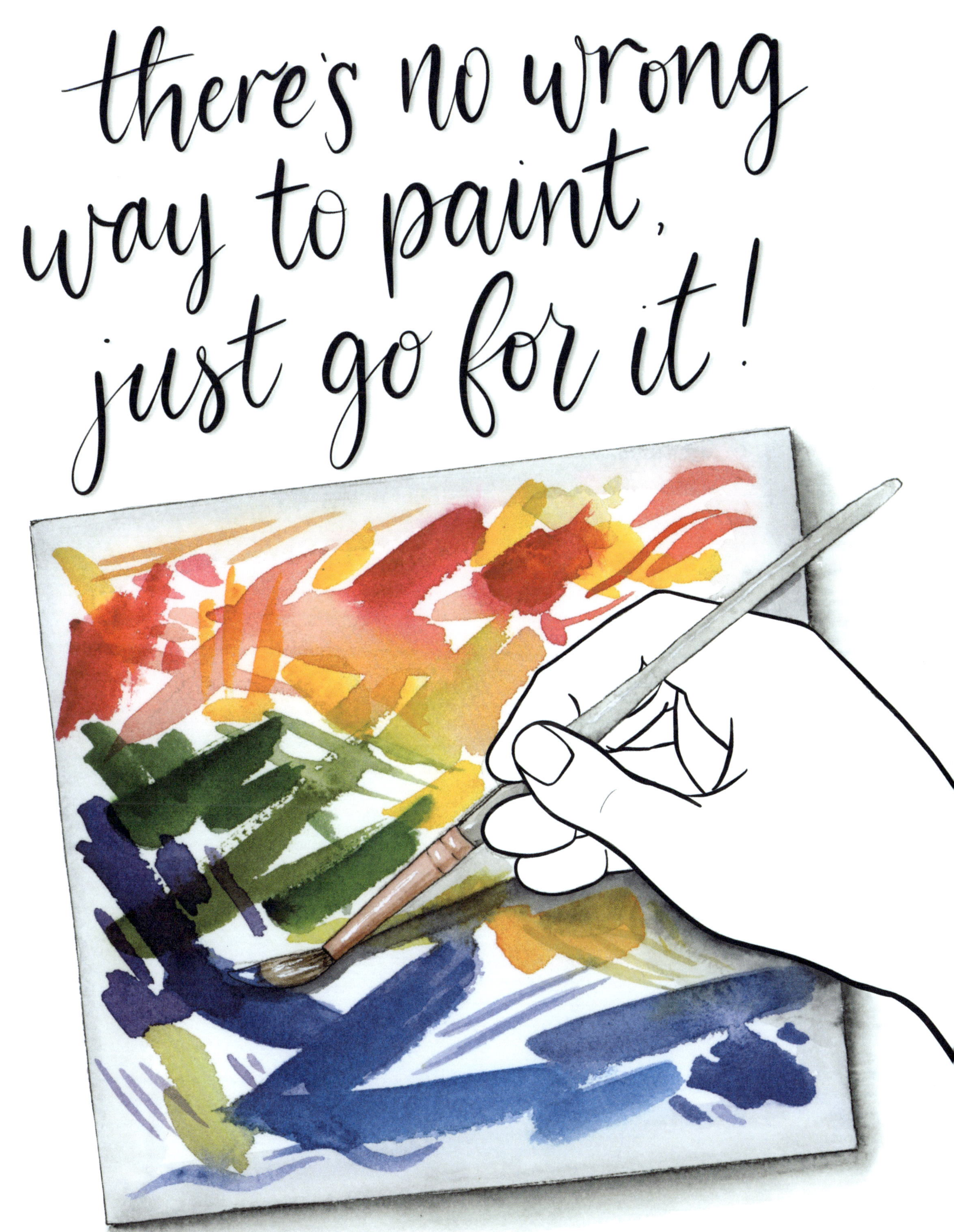
there's no wrong way to paint, just go for it!

TERMS AND TECHNIQUES

- **Value:** Refers to the lightness or darkness of a colour. By adding more water, you will achieve a lighter value. By adding more pigment, you will get a darker value.
- **Light Wash:** This is lightening a colour in your mixing well to achieve a light value.
- **Blending:** Refers to mixing two colours together on your paper to get a new hue. This is also a way to get two colours to mix into each other and achieve a soft gradient, rather than a sharp and defined line.
- **Gradient:** A gradual change in value or colour from one end of the spectrum to the next.
- **Colour Bleed:** This is when two colours slightly touch each other when placed side by side. One colour "bleeds" into the other.
- **Wet-on-Wet:** This technique involves adding wet paint to a wet surface on your paper.
- **Wet-on-Dry, or Layering:** This when wet paint is added to an already dried surface to create sharp lines and layers.
- **Blotting or Lifting Colour:** Using your paper towel to press down on the wet paint on your paper and lift the colour.
- **Negative or White Space:** Purposely leaving white areas of space throughout a painting to achieve defined shapes.
- **Mixing:** Adding colours together in a mixing well on your palette to create a new colour.

So, now that we have an idea of what techniques we are going to practice, let's jump right in.

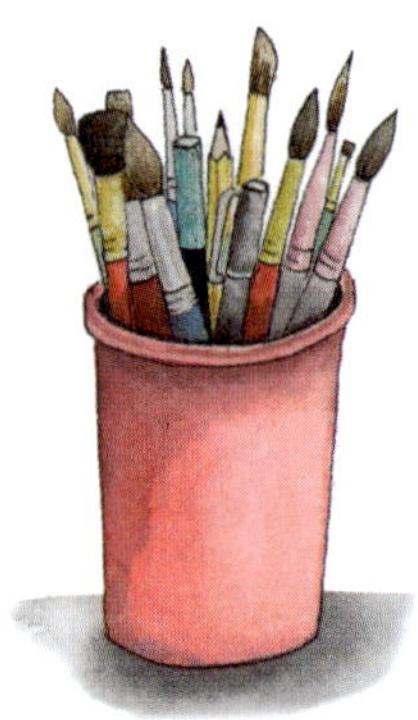

value scale

As mentioned in the definitions, value refers to the lightness or darkness of a colour. To practice our value scale, we are going to start off with a highly pigmented swatch of paint. To do this, pick a colour in your palette, create a puddle directly on top of that colour, and swish your brush around to pick up a lot of pigment. Once you feel like your brush has a good amount of paint, brush it on your paper. Now, you are gradually going to move to a slightly lighter value by dipping your brush into your water and running it against the side of your water jar. This will remove some of the pigment on the brush. Now, brush on the paint to reveal the darker value. Continue dipping your paint brush in your water, running it against the side, then brushing the colour over again, until you've reached the lightest colour value you can achieve. Your value scale should look something like this:

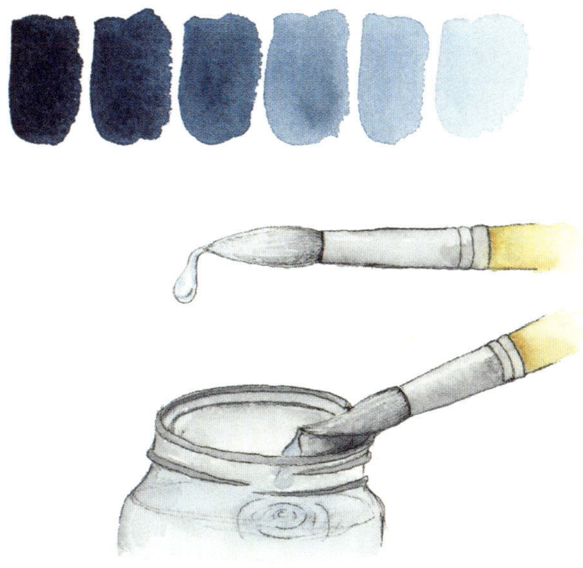

light wash

In my watercolour projects, I always start with a light wash. A light wash is basically skipping to the lightest value on your value scale without doing the whole process above. There are two ways you can achieve this. The first is to bring some of that saturated paint on your brush to a mixing well on your palette. Then, gradually bring clean water over to the mixing well to lighten the colour in your palette.

The second way, which is easier in my opinion, is take that brush that is saturated with colour and directly swish it around in your water jar a few times to take off the pigment. Then run it against the side of the jar to remove excess water. The more times you swish it around in the water jar, the lighter the colour will be.

To get used to using different values in your work, let's create a monochromatic painting. Choose one colour in your palette, and use as many different values as you can. You can use my sketch and example to do this, or create your own.

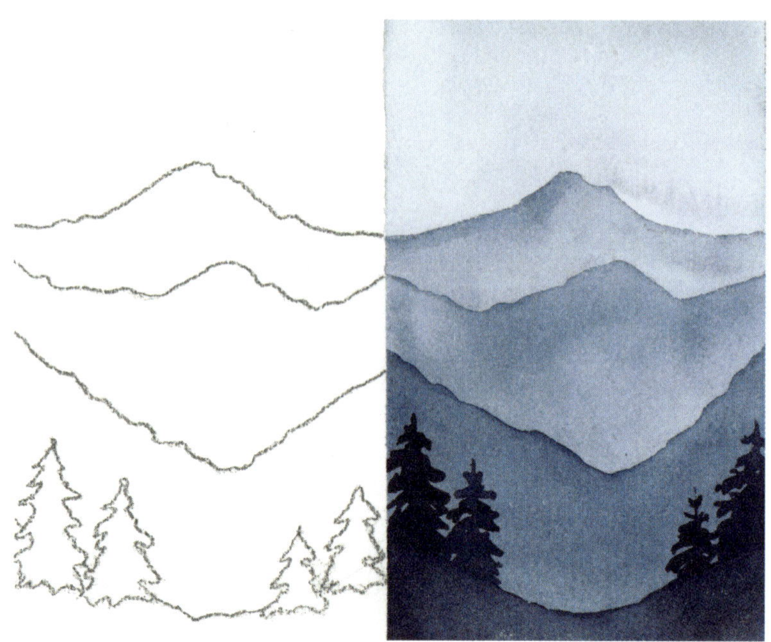

WATERCOLOUR LESSONS

blending

There are a couple of ways to achieve blending in watercolour. One involves mixing two colours together on paper to create a new one. To practice this, I often create a colour gradient that flows from one colour to the next. Let's try it.

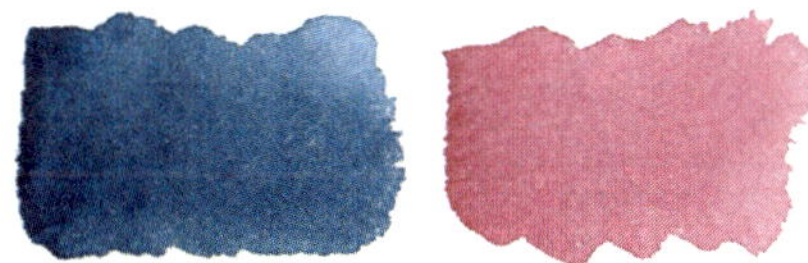

Pick two colours that will mix well together. In this example, I use blue and pink. Start by creating a saturated colour swatch with the blue, and leave white space beside it. Then wash off your brush and grab some pink. Place the pink swatch next to that white space.

Next, while they're still wet, gradually move the pigments to the middle white space one at a time. Move the pigments around, mixing them together. This will cause them to blend and create a purple in the middle. The paint should have a soft gradient from blue to purple to pink.

Another way to blend paint is by using a pulling method. This time let's try with only one co-lour: blue. Place some blue saturated pigment at the top of your page. Next, wash your brush completely of colour and dab a bit of the excess water on your paper towel (slightly drying it). Next, start to touch the edge of that swatch with the brush, and slowly pull down the colour. If the colour continues to be too saturated, continue to wash and dry off your brush and repeat it again. This should give you a soft gradient from a dark value to a light value. I use this method a lot in my work when creating skies or blending out hard lines for a soft edge.

To practice blending, let's create some fun sunset skies. I suggest starting with a smaller paper for faster blending and drying times.

Start with a pink colour at the top of your paper. Gradually move the pigment halfway down the page using the pulling method. Before it dries, add yellow to the bottom of the page, and start to gradually move it upwards to the middle of the page, meeting the pink. Once the two colours meet in the middle, start to blend them together.

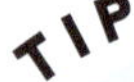

TIP

Save this practice painting for later. We will add to it when we learn the wet-on-dry technique.

**Scan QR code
for a tutorial**

colour bleed

Creating colour bleeds is one of my favourite things to do with watercolour paint. I use this technique a lot in my florals. A colour bleed happens when two wet pigments touch each other. With watercolour pigment, the paint naturally wants to travel to water. So, when two wet paints are placed side by side, one colour will run into the next, creating a colour bleed. The way this differs from a blend is that you see two distinct colours; the colours are not mixing together. Let's try it!

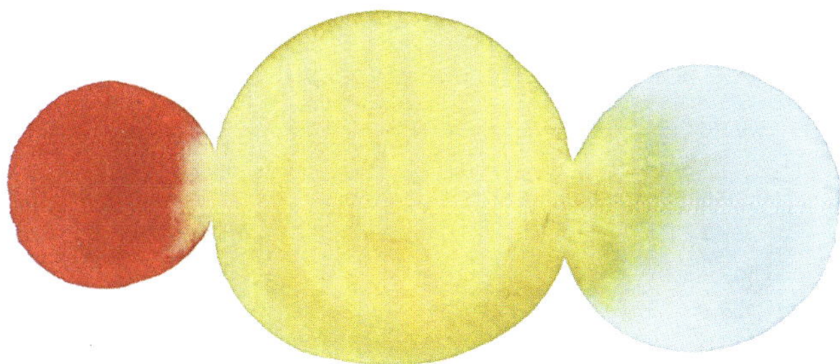

Paint a circle with one colour. Then, right beside that first circle, paint another one, with a small part of the two circles slightly touching. Watch as one of the colours bleeds into the next. The trick with this is to quickly graze the pigment—don't spend time touching them together over and over again. This will cause them to mix and blend. Now, create an abstract piece with this technique. You can use any kinds of shapes to do this; just remember, the bleed will only work when both shapes are still wet.

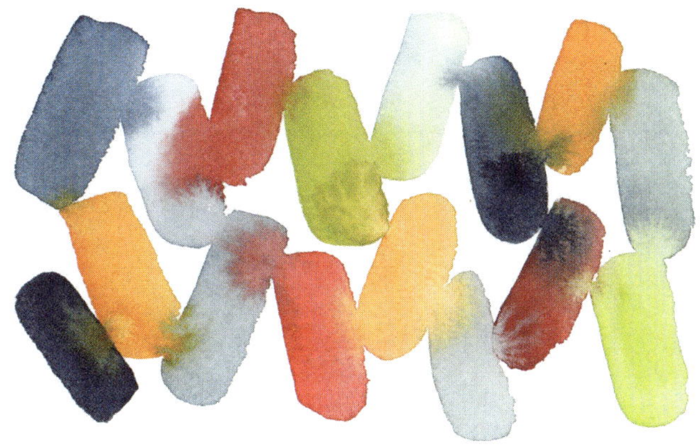

wet-on-wet

The wet-on-wet technique is probably the most famous watercolour technique. This technique is what makes this medium so special. Wet-on-wet is exactly what it sounds like: painting with wet pigment on a wet surface. The effects that happen when pigment touches a wet surface are truly magical. The colours explode and seem to almost dance on the paper. Some of the effects you can achieve with this technique are out-of-focus or blurred backgrounds, soft gradients, and deeper shadows. It also just looks cool. Let's have fun and experiment.

Take some clean water, or a light wash of pigment on your brush, and paint a circle. The amount of water that you are looking to have on your paper will create a light shine when you tilt the paper. This is referred to as the sheen. Now that you have a light sheen of water or colour on your paper, add more paint onto your brush. You can use any colour and drop it on to the wet surface. Watch that colour explode!

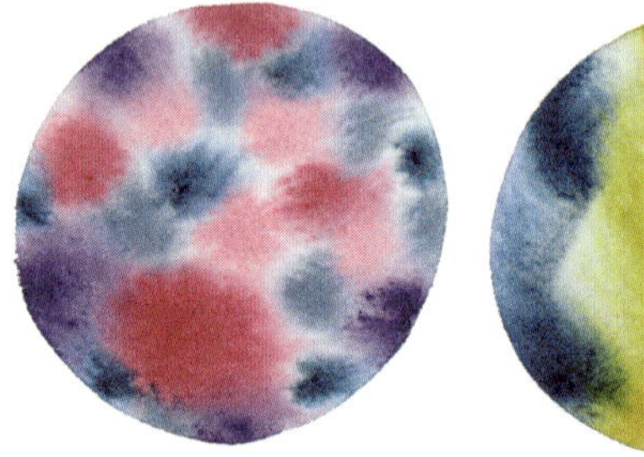

Here are a few tips for using the wet-on-wet technique: Try to be aware of how much water is on your brush and your paper. For wet-on-wet, you do not want a puddle of water on your paper. The colour won't move in the way you want it to if it is too wet. If your paper is too wet, take the corner of your paper towel and soak it up a little. Take notice of how much water is on your brush. If there is too much water, the droplets being placed on your paper will push the pigment away. Play around and get a feel for things that work for you and things that do not.

Scan QR code
for a tutorial

wet-on-dry

Wet-on-dry is a technique that is great for creating sharp lines and detail. Again, it is exactly what it sounds like: painting with wet paint on a dry surface. Because the surface you are painting on is dry, the pigment that you brush on will remain in that spot. It will not move as it does with wet-on-wet. This allows you to create detail over already dried paintings. Remember the blending practice painting we did of the sunset sky? Get out that painting and try painting something in the foreground. For this example, I'm going to paint a palm tree in black to create a beach view at sunset. Use your creativity and see what you come up with.

Make sure your
paper is fully dry before
you paint on top. If you add paint
to an area when parts are
still wet, you may get some funky
marks on your paper.

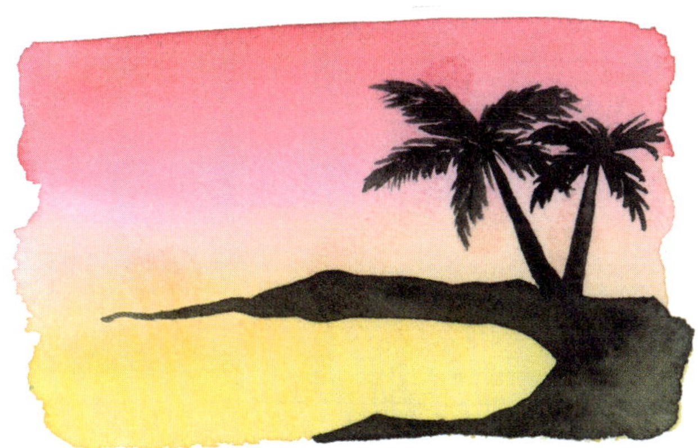

layering

The technique of layering, also known as glazing, is very similar to wet-on-dry. Essentially, what you are doing is the same thing: painting with wet paint on a dry surface. But, when it comes to layering, think of it as painting with a lighter value of colour to reveal part of the colour that is underneath. Layering with a light wash of a different colour on top of the first colour will create a new colour. This is a fun technique, and it can be great for abstract work, landscapes, or transparent-looking flowers. So, let's practice this!

First, pick a colour and paint any shape you'd like. Try to make a medium value of that colour, not too pigmented and not too light. Wait for it to fully dry. Once it's dried, pick another colour and layer another shape, partially covering the first shape. Again, use a medium wash that's not too pigmented and not too light. This will create a transparent, overlapping effect. Practice and see what you can do!

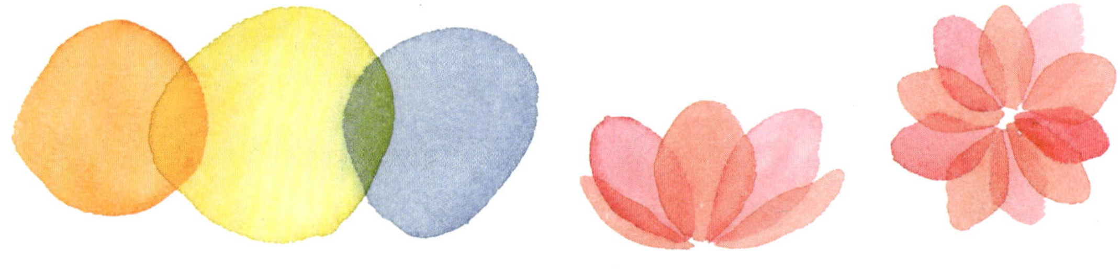

For more practice, do the same thing as the exercise above, but turn those shapes into flower petals.

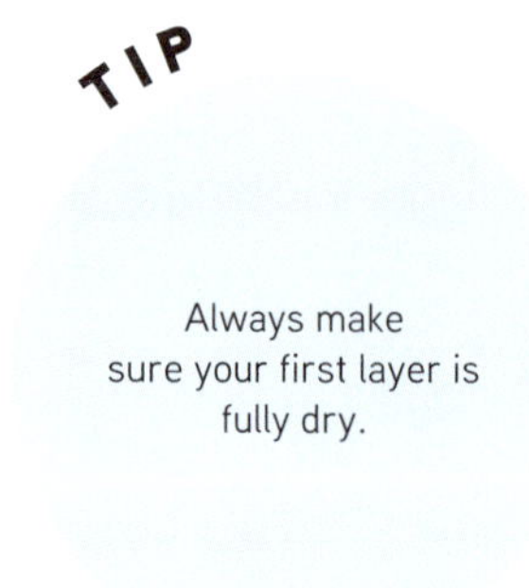

Always make
sure your first layer is
fully dry.

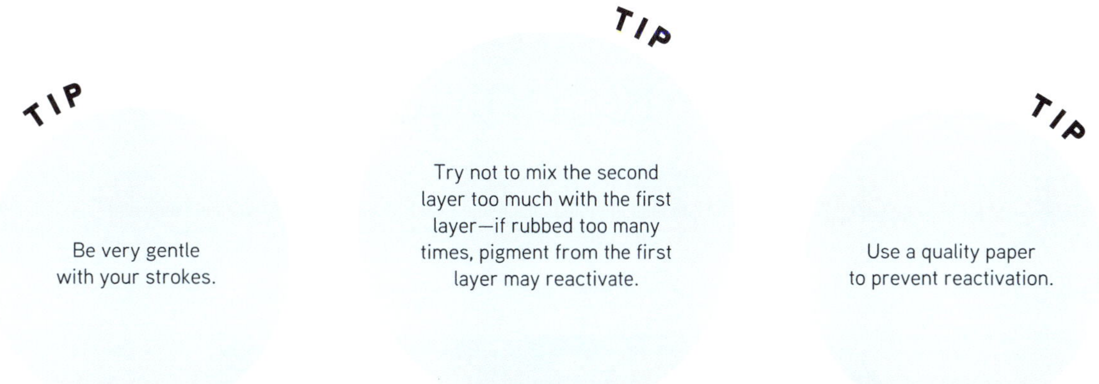

blotting/lifting

This technique can be used to create texture and fix mistakes. Blotting or lifting refers to taking your paper towel, pressing down on your painting, while it's still wet, and lifting colour. Sometimes, I will use this technique on a blue background to lift the colour and create some white, fluffy-looking clouds. Other times, I will use this method to fix a mistake, such as an accidental splash from my brush, or a stroke I didn't like. This will only work if the paint is freshly placed on the paper and is still wet. In most cases, after it has dried, it cannot be lifted. Some paints have more staining ability and are harder to lift. Create a blue background on your paper, then grab your paper towel and bunch up the end into a ball. Blot the areas where you'd like to create some clouds.

Test this out with other paint colours to get a feel for how they lift.

other fun techniques to try

SALT

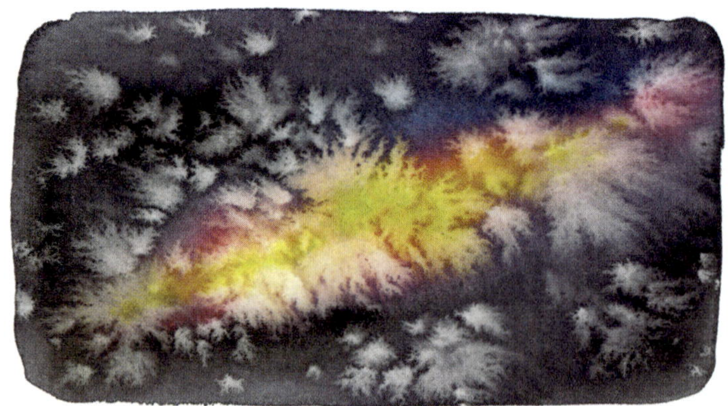

Try creating a wet background with lots of colourful pigment. Now sprinkle some salt onto the wet background and let it fully dry. Once it is fully dry, wipe the salt pieces off the paper to reveal the amazing texture underneath! This fun technique is great for painting a galaxy sky, or just adding texture to an abstract piece.

DRY BRUSH

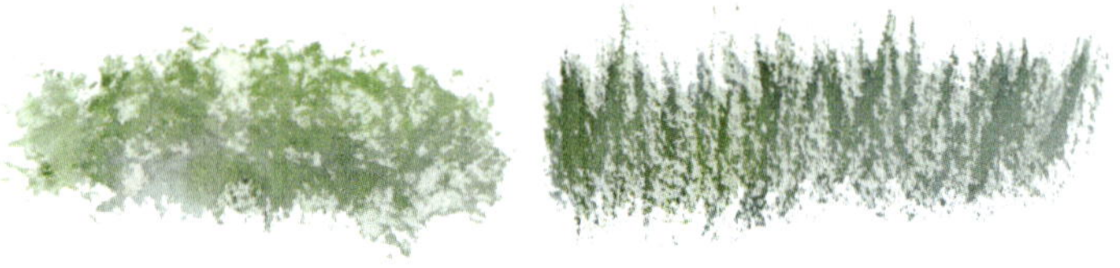

The dry brush technique can also create fun textures. Take your brush and dip it into water, then dry it on your paper towel. The brush should be damp, but not holding too much water. Now dab your brush into some paint in a mixing well in your palette. Pick up a little bit of pigment and separate your bristles. This may put a bit of strain on your brush, but just be sure to wash it and reshape the bristles when you're done. Try dabbing your brush on your paper now! You should be able to create small textures with the broken-up bristles. This technique is great for trees or bushes in distant landscapes, or it could be used for grass textures.

DROPPING WATER

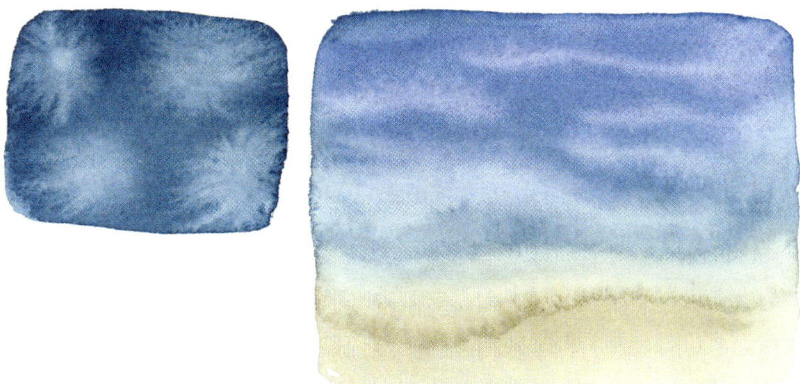

Dropping water onto your wet painting may sometimes be an "oopsie," but you can use this technique intentionally to create some amazing textures. Again, create a pigmented wet background with any colour you like. Now, take your clean wet brush, dip it into your water, and drop some clean water droplets onto the background. Watch as the water pushes away the pigment, creating a firework-like pattern! I may use this technique when I want to create ripples in an ocean landscape. I'll take my clean wet brush and drop some lines of clean water into the ocean. The water pushes away the pigment to create lighter, wave-like textures in the ocean.

beginner watercolour struggles

So, now that we have covered and tried all the important techniques, there is a good chance that there were a few struggles along the way. This is completely normal. Mastering watercolour is something that takes a lot of practice. Let's reflect on some of the struggles you may have encountered along the way.

WATER CONTROL

Water control is probably the most common struggle you will face. Trying to figure out how much water you need on a brush can be tricky.

First, let's discuss brush size. Determine the size of your brush based on the size of your piece, or the surface area you will be covering. When I'm painting a large watercolour background, I typically use a brush that's size 12 or larger. When painting smaller detail or medium-sized objects, I use a size 6 or 2. This is important because a larger brush will hold more water, while a smaller brush will hold less water. If you use a large brush with lots of water for small details, the watercolour may overpower the small details you are trying to paint.

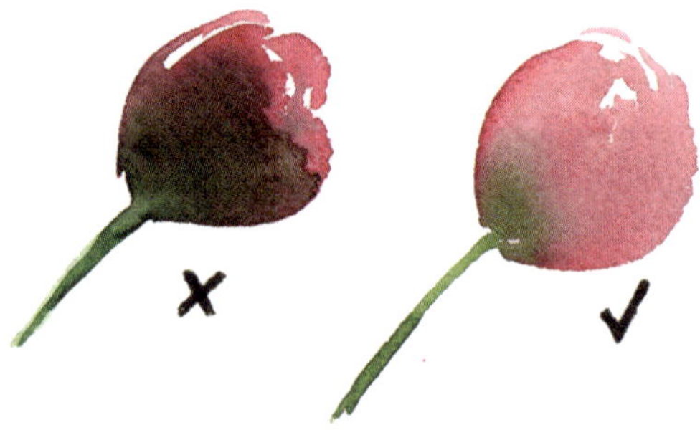

Here's an example: When painting small buds, I like to place a small colour bleed from the stem to the base of each bud in my floral paintings. If you use a larger brush, or too much water, the small bleed will most likely take over that bud. Not to worry, this can be fixed! Simply take your paper towel and press down over the bud, using the lifting technique. This will take up most of that colour. Add more pink colour to the bud and try the technique again, using less water or a smaller brush.

WATERMARKS OR WATERCOLOUR BLOOMS

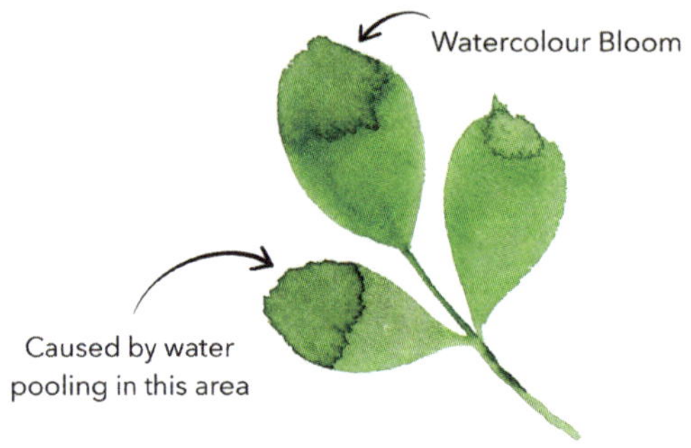

Getting a small pool of water in one spot in your painting is another common water control struggle. In this example, let's look at a leaf stroke. Sometimes, when we do our combination stroke of light to heavy, a part of the leaf will be left with a small pool of water. Once dry, this will cause a funky watermark called a bloom.

This happens because there is an uneven amount of water on parts of that stroke. The area with less water starts to dry faster than the pooled area. Ideally, you want the stroke to have the same amount of water distributed throughout the leaf. To avoid this problem, once you lay down your shape, move the colour and water around over the whole area to evenly distribute the water. If it still seems to be pooling in one spot, take your paper towel and gently touch that pool to soak up some of the water.

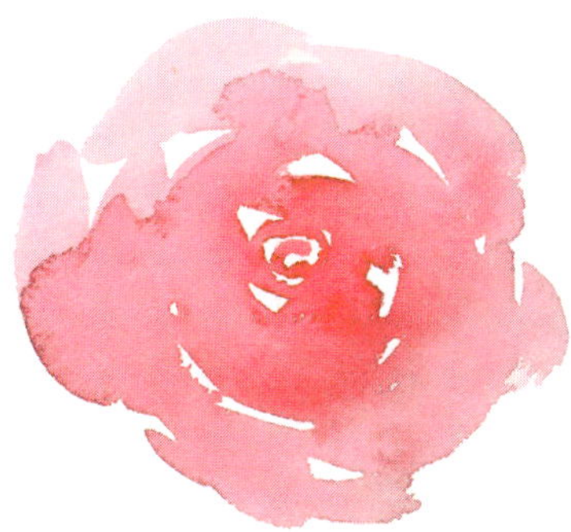

Let's look at another example of a watercolour bloom. This can happen when the wet-on-wet technique is used. When I want to create shadow and depth in my floral paintings, I will use a light wash to paint a rose, and then go in with some darker pigment in the centre of the rose. If the darker pigment has more water than the wet surface of the rose, I may get a watercolour bloom mark. To help you avoid the problem, when you are adding wet pigment to a wet surface, try to work quickly, so everything will remain as wet as the pigment you are dropping in. Also, make sure that your brush doesn't have too much water in it.

Water control is a common struggle all watercolourists deal with at times, but with lots of practice, you will get the hang of it. Here is a helpful tip to combat water control issues: After washing and loading your brush with paint, run your wet brush against the side of your jar, or gently tap your paper towel with the tip of your brush. This will take off any excess water.

chapter 4

COLOUR THEORY AND COLOUR MIXING

I have provided diagrams for each category of the colour wheel. To explore and get to know the colour wheel, let's make a wheel together!

Create a circle and section it into twelve slices.

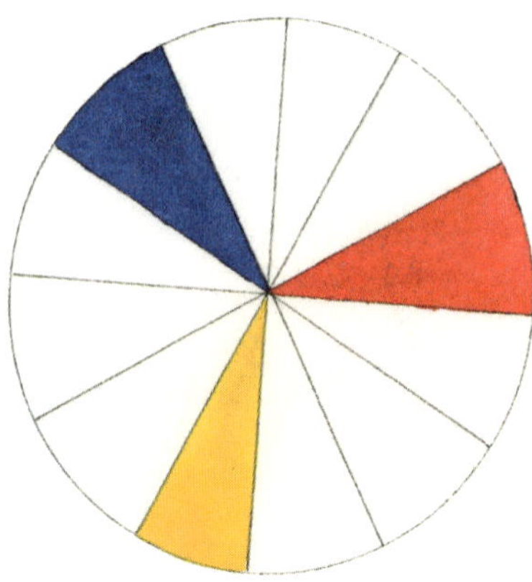

Using your primary colours, place red, yellow, and blue around the wheel, with three blank spaces in between each.

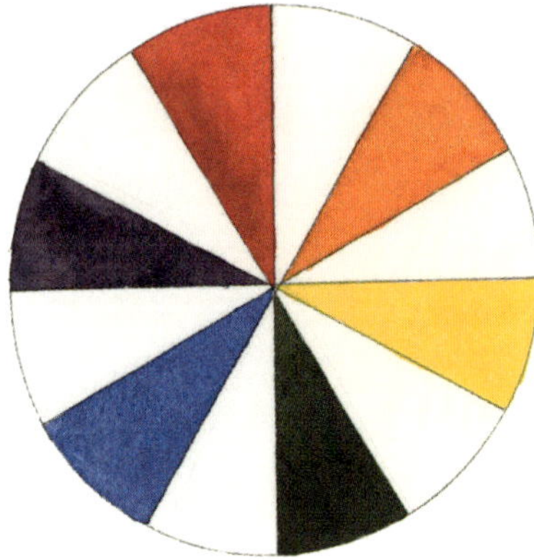

Next, mix two primary colours to create a secondary colour in your palette. Make sure you are using equal parts of both primary colours to get an accurate secondary colour. This colour is going to go directly in the middle between the two primary colours you mixed.

WATERCOLOUR LESSONS

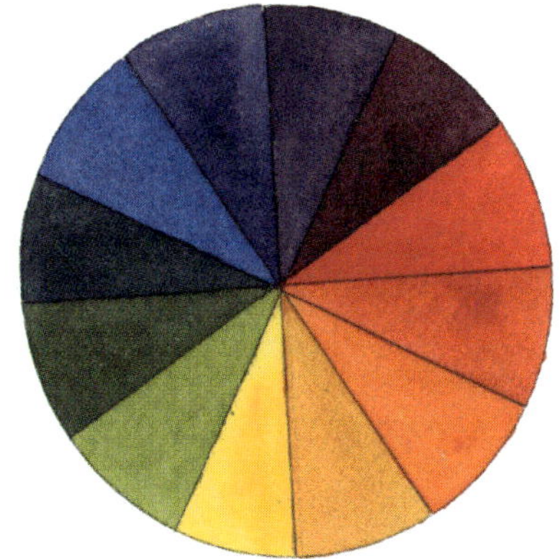

Lastly, we are going to create tertiary (or third-level) colours. These colours are made by mixing a primary colour and a secondary colour (blue and green, green and yellow, etc.). Place these colours in the spaces between the two (primary and secondary) colours you mixed to get them.

And there, you have created a basic colour wheel!

Now, let's talk about a few more important categories in our colour wheel.

analogous colours

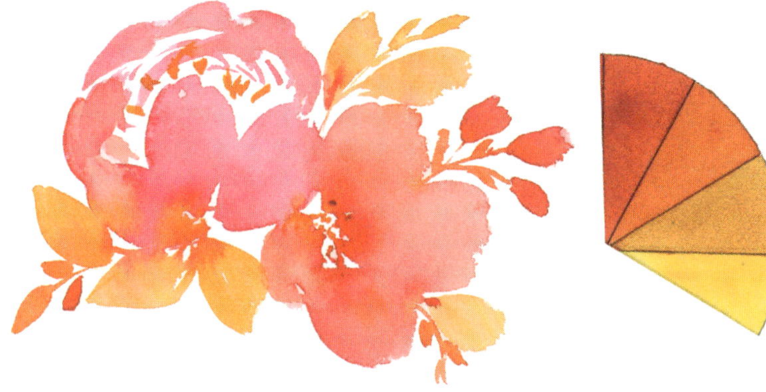

Analogous colours are three to four colours that sit next to each other on the colour wheel. Combining these colours in a painting can create a beautiful, rich, almost monochromatic look, which is pleasing to the viewer's eye.

complementary colours

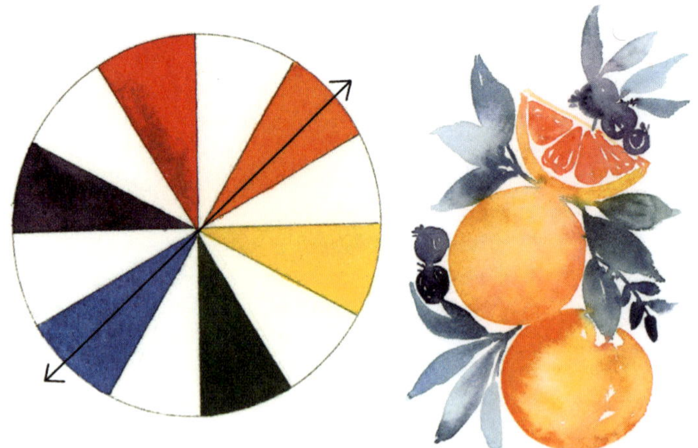

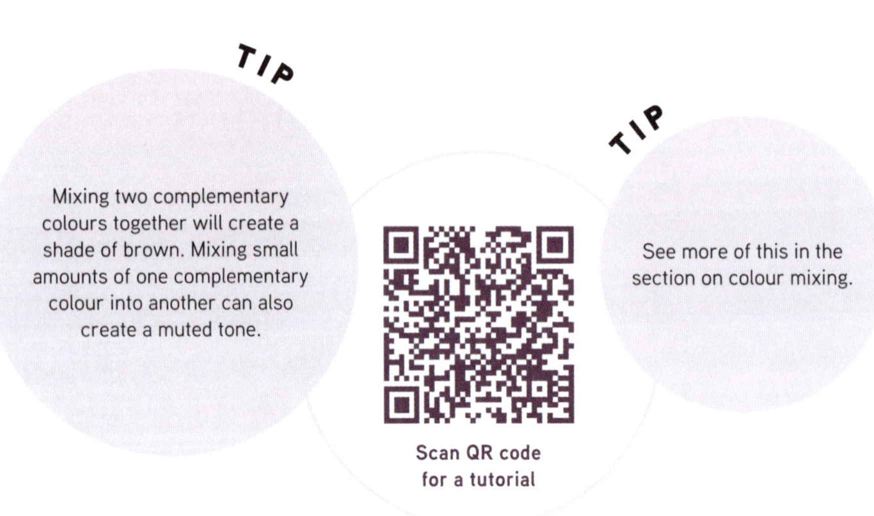

Complementary colours (also known as contrasting colours) are colours that sit across from each other on the colour wheel—for example, blue and orange, red and green, and purple and yellow. Using a pair of complementary colours together in a painting can create harmony and make the colours pop!

Scan QR code
for a tutorial

warm and cool colours

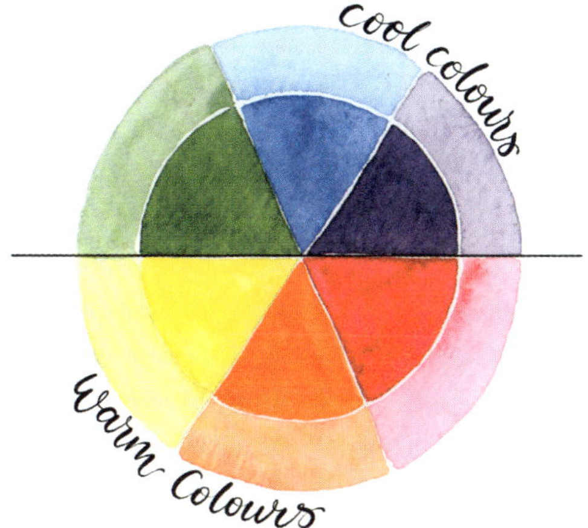

Identifying warm and cool colours is a skill that can help you mix beautiful, vibrant paints. While the concept may be tricky to grasp at first, it will become second nature with practice. When looking at your divided colour wheel, you can see that yellow, orange, and red are warm colours, while green, blue, and purple are cool colours.

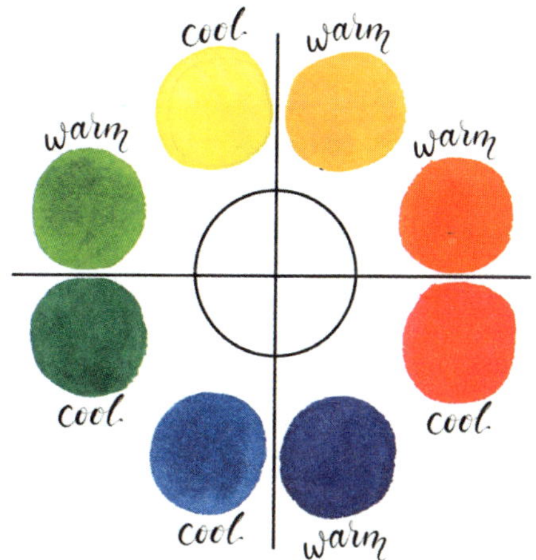

That may seem straightforward, right? Well, to make it a bit tricky, each of these colours has a warm or cool version. Looking at our warm-versus-cool chart, you will see two different hues of each colour. There is a warm yellow and a cool yellow. To identify whether a colour is cool or warm, you have to ask yourself, "Which secondary colour is it leaning more toward? Is it leaning more toward green, which is a cool colour, or orange, which is a warm colour?" Depending on the answer, it will determine whether that yellow is a cool yellow or a warm yellow. Looking at the red hues, you can see one is leaning more toward orange, which makes it a warm red, and the other is leaning more toward purple, or a blueish red, which makes it a cool red. Dissecting your different hues of paint colours can help you to understand which combinations are best for mixing.

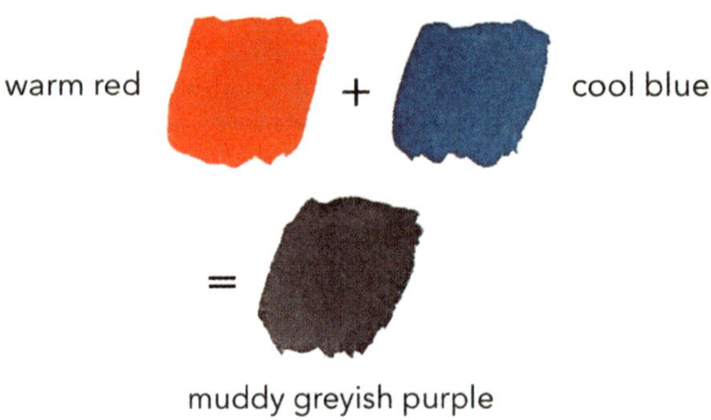

For example, let's take the colour purple. It can be quite easy to accidentally mix a muddy brownish-grey version of the colour. As we know, mixing red and blue creates a shade of purple. But what if we were to mix a warm red that's leaning more toward orange, and a cool blue that's leaning more toward green? We will end up with a muddy mess! Remember, contrasting colours, mixed together, make shades of brown. If the red has an orange tint to it and is mixed with blue, which are contrasting colours, it will make more of a brown or grey hue.

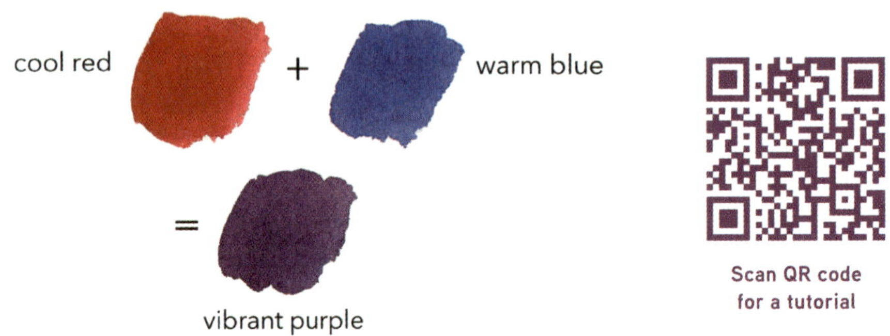

So remember, when choosing warm and cool tones to mix, you want to pick colours that have the same bias. To mix that perfect purple hue, you want to pick a cool red that is leaning more toward a reddish-purple and a warm blue that is leaning more toward a bluish-purple hue.

colour mixing

LIMITED PALETTE COLOUR CHART

Colour mixing is one of my favourite things about painting. I know it can seem a tad bit overwhelming, but there are certain exercises you can do to help you become more familiar with the process. The first one is making a colour chart. So, let's get started with a simple, limited-palette colour chart!

You can use as many of your paint colours as you'd like. In this example, I use six.

For my chart, I chose to use a limited palette that included a cool and a warm tone of each primary colour. I used Lemon Yellow, Cadmium Yellow, Winsor Red, Permanent Rose, French Ultramarine, and Phthalo Turquoise swatches of colour. Having a warm and cool tone of each colour in a limited palette will give you optimal mixing combinations. To make this chart, you will first need to make a square grid, with the number of squares depending on how many paint colours you are using. For my grid, I did six by six, making each square about an inch on a side.

To begin, list your paint colours along the top and side of the grid in the same order that you are painting them in.

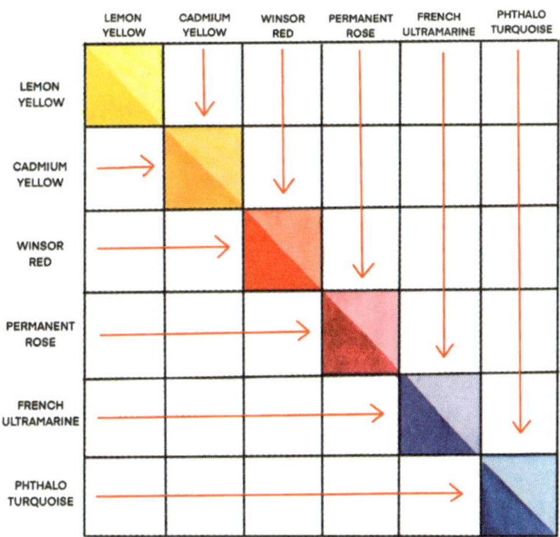

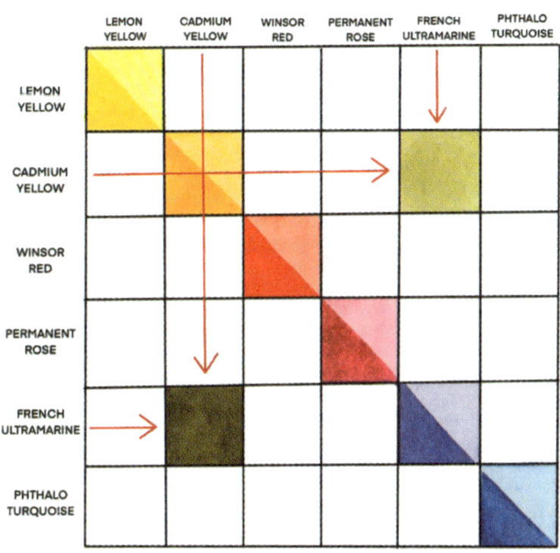

Now to fill in your chart! The pure colour swatch of each paint should land in a diagonal of the chart. As you can see, I created a dark value on the bottom corner of the square, using more paint than water, and a light value on the top of the square, using more water than paint. This will give you a good idea of how each of these colours would look in both values.

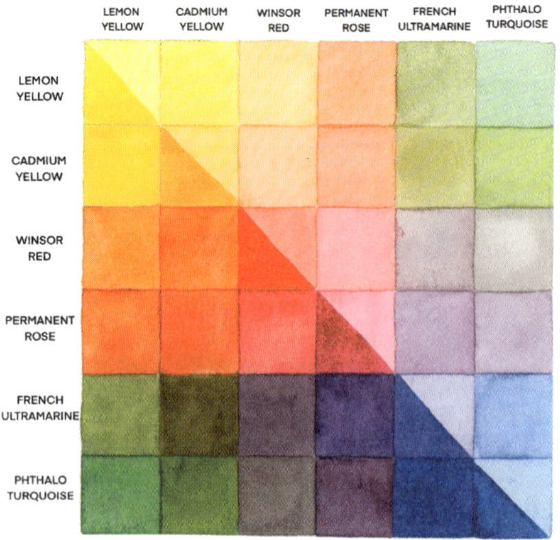

Next, one by one, mix equal parts of the corresponding colours where they meet in the chart. Instead of producing the same colour twice, I made the top of the grid the lighter value of the mix, and the bottom half the darker value. This exercise should be fun and relaxing, so take your time and enjoy the mixing process. Creating this chart will give you a great reference in the future. The practice will build your colour mixing skills.

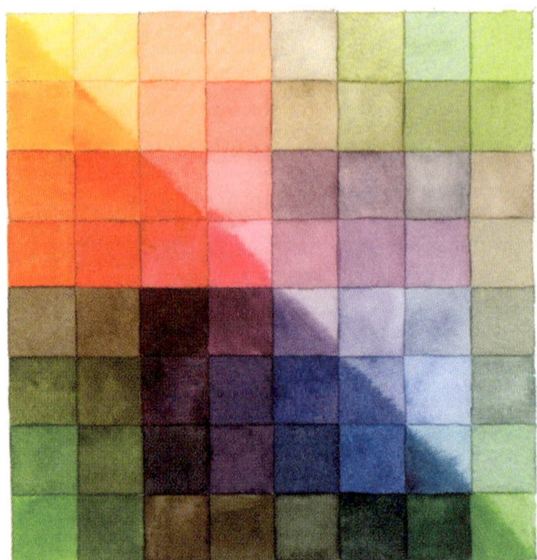

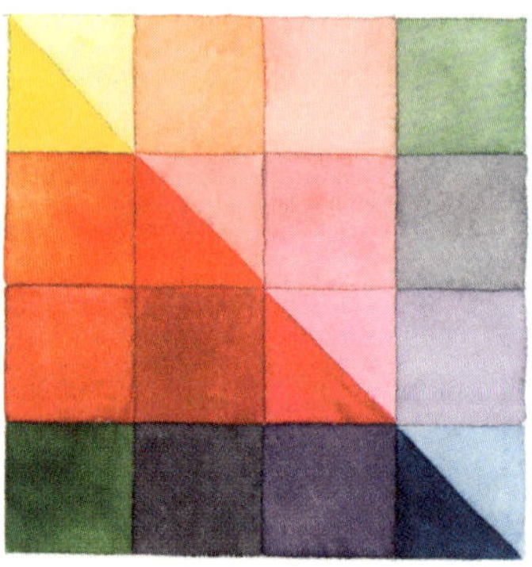

Scan QR code
for a tutorial

Here are two other examples of the same mixing chart with different numbers of paint colours. Work with what you have, and get to know your colour mixing possibilities!

value scale colour chart

Our next colour mixing exercise will focus more on the value scale and the possibilities that using only two colours can create! This is one of my favourite exercises, and it can create a beautiful piece to hang in your room.

First, pick two colours. The example I have created is a combination of Permanent Rose and Cadmium Yellow. Start by placing each pure colour at opposite sides of the paper. Next, mix equal parts of each colour, and place that right in the middle. Lastly, mix two more swatches, each favouring one of the colours. One will have a bit more yellow to it, and the other will have a bit more pink to it. You should end up with five colour swatches in a gradient moving from one colour to the next. You have just created three new hues using only two colours! But we're not finished.

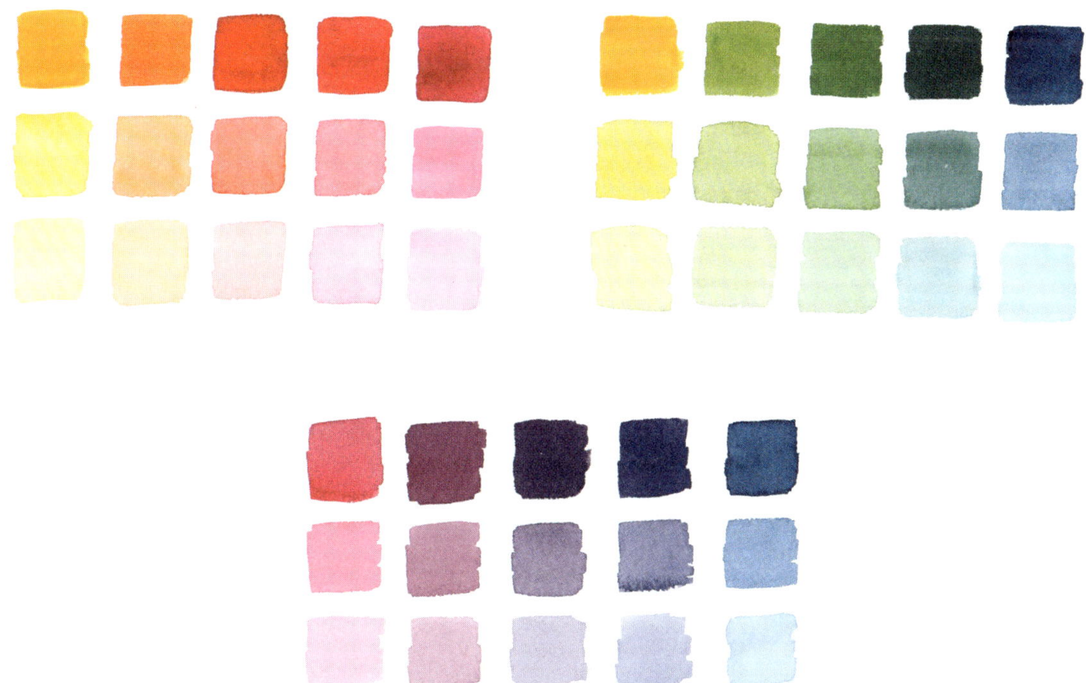

Now, add slightly more water to each colour mixture, to make a medium value of each colour, and place it below the darker value line above. You have five more new hues! And lastly, create another line of an even lighter value by adding more water to those mixtures. Using only two paint colours, you have now created fifteen new hues! Try this exercise with as many different paint combinations as you'd like.

mixing complementary/ contrasting colours

For this exercise, we are going to be focusing on mixing contrasting colours. Reminder: Contrasting colours are two colours that sit opposite each other on the colour wheel.

Mixing contrasting colours will achieve two things: It will either create a shade of brown, or mute or tone down vibrant colours. For this exercise, we will use the same five-swatch gradient format used in the last exercise.

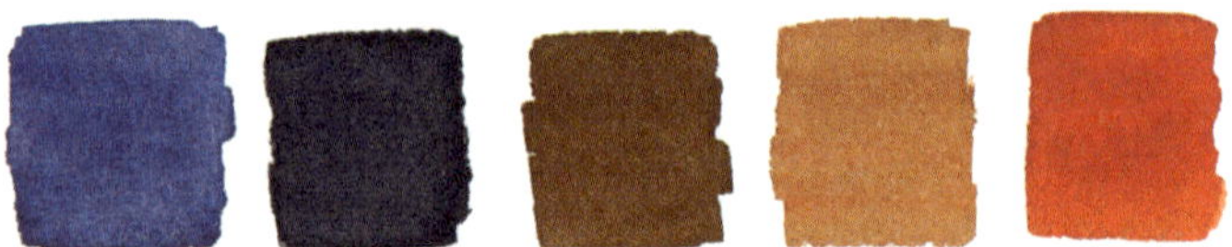

Start by placing two contrasting colours on opposite ends of the paper. The first combination I used in the example is Ultramarine and Orange, which I created by mixing Winsor Red and Cadmium Yellow. Next, mix two equal parts of the colours together, and place it in the middle. This should create a shade of brown. For the next two swatches, mix a little more of each colour, favouring one side of the scale, then the other. You should end up with a darker, muted blue and a rusty-coloured muted orange.

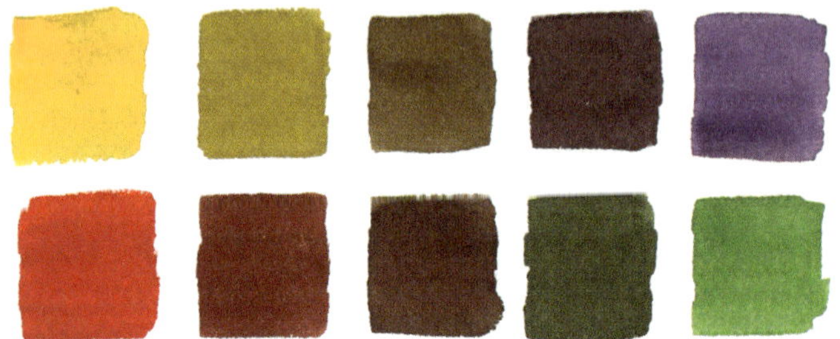

Now, create two more mixing scales with the last two contrasting colour combinations: yellow and purple, and red and green. Learning to mix muted colours is great for creating shadows in your watercolour pieces.

Now that we've learned to mix colours like a pro, I suggest that you dedicate a sketchbook (remember, inexpensive watercolour paper will be just fine for now) to mixing as many different combinations as you can. Practicing colour mixing is also a great way to relax and get yourself motivated to paint. Try adding a third colour into some of your mixes and see where it takes you.

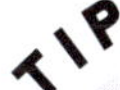

If you're new to colour mixing and still getting to know the colours in your palette, write the names of the colour mixes along with the swatches for future reference.

Scan QR code for colour mixing YouTube playlist

favourite mixing combos

Here are some examples of my favourite colour mixes that I love to use in my work.

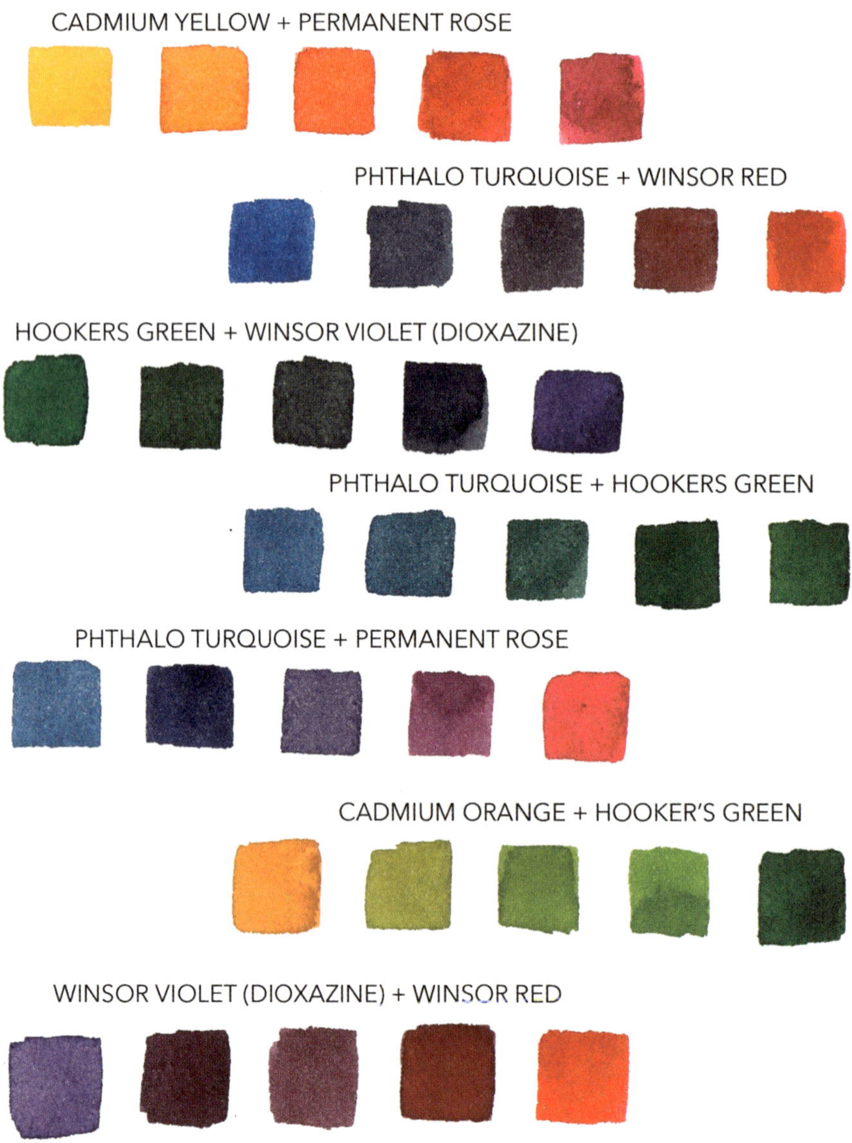

With every
mistake
you learn
something
new!

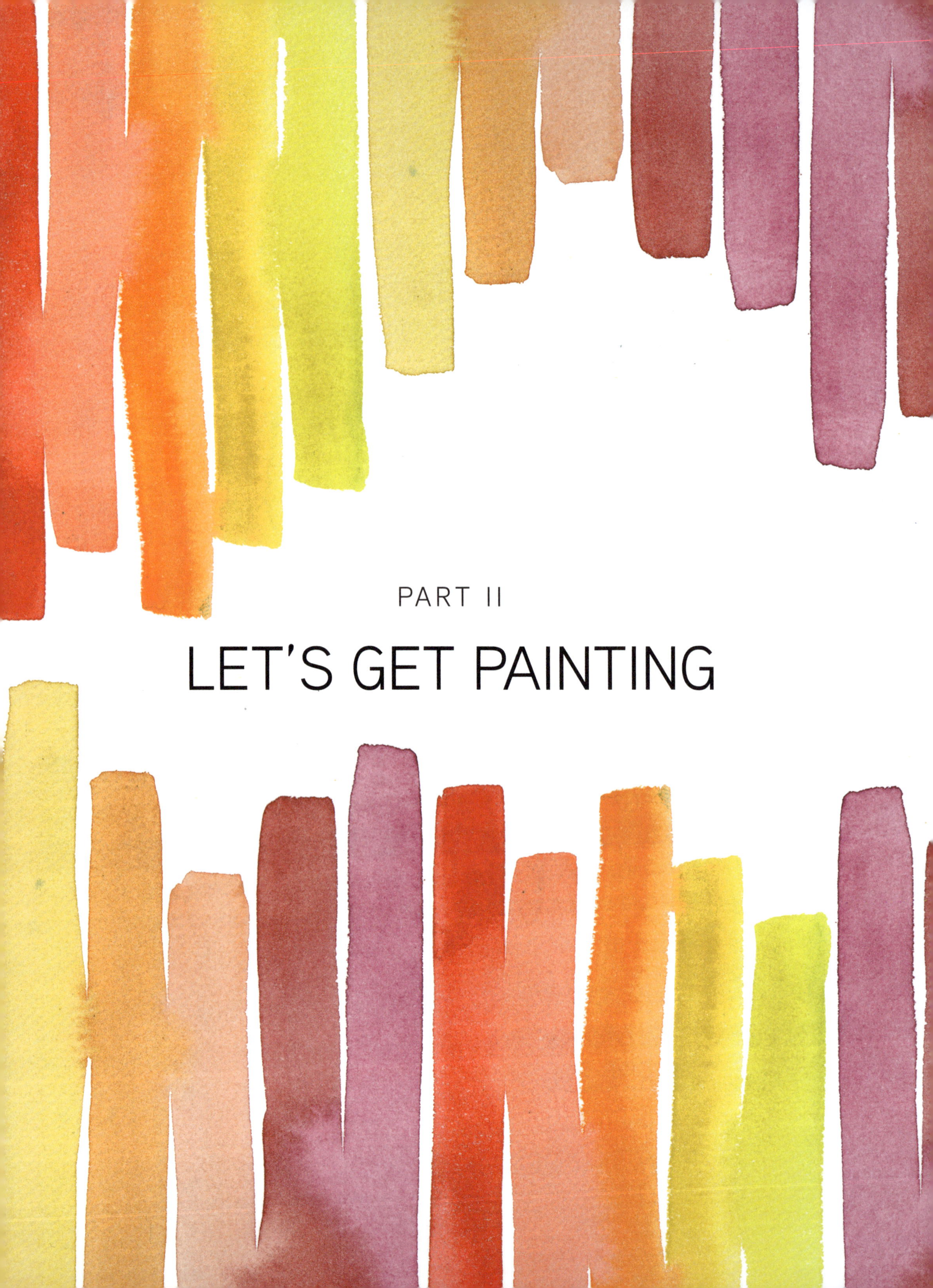

LET'S GET PAINTING

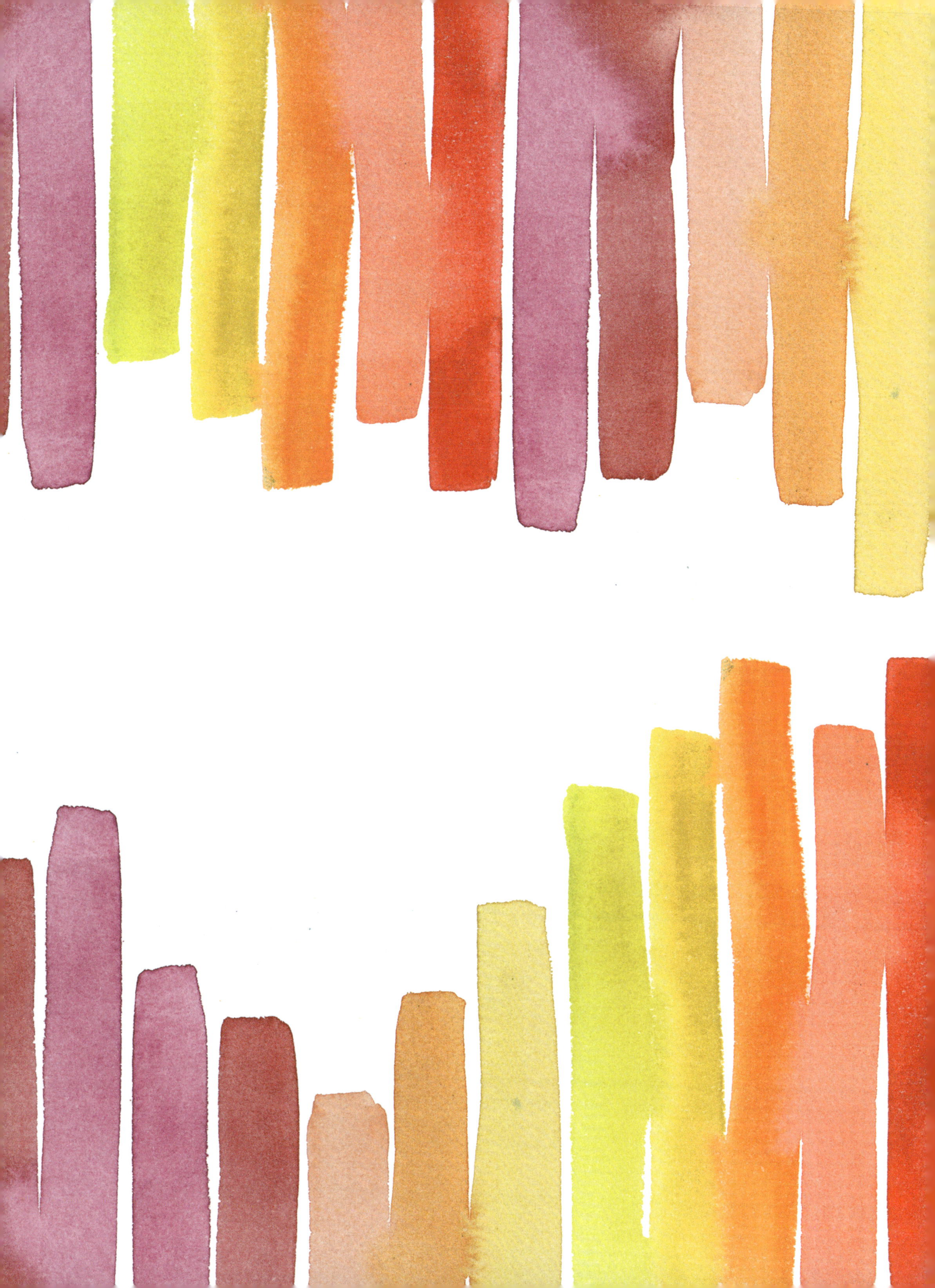

chapter 5

BEFORE YOU BEGIN

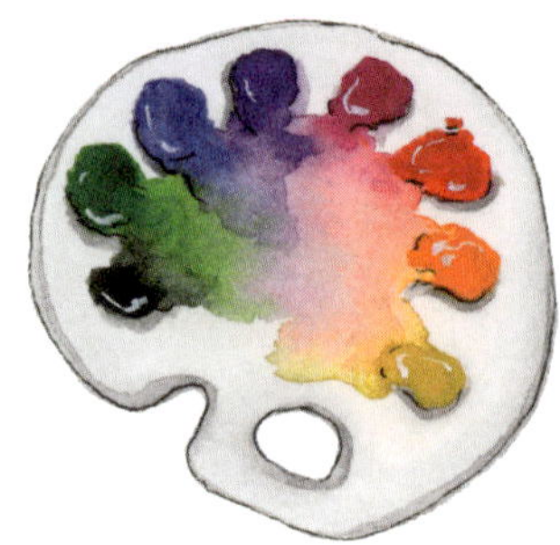

1. Be aware of which steps need to be completely dry before continuing to the next step. Also, know which steps need to remain wet when continuing to the next step. There will be a lot of wet-on-wet as well as wet-on-dry techniques used in these paintings. Read through all of the project first to prepare yourself, then set up your materials before you start.

2. The more detailed projects require a pencil sketch beforehand. I have supplied you with some sketches at the back of the book that you can trace before starting a project. Feel free to free hand-sketch your own instead!

3. Your first attempt won't always be perfect. If you are new to watercolour painting, please give yourself some grace. I believe that becoming a good watercolour artist can happen for anyone, but, like everything, it takes practice. I wasn't the best painter my first, second, or third time around. This is a skill I have developed over the years, and even now, I am learning new things and progressing with practice.

4. Don't throw away your first attempts. Looking back and tracking your progress through this journey is one of the most satisfying things about the process. I still look at some of my work from when I first started and can't believe how far I've come. Starting a watercolour sketchbook is a great way to track your progress.

5. Do not give up halfway through. It can be perfectly normal to get frustrated mid-painting or second-guess yourself. I still do. If you need to, take a break, and come back when you're ready to finish. An important thing to remember is that there is almost always an awkward stage in every painting. When the painting is done, you may think, "Hey, that turned out better than I thought it would!"

6. Have fun! Painting should be enjoyable and relaxing. The wonderful thing about watercolour is that you can create beauty just by watching your colours dance on the page. Don't think about creating something perfect—just create for the enjoyment of it. You've got this!

The colours used in these projects are just for reference. Feel free to change up the colour palettes and mixtures and use whatever you have! I am all about being budget-friendly, so do what's best for you!

The colours listed here are from the Winsor & Newton professional line:

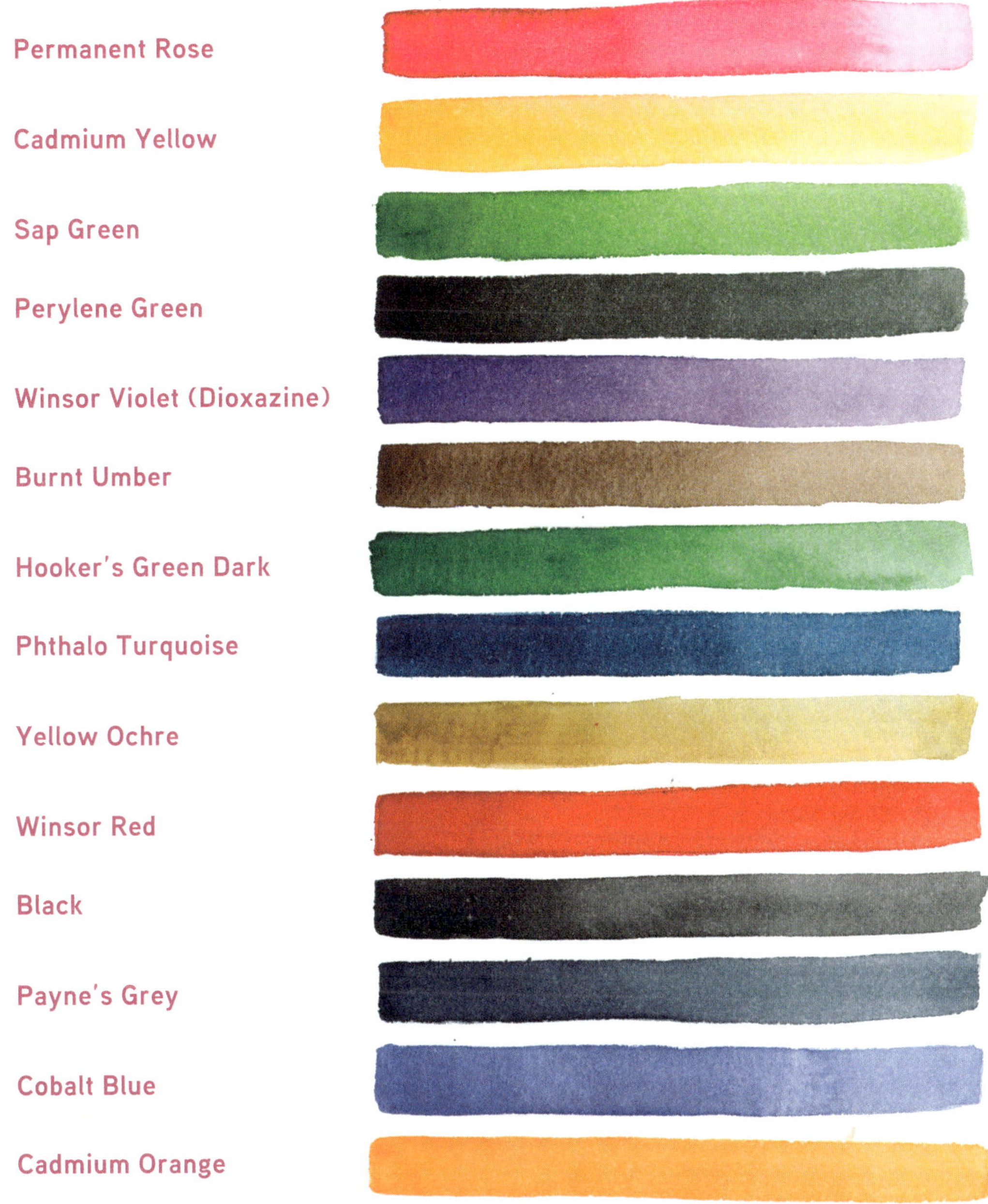

Permanent Rose

Cadmium Yellow

Sap Green

Perylene Green

Winsor Violet (Dioxazine)

Burnt Umber

Hooker's Green Dark

Phthalo Turquoise

Yellow Ochre

Winsor Red

Black

Payne's Grey

Cobalt Blue

Cadmium Orange

chapter 6

BOTANICAL PAINTING PROJECTS

project one: loose florals

Painting loose florals is what got me into watercolour. I love the seemingly effortless strokes that bring a painting to life. For the first project, you are going to learn how to paint my two favourite flowers and some leaves.

the rose

Techniques Used:

- Value scale
- Light wash

Materials Needed:

- Watercolour paper
- Round brush size 12
- One paint colour
- Clean jar of water
- Paper towel

Paint Colours:

- Permanent Rose

Step 1: Using the tip of your brush and light pressure, create some circular scribbles in the centre. Have some circles overlapping each other—it shouldn't look like a perfect spiral.

Step 2: Referring back to our basic strokes section, we are going to create three C-curves around our centre scribbles. One part of each curve should be touching a part of another stroke.

Step 3: Next, with a slightly lighter wash of colour, create a larger C-curve over a place where two smaller curves meet. Repeat two more times. Remember to leave a bit of white space to give the illusion of separated petals.

Step 4: Using an even lighter wash of pigment, create larger and fatter curves around the outside.

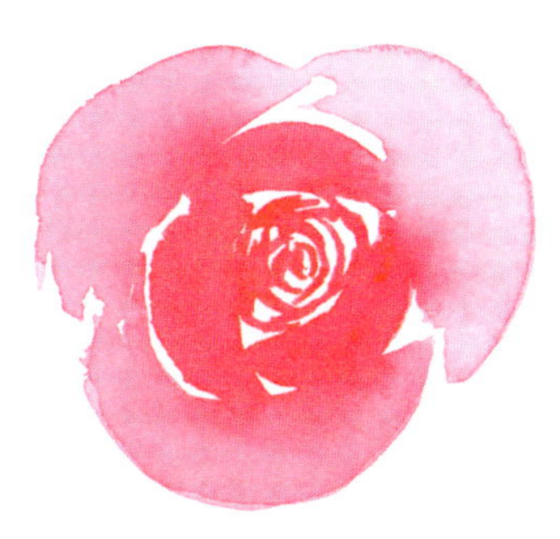

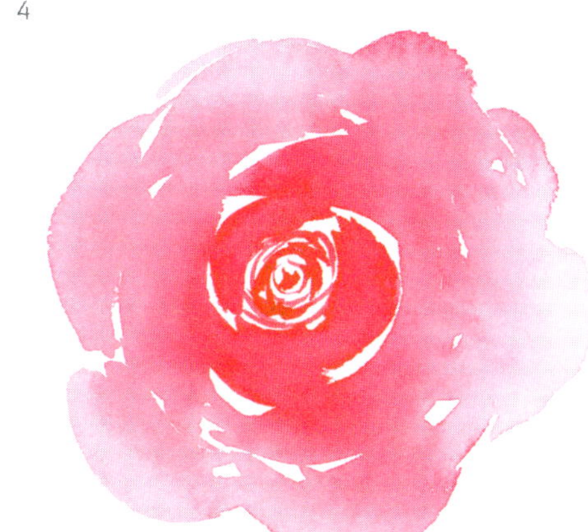

TIP

Do not create high-arched C-curves with lots of white space in between. Keep them close with white space and smaller-arched strokes.

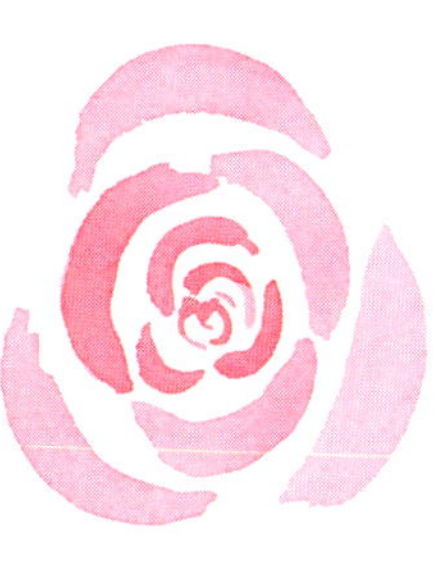

the peony

Techniques Used:

- Light wash
- Blending
- Wet-on-wet

Materials Needed:

- Watercolour paper
- Two paint colours
- Paper towel
- Round brush 6 or 12
- Clean jar of water

Paint Colours:

- Permanent Rose
- Cadmium Yellow

Colour Mixing Recipes:

- Permanent Rose and Cadmium Yellow 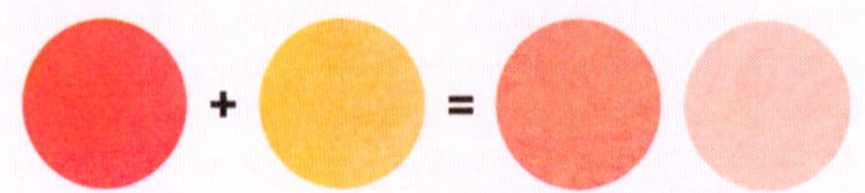

Step 1: Using a light wash, create a round petal shape. The tips of these petals do not have to be perfect; in fact, they look better when they have a bit of a jagged edge.

Step 2: To the right side of the petal, create another petal shape on an angle beside it. Have them touching slightly.

Step 3: Create two smaller, thicker C-curve-shaped petals on either side of the two centre petals. Add some scribble curved shapes over top of the petals, using light pressure and the tip of your brush.

Step 4: Next, add four messy C-curve petals over top of the peony. They should all be touching at least one area of another petal, leaving a bit of white space.

Step 5: Add some pigment onto your brush that is darker than your first light wash, and tap it to the base parts of the petals. This will create dimension. Make sure your first layer is wet before doing this, so you can get a nice seamless blend.

Step 6: Lastly, add some yellow dots to the thin curved lines in the centre of the Peony.

TIP

Leaving the right
amount of white space in
between each petal and the
next is crucial when creating
the flower. Leaving too much
white space can disconnect the
look of the flower, but leaving
too little can make the
flower lose its shape.

1

2

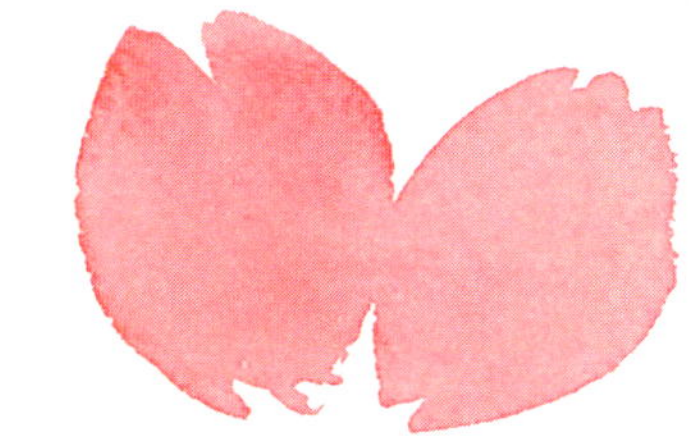

TIP

Don't get
frustrated;
just keep on
practicing.

3

4

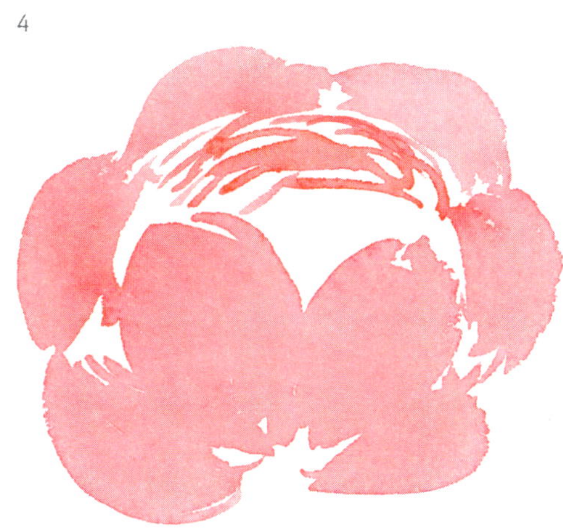

5

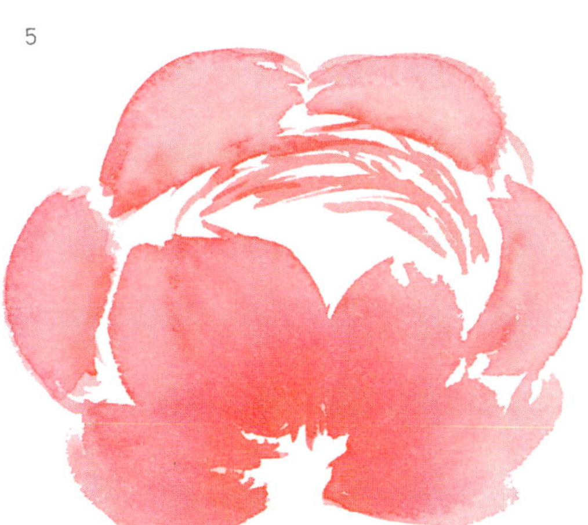

6

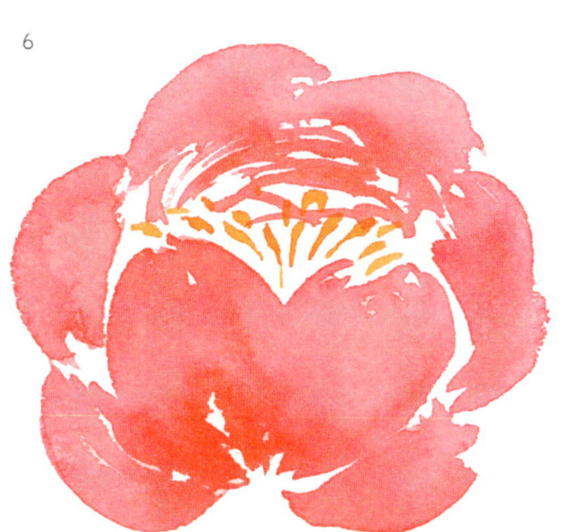

leaves

Techniques Used:

- Wet-on-wet
- Colour bleed

Materials Needed:

- Watercolour paper
- Round brush 6 or 12
- Two paint colours
- Clean jar of water
- Paper towel

Paint Colours:

- Sap Green
- Perylene Green

Step 1: Start by creating a long curved stem using the tip of your brush and light pressure. I started with the colour Sap Green for these leaves.

Step 2: At the top of the stem, create half of the leaf by using the "light pressure, heavy pressure, light pressure" stroke we learned back in chapter 2.

Step 3: Create the other half of the leaf by meeting the bottom of the first stroke at the base and curving your stroke to meet at the top.

Step 4: Create two more leaves, repeating these steps. Have them staggered down the stem.

Step 5: While the leaves are still wet, add a small amount of your darker green to the stem and the base of the leaves to give them depth.

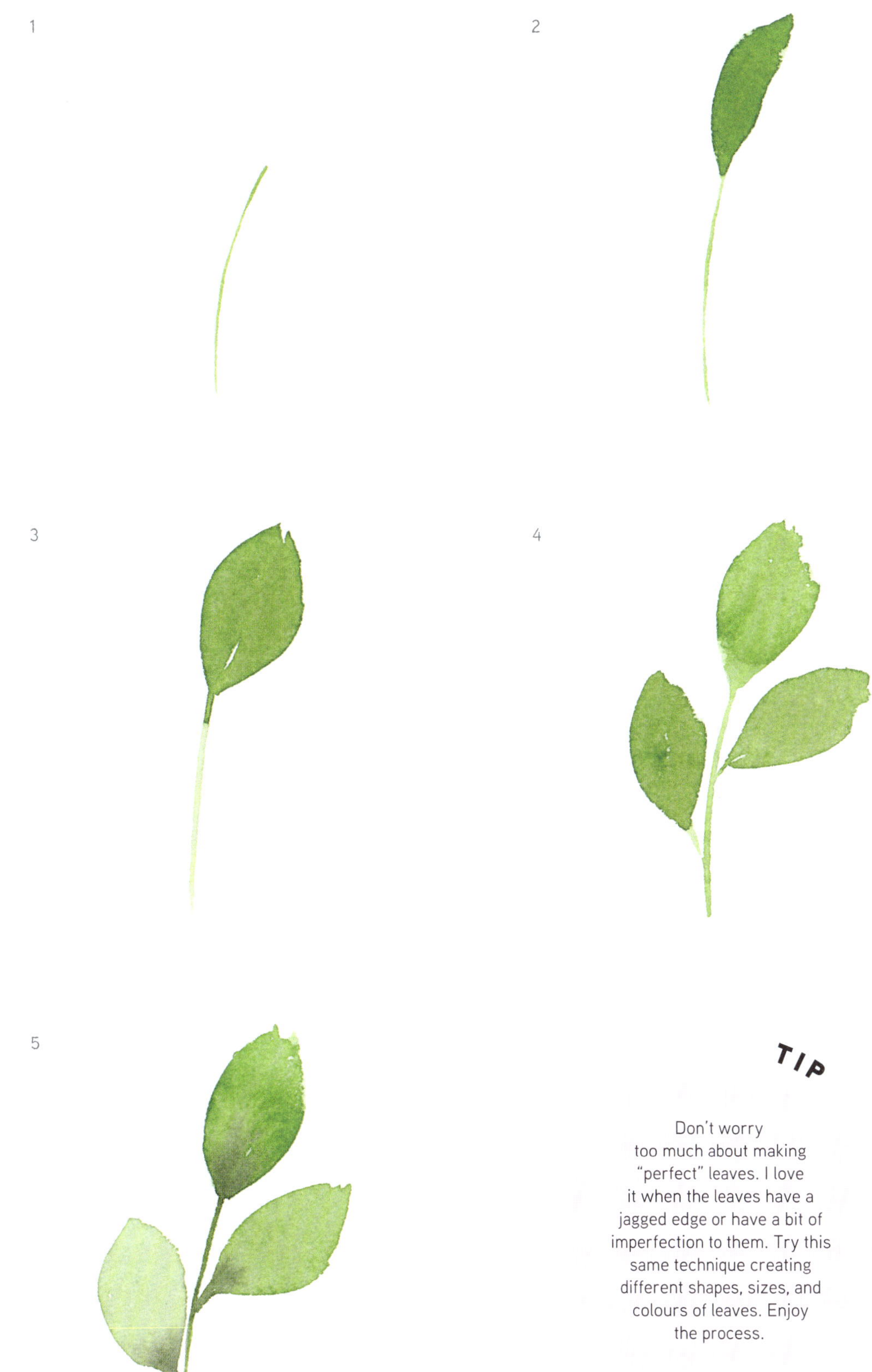

TIP

Don't worry
too much about making
"perfect" leaves. I love
it when the leaves have a
jagged edge or have a bit of
imperfection to them. Try this
same technique creating
different shapes, sizes, and
colours of leaves. Enjoy
the process.

a bouquet-putting it all together

Let's take what we have learned and put these loose florals together!

Techniques Used:

- Colour bleeds
- Wet-on-wet
- Light wash

Step 1: Create your peony and add some leaves to the bottom and the left of the flower. I enjoy it when the green leaves bleed into parts of the flower, so I make sure to add the leaves while the peony is still wet.

Step 2: Add your rose to the other side of the peony. Again, I love the look of a colour bleed, so I will add a small cluster of leaves to the side of the rose while it's still wet.

Step 3: Add some more leaves around the flowers in the bare spaces. Add different values and sizes of leaves to make the piece look more interesting.

TIP

Have the stems of leaves curving around the flowers, rather than sticking straight out. The bouquet will flow better, rather than looking stiff and rigid.

TIP

Working quickly on 100 percent cotton paper gives the best results when trying to achieve colour bleeds. Try not to get frustrated if the colour bleeds are not working as shown. It takes a lot of practice to understand how to keep your paper wet enough to allow this to happen effortlessly.

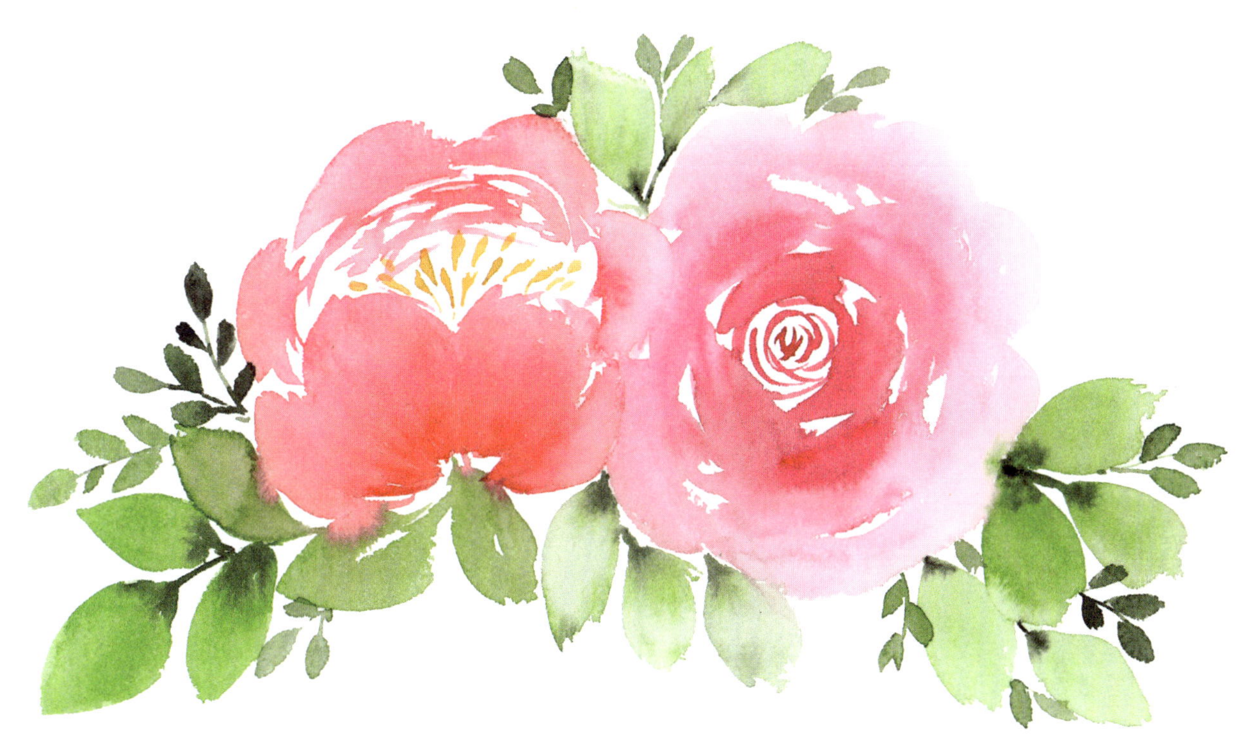

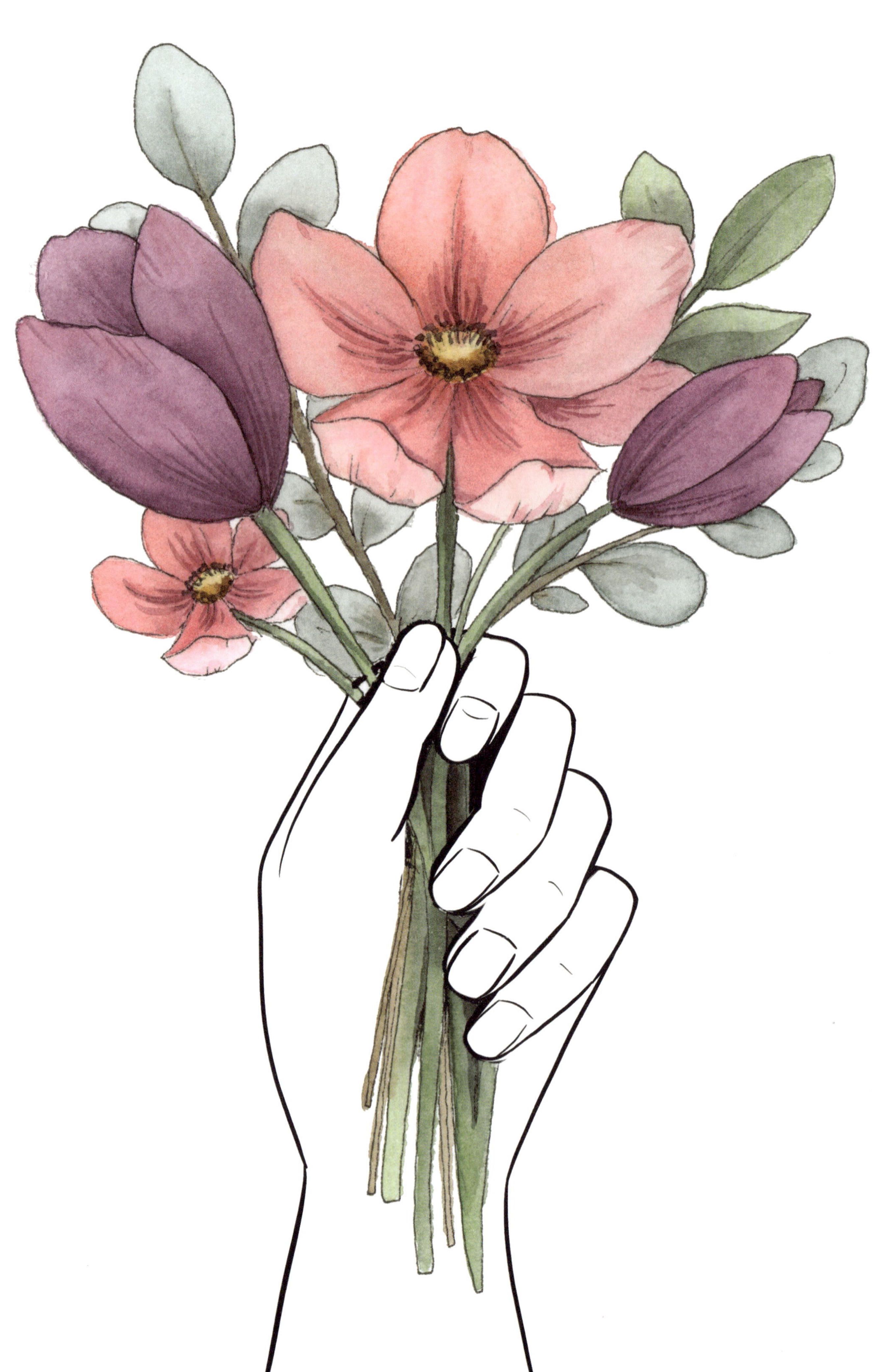

project two: detailed florals

Detailed florals are quite different than the previous lesson of loose style florals. While loose flowers all tend to be done in one quick motion, detailed work takes more time, more layers, and longer dry times. With this technique, you can take your time with each layer, rather than rushing to get the perfect colour bleeds. In this section, we will be painting two different detailed flowers and a stem with leaves. A major part of working with layers is working on blending and gradients. See Part III (starting on page 142) for tracing pages for some of these projects.

tulips

Techniques Used:

- Blending
- Dark-to-light gradient
- Wet-on-dry

Materials Needed:

- Watercolour paper
- Round brush 6 and 2
- Five paint colours
- Clean jar of water
- Paper towel

Paint Colours:

- Winsor Violet (Dioxazine)
- Permanent Rose
- Sap Green
- Perylene Green
- Cadmium Yellow

Colour Mixing Recipes:

- Winsor Violet (Dioxazine) and Permanent Rose

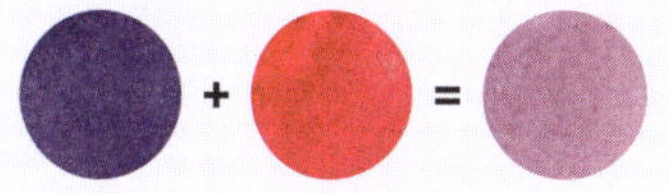

Step 1: Using your size 6 brush, start by painting a light wash of our purple and pink colour recipe over the whole heads of both tulips. Let it completely dry.

Step 2: Next, working on one flower at a time, paint a light layer of clean water over the centre petals of each tulip. While the petal is still wet, add some darker, saturated paint of our colour mixture to the base of the petal. Gradually move the colour upwards to create a dark-to-light gradient. If you see any harsh lines in the gradient, wash and dry off your brush, then use it to help the colour along and blend out those harsher edges. Because the petal on the first flower is smaller, it will most likely end up being a darker colour all over, which is perfectly fine. Let it dry completely.

Step 3: Again, working on one petal at a time, follow the same steps for the left petal in each flower. This time, while the petal is still wet, tap a small amount of pink to the top of the petal.

This should create a soft gradient from a pinkish purple to a dark purple on the petal. To achieve a soft gradient from one colour to the next, again, wash off your brush, dry it, and use it to help move the colours along.

Step 4: Repeat the previous step to the last petals. Make sure your previous step is dry first.

Step 5: Once dry, take your size 2 detail brush and create small, curved lines on the petals using the tip of your brush and light pressure. Make sure the lines curve with the shape of the petal.

Step 6: Paint a wash of Sap Green over both stems and leaves. Let completely dry.

Step 7: Working on each leaf individually, paint a medium-value wash over the full leaf with Sap Green. While it's still wet, add some darker green to the base of the leaf, and anywhere else the tulip petals may cast a shadow. Once dry, take your size 2 brush and the darker green to create some small, detailed line from the base of each leaf. Lastly, add a small amount of yellow to your green and fill in each tulip stem.

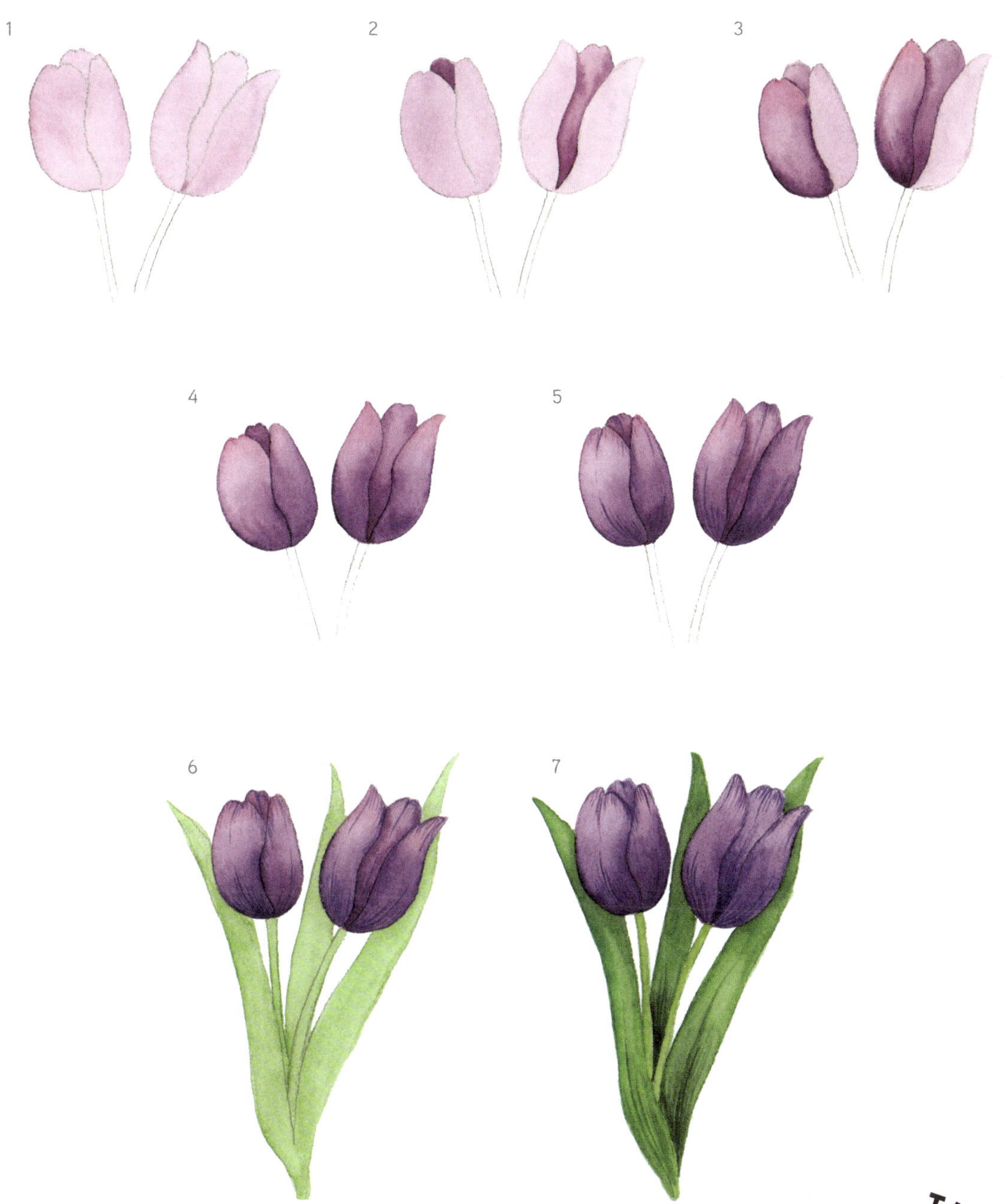

TIP

While blending out the colours, make sure there is no excess water in your brush; this will cause water to drop on the petal, creating water marks.

cosmos

Techniques Used:

- Light wash
- Blending
- Wet-on-dry

Materials Needed:

- Watercolour paper
- Round brush 6 and 2
- Four paint colours
- Clean jar of water
- Paper towel

Paint Colours:

- Permanent Rose
- Cadmium Yellow
- Sap Green
- Black

Colour Mixing Recipes:

- Permanent Rose and Sap Green
- Permanent Rose and Black

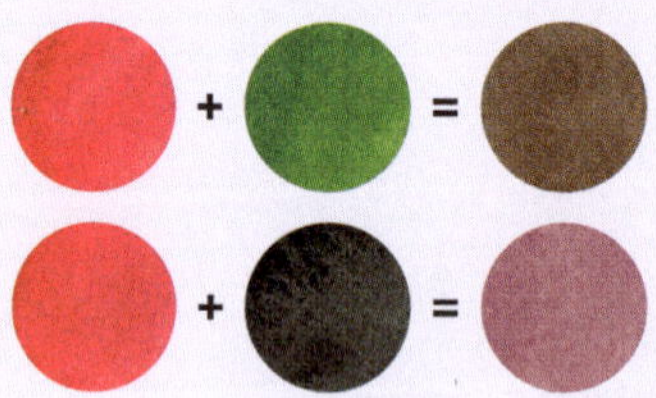

Step 1: Using your size 6 brush, paint a light wash of Permanent Rose over all the petals. Let it dry completely.

Step 2: Then, starting with three petals that are not touching each other and working on one petal at a time, paint a layer of clean water over the petal. While the petal is still wet, add some darker pigment to the base, gradually moving it toward the tip to create a dark-to-light gradient. If you find there is a harsh line, wash and dry off your brush and blend it out.

Step 3: Next, repeat the same step with the four remaining petals. Make sure to leave the undersides of the two bottom petals light. While adding the darker pigment, I like to drag a bit of it up the centre to create a bit more depth. Let dry completely.

Step 4: Once all the petals are dry, grab your size 2 brush and pick up a medium wash of the pink. Using the tip of your brush and light pressure, create small delicate lines from the base of the petals and the top of the petals. Make sure your lines are following the curve of the petal.

Step 5: Next, add some Cadmium Yellow to the centre of the flower. Then tap a small amount of your brown mixture along the bottom of the stamen while it's still wet to create a shadow. Once dry, grab a small amount of the dark pink mixture and add smaller textured lines on the petals around the stamen, and a few on the tips of the petals.

Step 6: Take a small amount of black on your brush and create tiny lines around the stamen, and add a bit of darkness to the underside of the stamen to create a deeper shadow. Next, saturate your brush with yellow pigment and create some dots on top of the small black lines of the stamen.

Step 7: Lastly, paint your flower stem with a light wash of Sap Green. Add some darker pigment of green to one side of the stem to create a bit of a shadow.

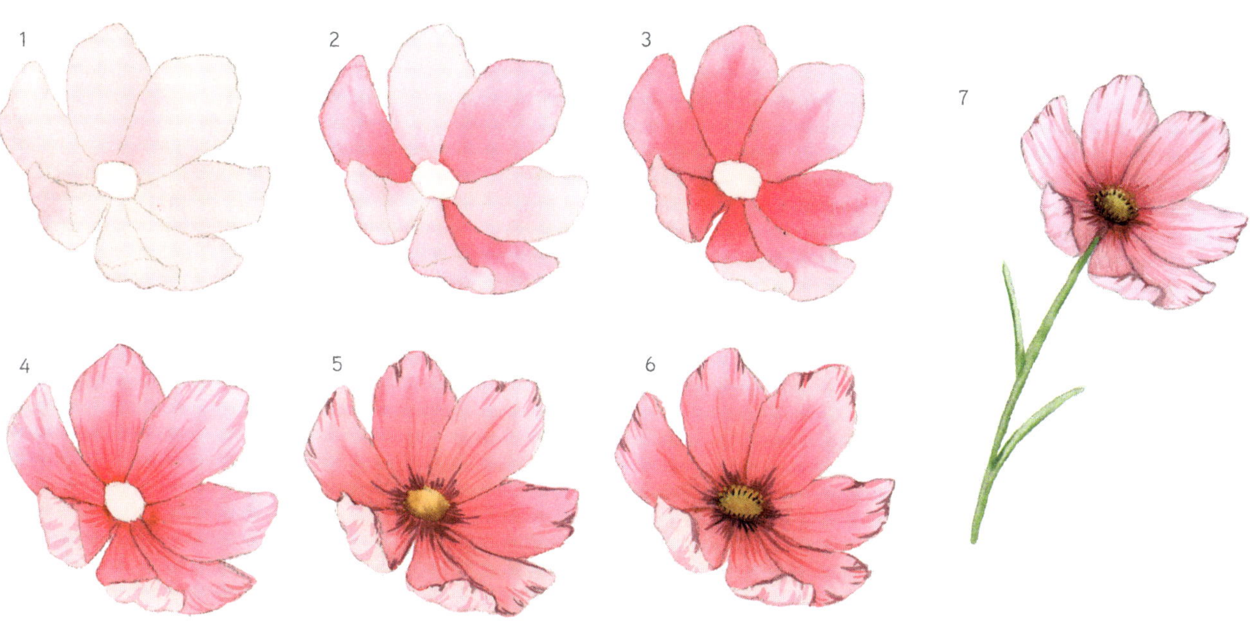

eucalyptus

Techniques Used:

- Light wash
- Blending
- Wet-on-dry
- Colour bleed

Materials Needed:

- Watercolour paper
- Round brush size 6
- Three paint colours
- Clean jar of water
- Paper towel

Paint Colours:

- Winsor Violet (Dioxazine)
- Hooker's Green
- Phthalo Turquoise
- Burnt Umber

Colour Mixing Recipes:

- Winsor Violet (Dioxazine), Hooker's Green, and Phthalo Turquoise

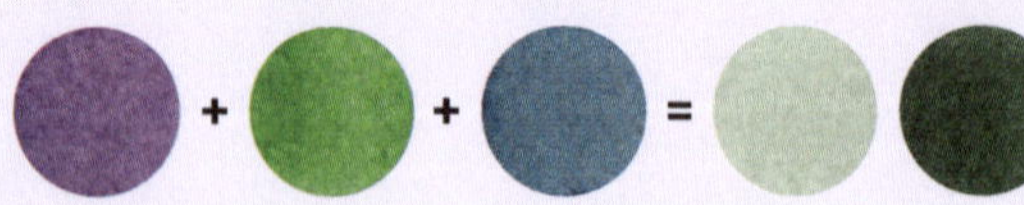

Step 1: Use a light wash of your eucalyptus colour mixture to paint all the leaves. Let them fully dry.

Step 2: Working on one leaf at a time, paint the leaf with a clean base of water. Next, tap a darker value of the colour to the base and the tip of the leaf. I like to drag a line up the middle for more definition. Blend out any harsh edges between the light and dark washes. If any two leaves are touching, wait till one of the leaves dries, so they don't bleed together. Notice that I have added a darker wash to the leaves that are slightly behind another.

Step 3: Lastly, with your size 2 brush, add a wash of Burnt Umber to the stem using the tip of your brush and light pressure. Once dry, then add a darker wash to one side of the stem to create a shadow.

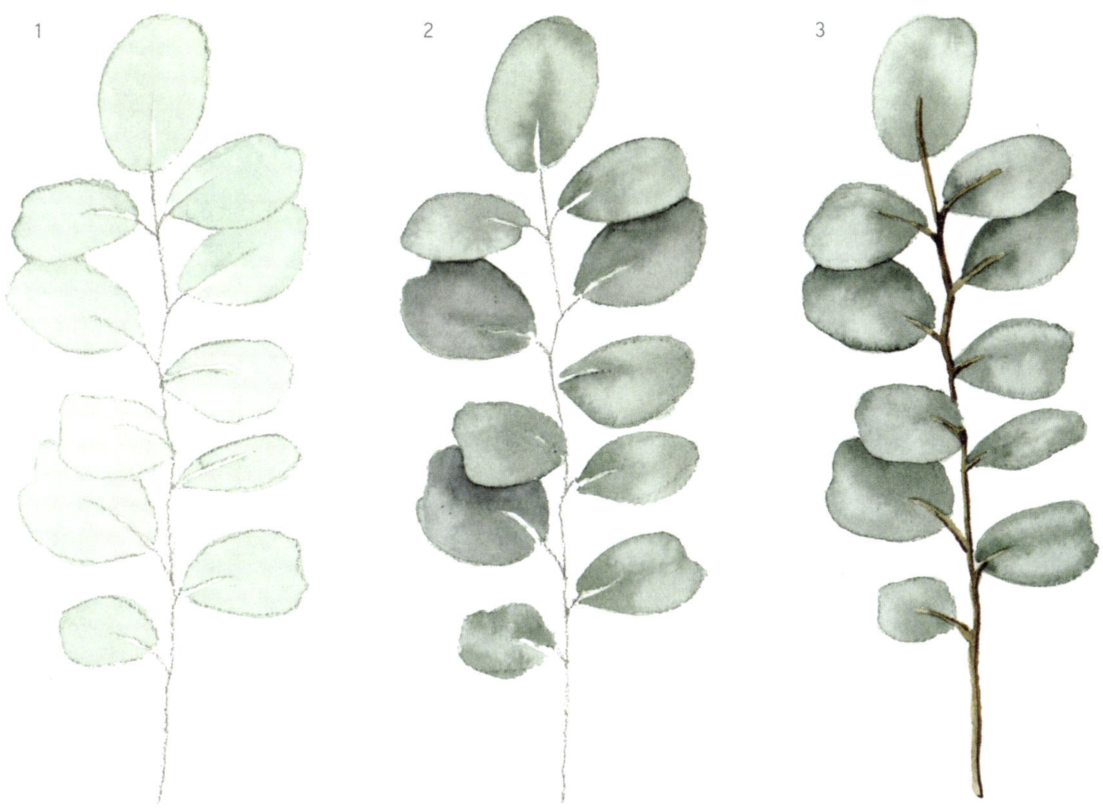

project three: trees

Trees are a lot of fun to and relaxing to paint. They also come in different shapes that we will explore. When painting the following trees, loosen your grip on your paint brush and have fun with it.

DIFFERENT TREE SHAPES

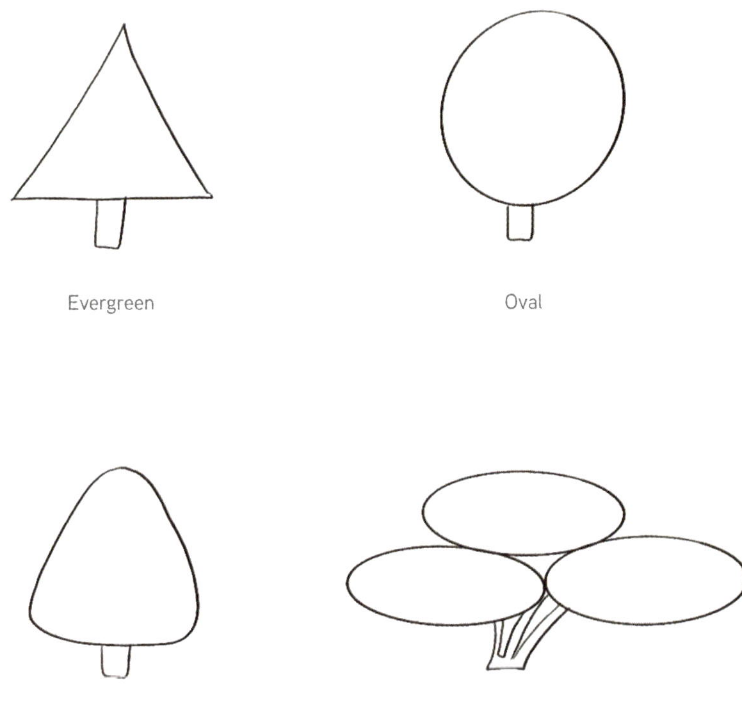

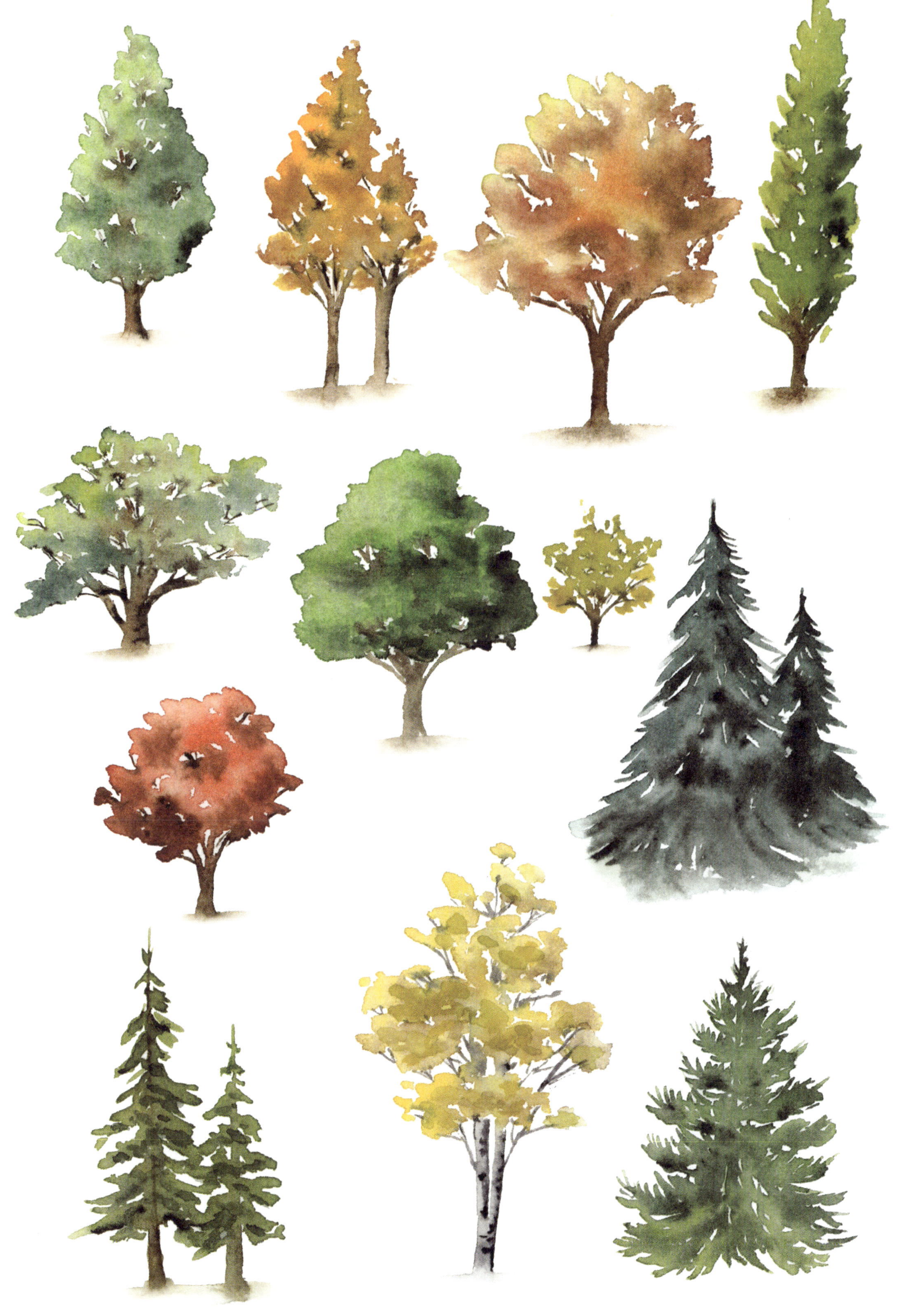

evergreen tree

Techniques Used:

- Wet-on-wet

Materials Needed:

- Watercolour paper
- Round brush size 6
- Two paint colours
- Clean jar of water
- Paper towel

Paint Colours:

- Winsor Violet (Dioxazine)
- Hooker's Green

Colour Mixing Recipes:

- Winsor Violet (Dioxazine) and Hooker's Green

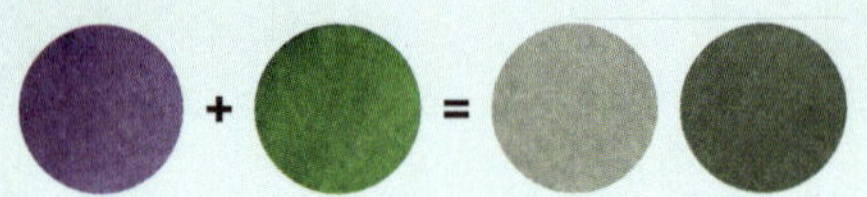

Step 1: Using the tip of your brush and light pressure, paint a line using a light wash of your green mixture. Continuing to use light pressure and the tip of your brush, create small V shapes at the top of the line. Try not to make them look too perfect or symmetrical.

Step 2: Start to paint angled tree branches moving down the trunk. The branches should have a slight curve to them. Then create wispy lines coming off the branches. The branches toward the top of the tree should be shorter and gradually get longer as you move down the tree.

Step 3: Finish the shape of the tree following the previous steps. As you reach the bottom, have some of the branches pointing down.

Step 4: While the full tree is still wet, take some darker pigment and add it to the undersides of the branches to create a shadow effect all over the tree. Make sure to have some of the darker shade in the middle of the tree, so it looks like branches are coming out from all angles of the tree, rather than just the sides.

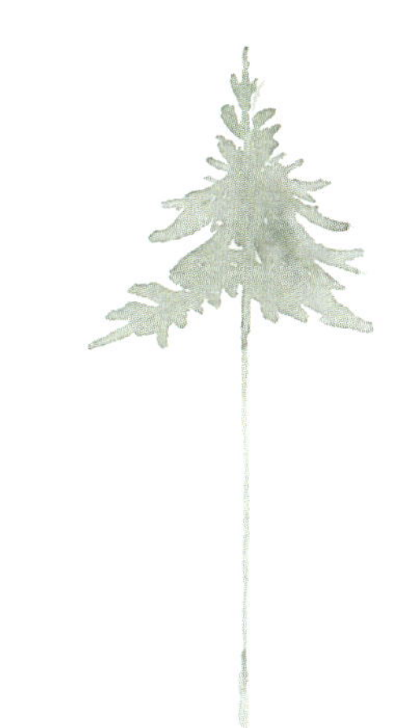

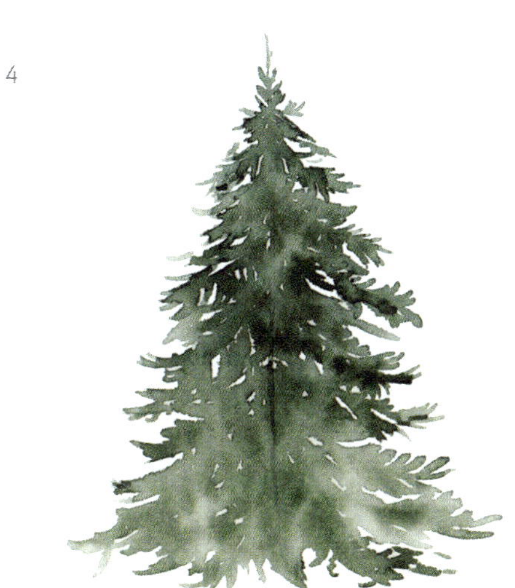

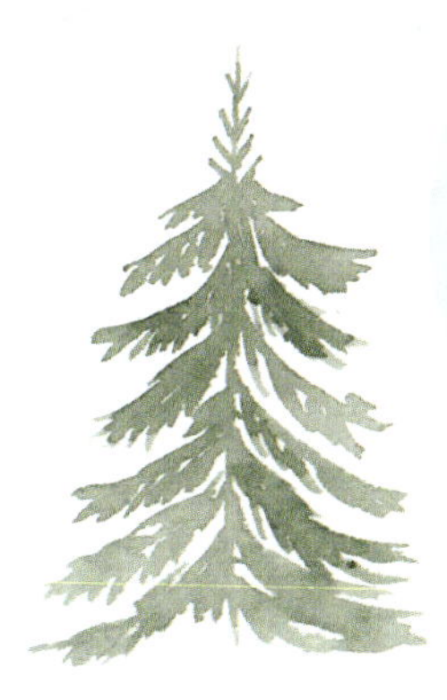

When painting your tree,
try not to leave too much
white space between branches
or have them be too symmetrical.
Trees are not perfect and have a
lot of asymmetries; embrace their
imperfections. Fill in those white
spaces by having some branches
coming down in front at
all angles.

oval-shaped tree

For this technique, I like to have my size 6 round brush on a forty-five-degree angle. You can choose whatever colour you'd like to paint your trees.

Techniques Used:

- Wet-on-wet
- Wet-on-dry

Materials Needed:

- Watercolour paper
- Round brush size 6
- Three or four paint colours
- Clean jar of water
- Paper towel

Paint Colours:

- Sap Green
- Perylene Green
- Burnt Umber

Step 1: Start by painting small dabbing and scrubbing marks into an oval shape using a light wash of Sap Green. Make sure to leave some small white spaces throughout the tree. Have some smaller dab marks coming out of the oval shape to create a bit more asymmetry.

Step 2: While the first wash is still wet, using the wet-on-wet technique, add a darker value of Sap Green to one side of the tree, horizontally along the middle, and along the bottom of the tree. Then, while still wet, take your darkest green and do the same. This will create the illusion of a shadow.

Step 3: Once the tree is completely dry, take some Burnt Umber and create your tree trunk. Using the tip of your brush, have some thinner branches coming out the side and running throughout the tree. To add some definition, take a darker value of the brown, or mix in a bit of black, and add some darker shadows down one side of the trunk.

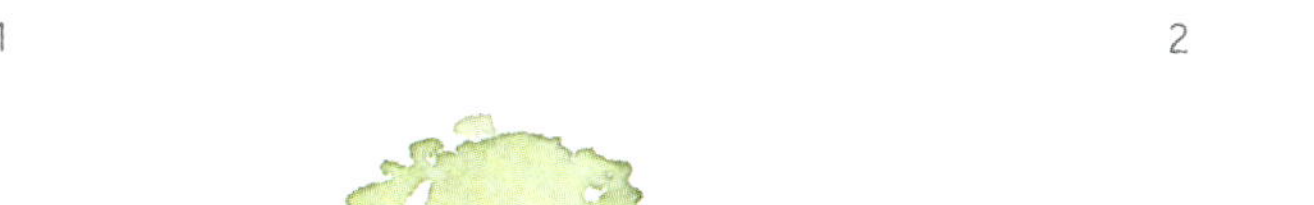

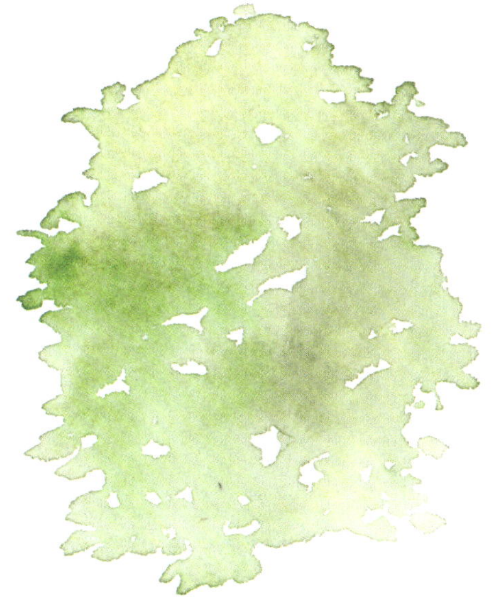

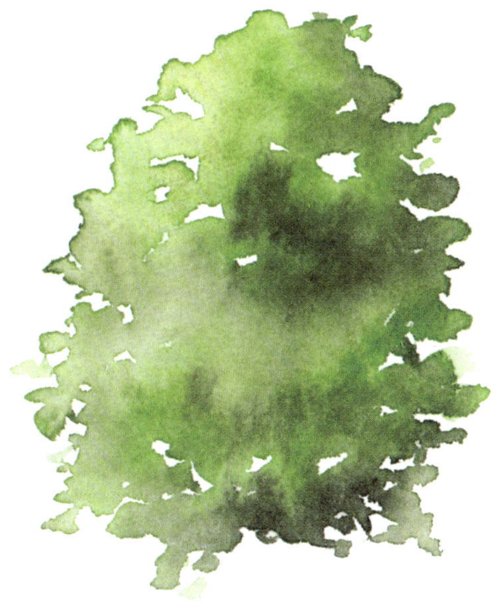

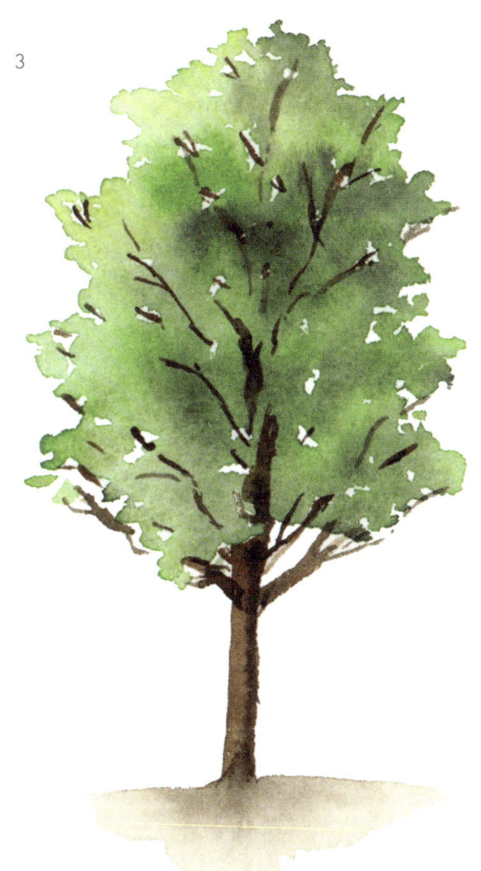

cone-shaped tree

For this tree, you will use the same technique as used for the Oval-Shaped Tree. I find my size 6 round brush on a forty-five-degree angle works best. Again, you can choose whatever colour you'd like to paint your trees. For the example, I used the following:

Paint Colours:

- Cadmium Yellow
- Yellow Ochre
- Burnt Umber
- Black

Step 1: Paint small dabbing and scrubbing marks into a cone shape using a light wash mixture of Cadmium Yellow. Make sure to leave some small white spaces throughout the tree. Create some smaller dab marks coming out of the cone shape to create a bit more asymmetry.

Step 2: While the first wash is still wet, using the wet-on-wet technique, add some Yellow Ochre to one side of the tree, horizontally along the middle, and along the bottom of the tree in three sections. Then take your Burnt Umber and do the same.

Step 3: Once the tree is completely dry, take a light wash of black to create a light grey and create your tree trunk. Add some small black lines on the trunk to emulate a birch tree trunk. Using the tip of your brush and a medium wash of grey, have some thinner branches coming out of the side and running throughout the tree.

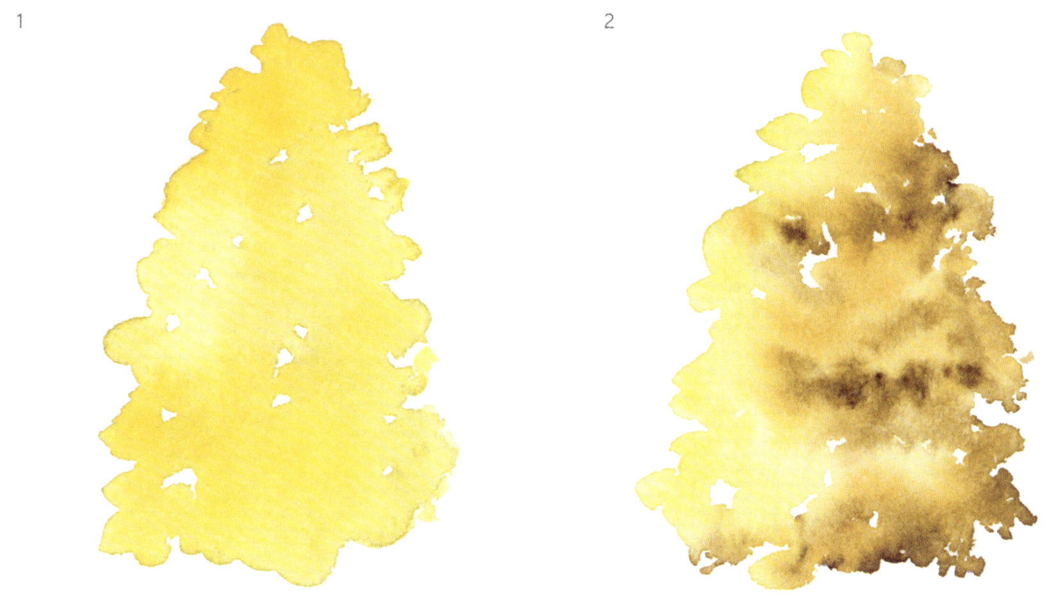

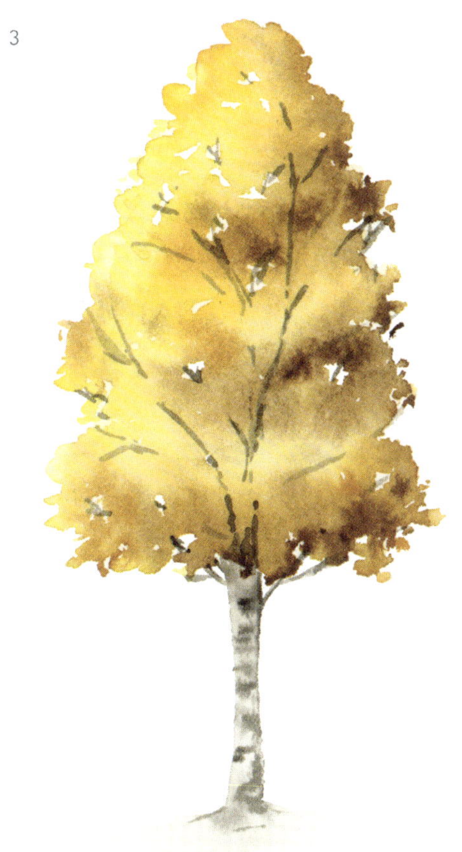

long-shaped tree

For this tree, you will use the same technique as used for the Oval- and Cone-Shaped Trees. I find my size 6 round brush on a forty-five-degree angle works best. Again, you can choose whatever colour you'd like to paint your trees. For the example, I used the following:

Paint Colours:

- Sap Green
- Perylene Green
- Burnt Umber

Step 1: Paint small dabbing and scrubbing marks into an elongated tree shape using a light wash mixture of Sap Green. Make sure to leave some small white spaces throughout the tree. Create some smaller dab marks coming out of the tree shape to create a bit more asymmetry.

Step 2: While the first wash is still wet, using the wet-on-wet technique, add some more pigmented medium green to one side of each of the three oval shapes. Then take your darker green and do the same.

Step 3: Once the tree is completely dry, use some brown to create your tree trunk. With this tree, I decided to paint multiple trunks. Next, add a darker wash of brown, or mix it a bit with black, to create a shadow down one side of the trunks. Using the tip of your brush, have some thinner branches coming out the side and running throughout the tree.

1

3

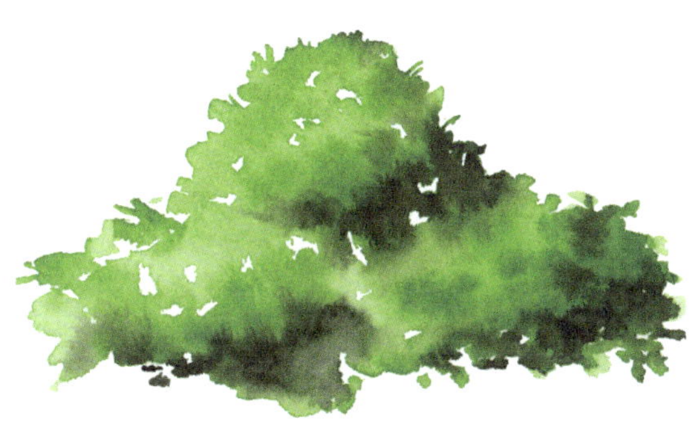

5

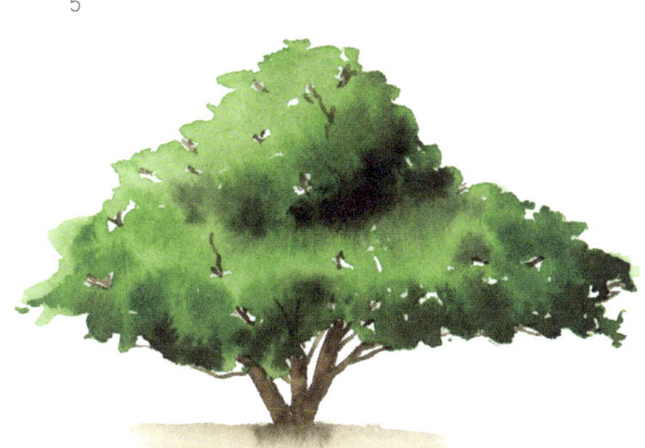

project four: plants

In this section, we will be painting potted house plants. Please feel free to switch it up and use your own creativity to create fun patterns, shapes, and colours for the pots! See Part III (starting on page 142) for tracing pages for this project.

cactus

Techniques Used:

- Wet-on-wet
- Wet-on-dry

Materials Needed:

- Watercolour paper
- Round brush size 6
- Seven paint colours (modify colours with what you have)
- White ink (I used Dr. Ph Martin's Bleedproof White ink. Other great options are a white gel pen or white gouache)
- Clean jar of water
- Paper towel

Paint Colours:

- Sap Green
- Phthalo Turquoise
- Payne's Grey
- Permanent Rose
- Hooker's Green Dark
- Burnt Umber

Colour Mixing Recipes:

- Permanent Rose and Hooker's Green Dark 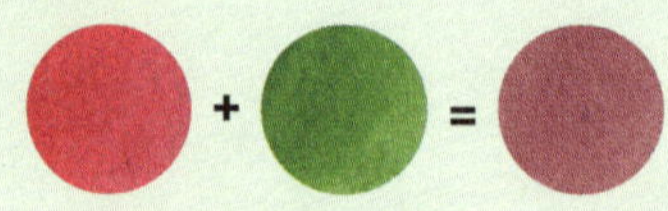

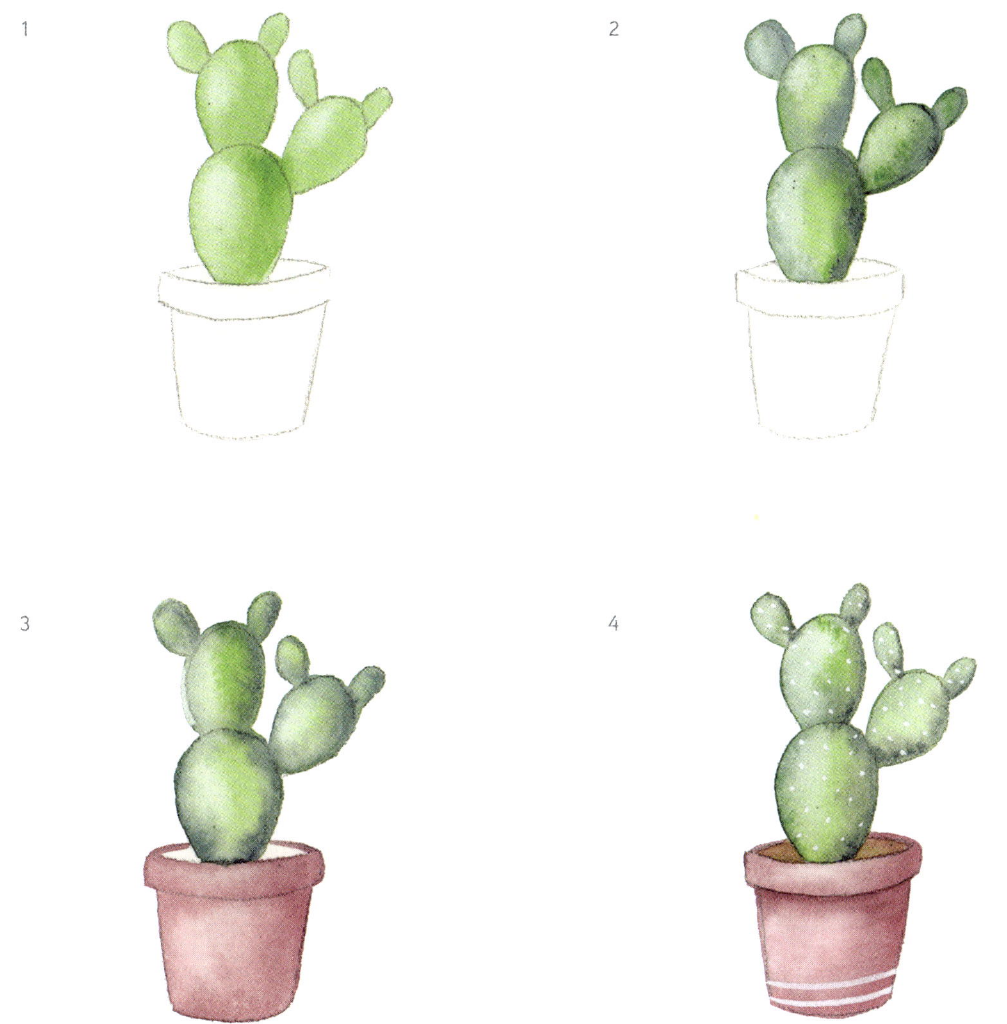

Step 1: Paint a light wash of Sap Green all over the cactus. While it's still wet, add a slightly more pigmented wash of Sap Green to the right side of the cactus.

Step 2: While the cactus is still wet from the previous step, tap a small amount of Phthalo Turquoise along the left side of the cactus, and tap a small amount of Payne's Grey along the right side of the cactus.

Step 3: Once our cactus is dry, paint a light wash all over the pot, using our colour recipe mixture. While still wet, add a darker value of the mixture to the right side of the pot to create a bit of shadow.

Step 4: Once everything is dry, paint the soil in the pot using Burnt Umber. Lastly, add some detail to your pot and cactus. I used my white ink to add dots to the cactus and lines along the pot. I also added a darker shadow under the lip of the pot, then blended it out to add a bit more depth.

monstera plant

Techniques Used:

- Wet-on-wet
- Wet-on-dry

Materials Needed:

- Watercolour paper
- Round brush sizes 6 and 2
- Four paint colours (modify colours with what you have)
- White ink (I used Dr. Ph Martin's Bleed-proof White ink. Other great options are a white gel pen or white gouache)
- Clean jar of water
- Paper towel

Paint Colours:

- Sap Green
- Perylene Green
- Payne's Grey
- Burnt Umber

Step 1: Working on one leaf at a time, paint a medium wash of Sap Green all over the leaf. While it's still wet, take your Perylene Green and paint around the outline of the leaf. This will create a beautiful wet-on-wet effect.

Step 2: Once all the leaves are painted and dry, fill in your stems with dark green. Then take your Payne's Grey and paint a light wash all over the pot. While it's still wet, add a darker value of the grey to the right side, and around the base and lip of the pot. Let it dry completely.

Step 3: Paint the soil in the pot brown. Lastly, add some detail to the leaves and pot. I took my size 2 brush and some dark green to paint some thin lines for the veins of the leaves. Then I used my white ink to add some fun patterns to the pot.

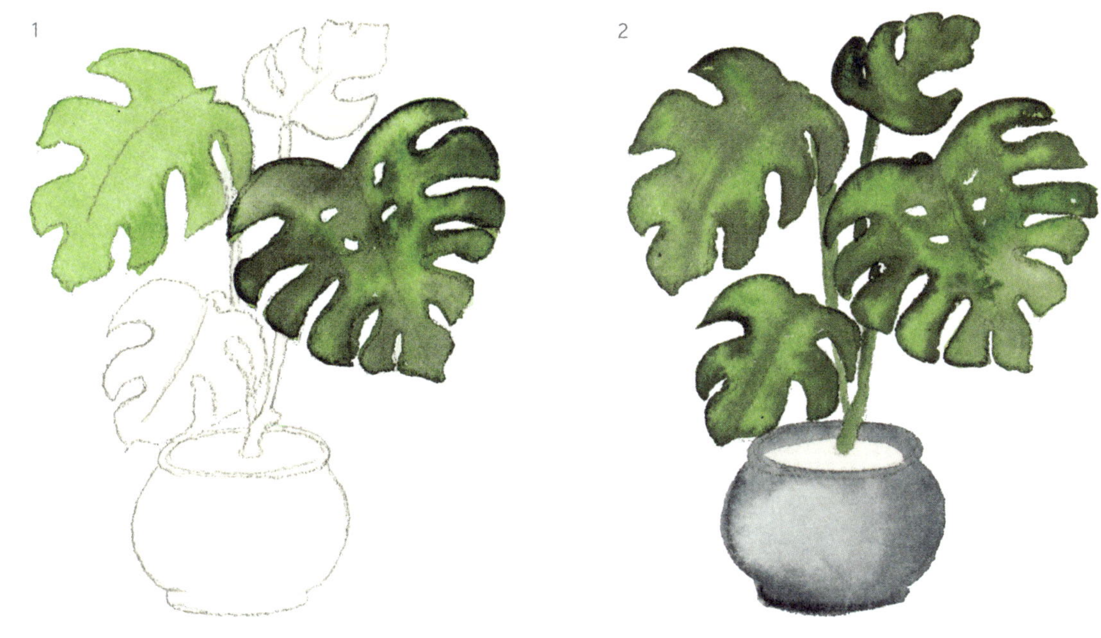

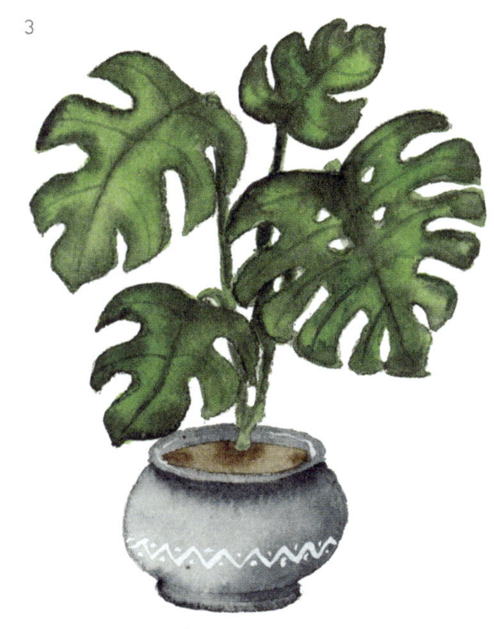

snake plant

Techniques Used:

- Wet-on-wet
- Wet-on-dry

Materials Needed:

- Watercolour paper
- Round brush size 6
- Six paint colours (modify colours with what you have)
- White ink (I used Dr. Ph Martin's Bleed-proof White ink. Other great options are a white gel pen or white gouache)
- Clean jar of water
- Paper towel

Paint Colours:

- Sap Green
- Cadmium Yellow
- Perylene Green
- Winsor Red
- Burnt Umber
- Black

Colour Mixing Recipes:

- Cadmium Yellow and Sap Green

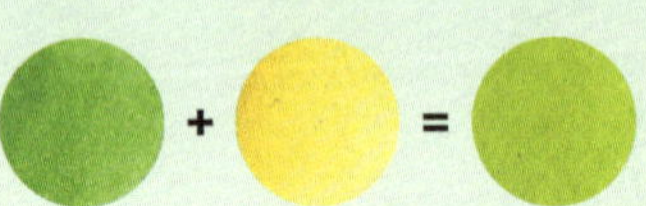

- Winsor Red and Burnt Umber

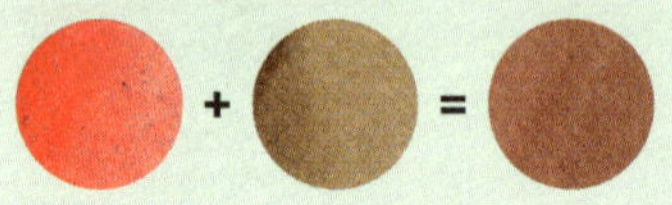

Step 1: Using our yellow and green mixture, paint a light wash over all the leaves. Let dry.

Step 2: Painting one leaf at a time, paint an inner wash of Sap Green, leaving a border of the first colour around the leaf. This will create separation between the leaves. While the Sap Green is still wet, take a small amount of Perylene Green and tap some lines horizontally across the leaf.

Step 3: Using a light wash of our red and brown colour recipe, paint the pot all over. Then tap a darker value of the colour to the right side of the pot. Let it dry completely.

Step 4: Lastly, create some detail on the pot. I added a bit of a darker pigment to the inside of the pot for some shadow. I then added some black and white detailed lines on the pot.

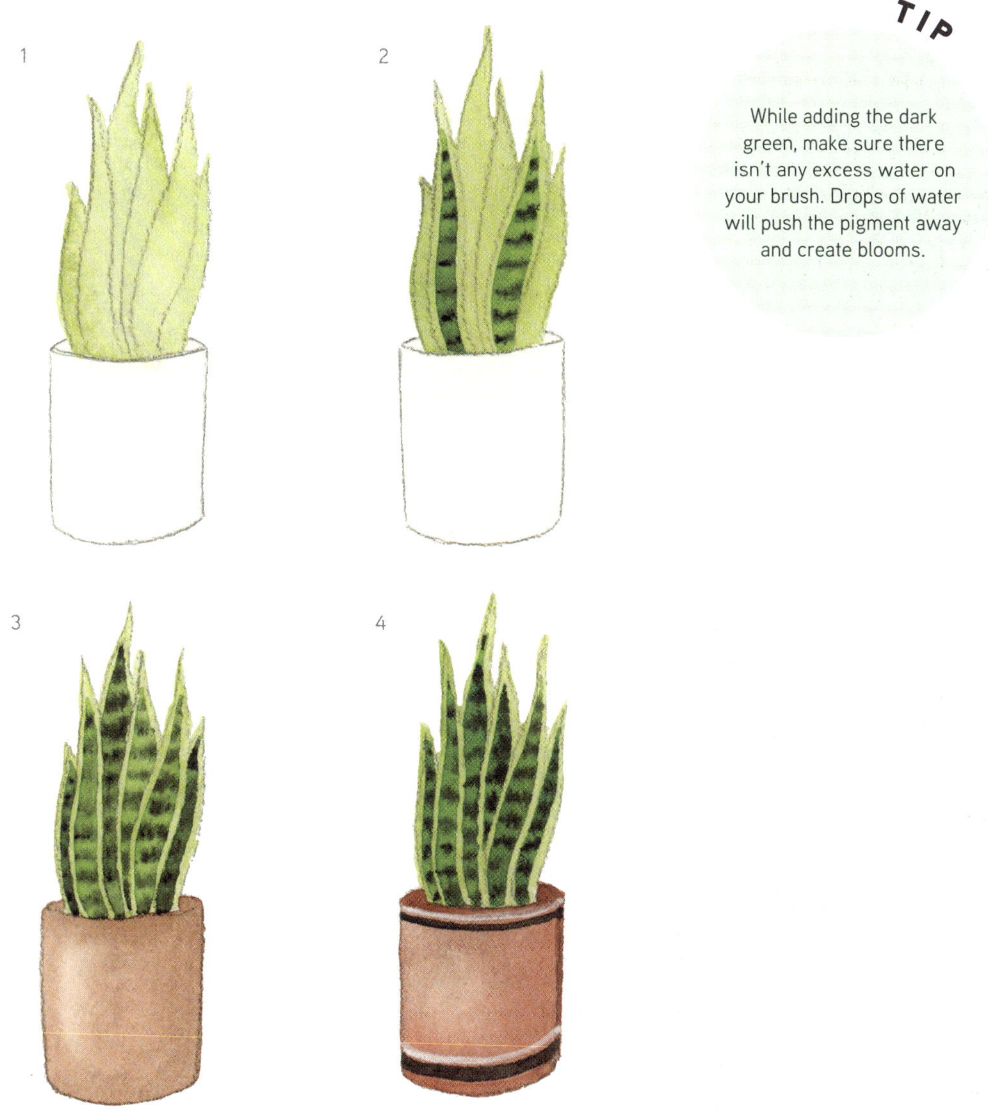

TIP

While adding the dark green, make sure there isn't any excess water on your brush. Drops of water will push the pigment away and create blooms.

chapter 7

LANDSCAPES

project one: snowy forest

Techniques Used:

- Dark-to-light gradient
- Wet-on-wet
- Wet-on-dry
- Blending

Materials Needed:

- Watercolour paper
- Wash brush, round brush size 6
- One paint colour (modify colours with what you have)
- White ink (I used Dr. Ph Martin's Bleed-proof White ink. Other great options are a white gel pen or white gouache)
- Clean jar of water
- Paper towel

Paint Colour:

- Payne's Grey

Step 1: Using your wash brush, take some clean water and wet the background two-thirds of the way down with your wash brush. Then take your Payne's Grey colour and create a dark-to-light gradient for the sky. I like to start at the top with the most saturated dark value, and then slowly move it down toward the horizon line. If you feel there is too much of the saturated colour moving toward the horizon line, wipe your paint brush off on your paper towel and take off some of that colour.

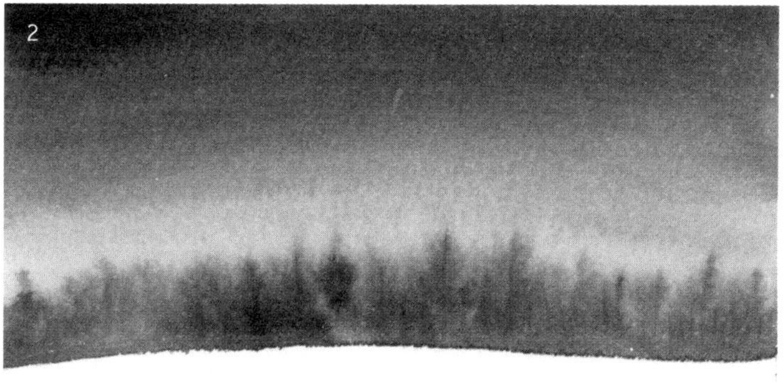

Step 2: While the sky is still wet, pick up some darker saturated colour on your size 6 round brush. Create some evergreen tree shapes in the background, close together. Because your sky is still wet, the trees will look fuzzy and out of focus. Don't focus too much on the detail of these background trees, as they will most likely blur together. Leave to dry.

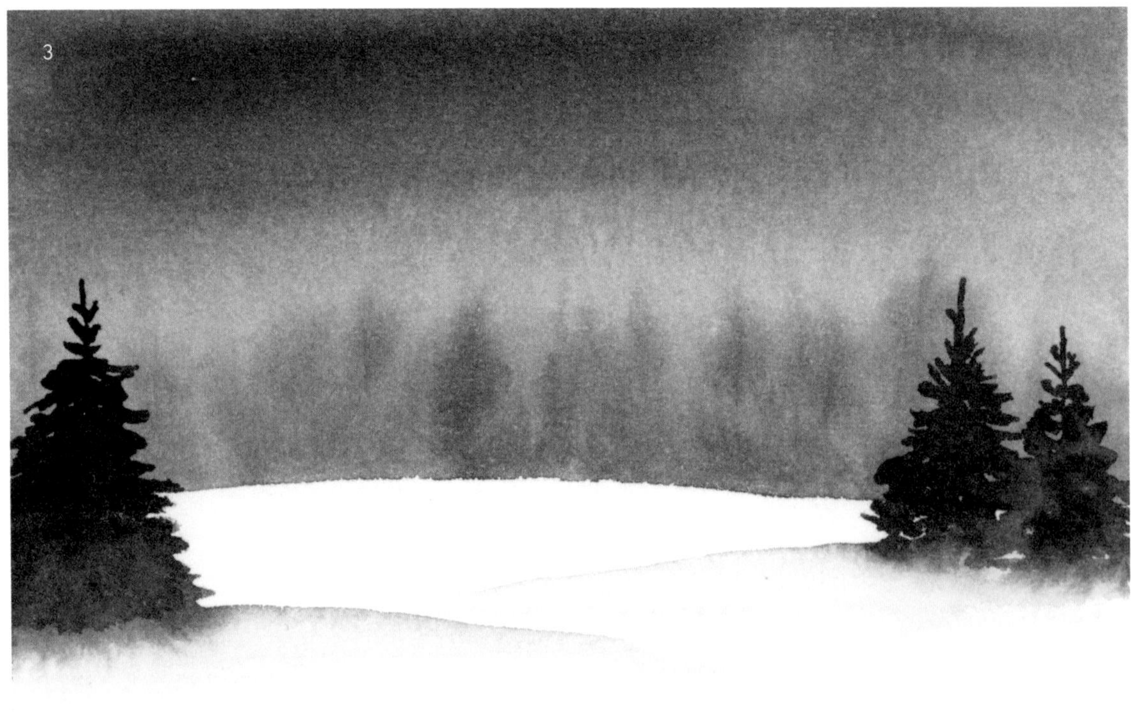

Step 3: Once the background is completely dry, pick up some more of the darkest value of your Payne's Grey colour. Create two trees to the right side of the painting that fall just below the horizon line. This will create a middle ground. While the two trees are still wet, wash and dry off your brush and slightly touch the bottom of the trees, then drag toward the middle of the painting. Some of the colour will bleed out into the snow and create a light wash of shadow appearing underneath the trees. Do the same thing on the left side, creating one tree that is slightly farther down than the last two. This will give the illusion of the single tree being in the foreground. Create the same shadow line, dragging it to the middle underneath the ones above.

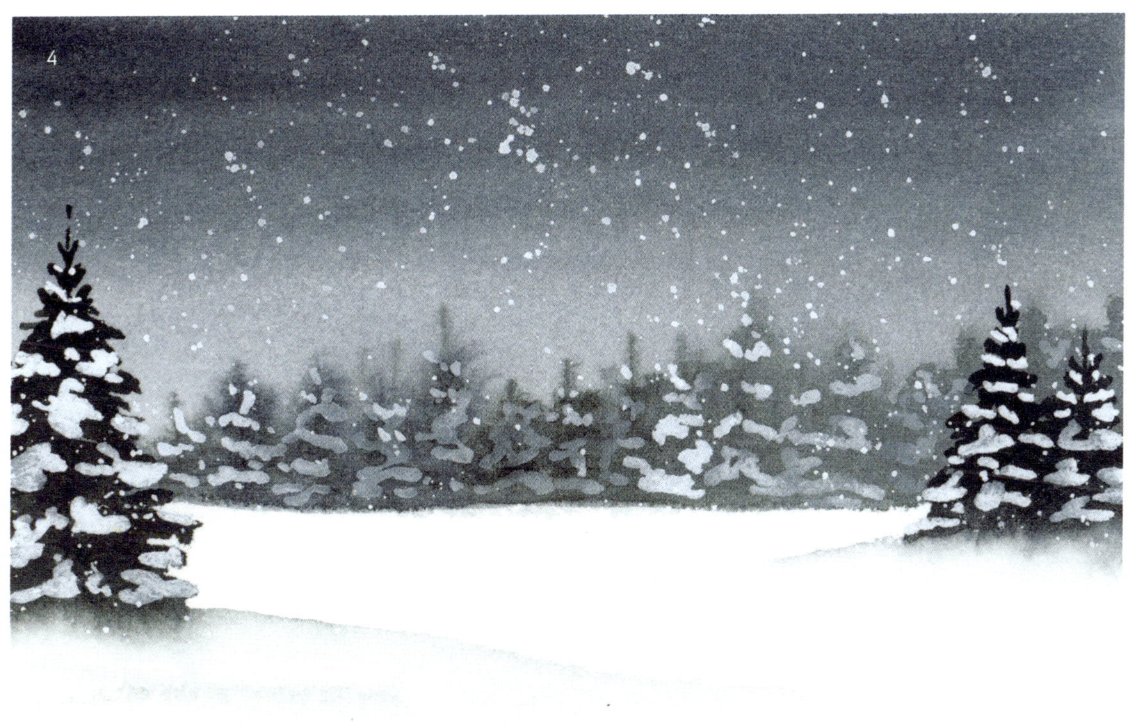

Step 4: Using some of your white ink, create some snowfall strokes on the background trees by loosely dabbing your brush. I added a bit more water to my ink to make it less opaque. Next, use a more pigmented wash of white ink on your brush to make it more opaque, and add some loose snowfall strokes to the trees in the foreground. Lastly, flick your brush to create some splatter marks all over the painting. This will add a snowfall effect.

project two: sunset field

Techniques Used:

- Blending
- Wet-on-wet
- Wet-on-dry
- Dropping water

Materials Needed:

- Watercolour paper
- Wash brush, round brush sizes 2 and 12
- Six paint colours (modify colours with what you have)
- White ink (I used Dr. Ph Martin's Bleed-proof White ink. Other great options are a white gel pen or white gouache)
- Clean jar of water
- Paper towel

Paint Colours:

- Cadmium Yellow
- Permanent Rose
- Cobalt Blue
- Sap Green
- Perylene Green
- Cadmium Orange

Step 1: Start by wetting the background two-thirds of the way down the paper with some clean water and your wash brush. While still wet, pick up some yellow paint with your size 12 round brush, apply it to the horizon line, and gradually move it to the middle of the sky. Next, add some Permanent Rose and dab it to either side of your sky by moving your brush in a soft and loose movement from side to side. Then take some Cobalt Blue and apply it to the top of the sky, gradually moving it down to meet the yellow. Try not to mix the yellow and the blue, but rather have them slightly touch. To achieve a seamless gradient, wash and dry off your brush to slowly blend. Continue to take some more pink and add it to the top of the sky, mixing with the blue to create a light purple. Take some more of that light purple mix and add to the bottom of the middle pink strokes. The trick to having this beautiful gradient from one colour to the next is making sure you don't have a lot of water or pigment on your brush. Remove any excess water or paint by consistently dabbing your brush on your paper towel.

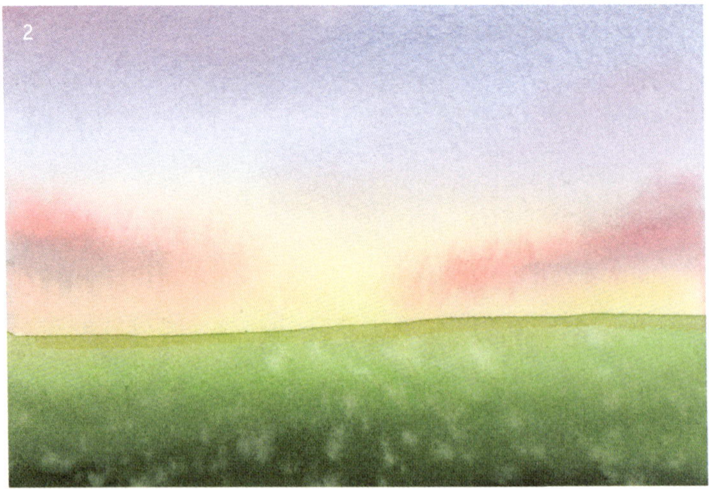

Step 2: Once the sky is completely dry, paint the bottom half using Sap Green. While still wet, add a small amount of Cadmium Orange to where the grass meets the sky. Then, take some dark green and add it to the foreground of the grass. This should create a gradient of a light greenish orange into a dark green. While still wet, take some clean water on your brush and flick some water splatter marks onto the grass. The clean water droplets will push the pigment away and create some beautiful white, out of focus splatters. Leave to dry completely.

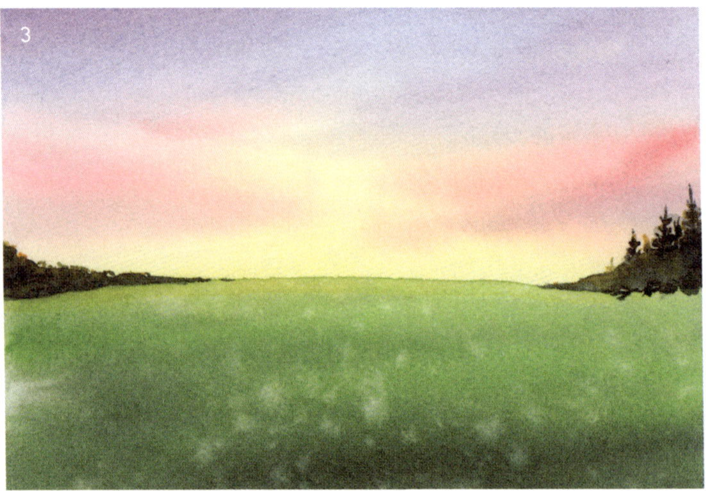

Step 3: Using your size 2 brush and your dark green, paint some tiny trees to both the left and right sides of the landscape. I also added a small amount of orange by mixing Permanent Rose and Cadmium Yellow to add some light from the sunset hitting the trees.

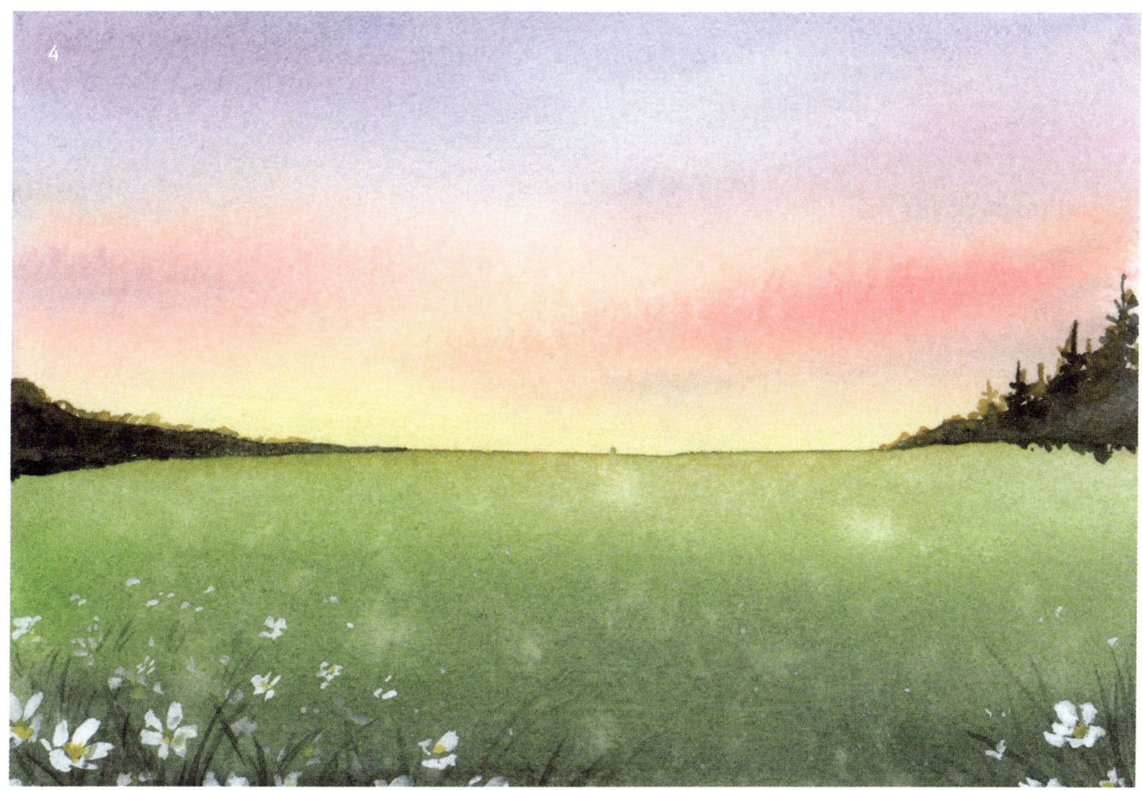

Step 4: Lastly, take your white ink and create some daisies in the foreground of the field. Daisies that are closest to the bottom of the page should be the largest, and any others behind should gradually get smaller to show depth. I then added some small yellow dots to the centres of the white petals and some thin green lines to create grass and stems.

project three: the beach

Techniques Used:

- Blotting/lifting
- Blending colour gradient
- Dropping water
- Wet-on-dry

Materials Needed:

- Watercolour paper
- Round brush sizes 6 and 12
- Five paint colours (modify colours with what you have)
- Clean jar of water

Paint Colours:

- Cobalt Blue
- Sap Green
- Phthalo Turquoise
- Burnt Umber
- Yellow Ochre

Colour Mixing Recipes:

- Phthalo Turquoise and Sap Green

- Yellow Ochre and Burnt Umber

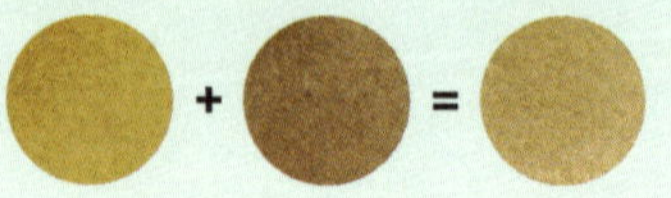

Step 1: Using your size 12 brush, paint a light wash of Cobalt Blue for the sky. Before it dries, use your paper towel to roughly dab and lift some of the colour to reveal the white paper underneath. This will give the illusion of clouds. Let fully dry.

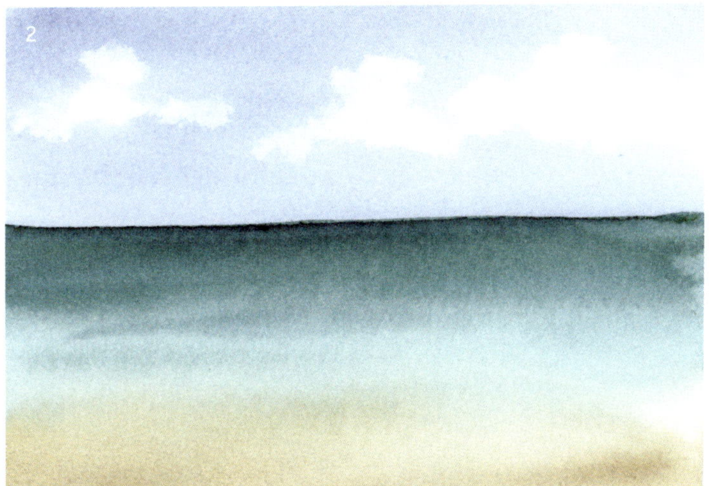

Step 2: Create a gradient of your sea mixture to sand. To do this, lay some clean water over the whole area first. This will help the colours blend smoothly. Then take a dark wash of your sea mixture and start applying to the horizon line. Slowly move your brush halfway down. Remove some pigment from your brush by dabbing on your paper towel or slightly washing it off to create a lighter gradient once the sea colour meets the middle. Once you have a light wash toward the middle, wash and dry off your brush and pick up some of your sand colour mixture. Start applying the sand colour to the bottom of the page and slowly start to move it up to meet the light wash of the water. To get the best results of an even gradient, have a light wash of both the sea and sand meet toward the middle without mixing. If there's too much pigment of either colour, they could mix together and create an undesired look.

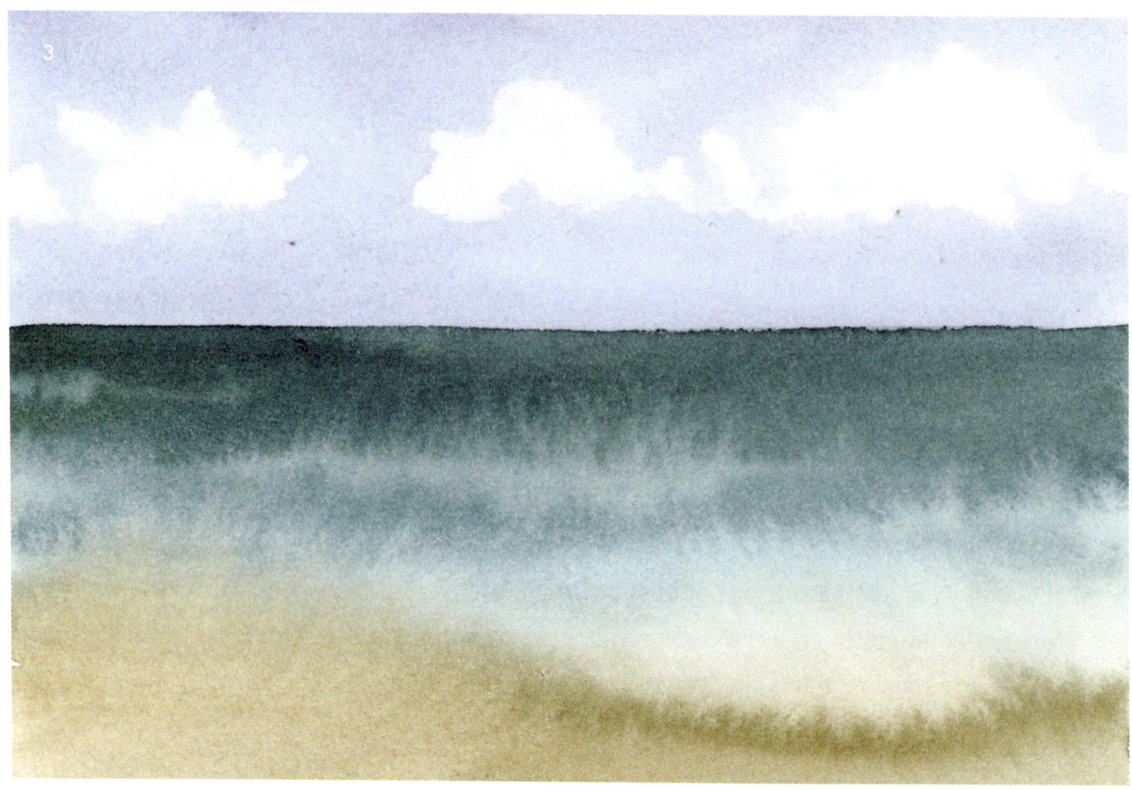

Step 3: While the sea and sand are still wet, take some clean water on your size 6 brush and drop it where you would like to create waves. The clean water will push the pigment away and create some blooms that resemble waves. Let fully dry.

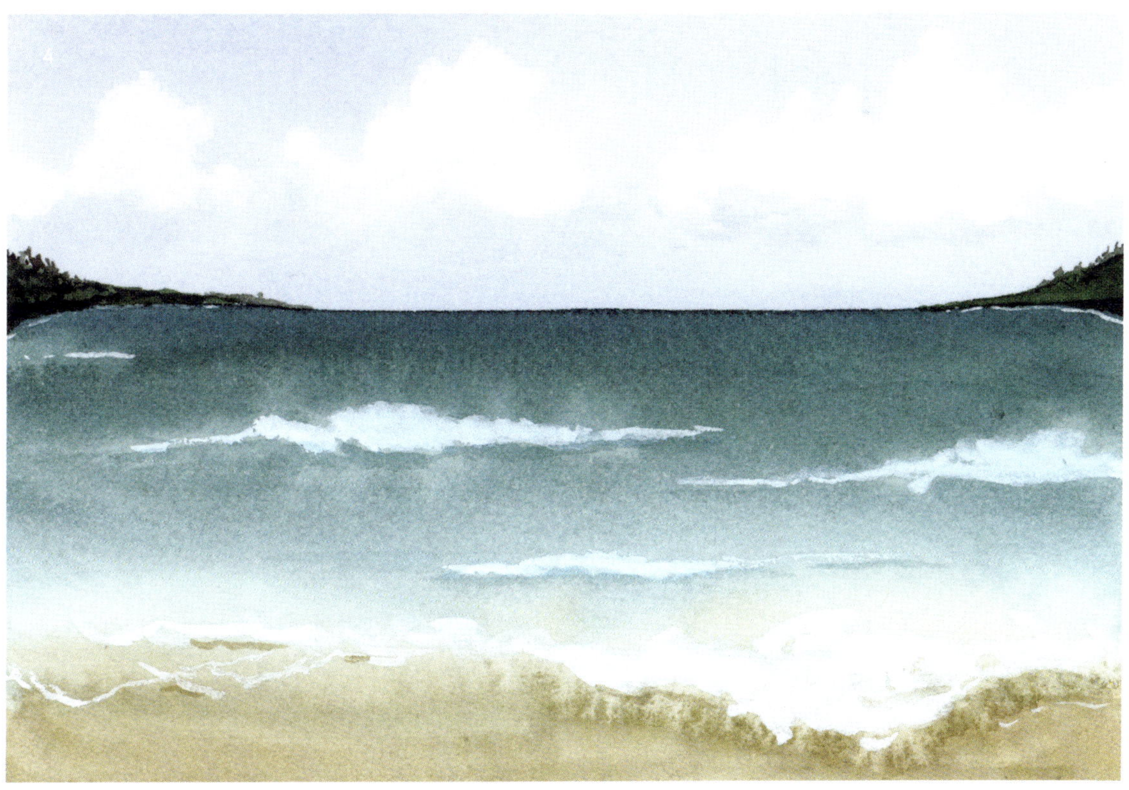

Step 4: To add some final details to your painting, take some white ink on your size 6 brush and dab where you would like to accentuate the waves. Lastly, take some Sap Green and create some distant land pieces on the horizon line on either side of the water.

project four: ocean waves

Techniques Used:

- Light-to-dark gradient
- Blending

Materials Needed:

- Watercolour paper
- Wash brush, round brush size 6
- One paint colour (modify colours with what you have)
- Clean jar of water

Paint Colour:

- Payne's Grey

 Step 1: Create a light-to-dark gradient over the whole background using Payne's Grey. Let fully dry.

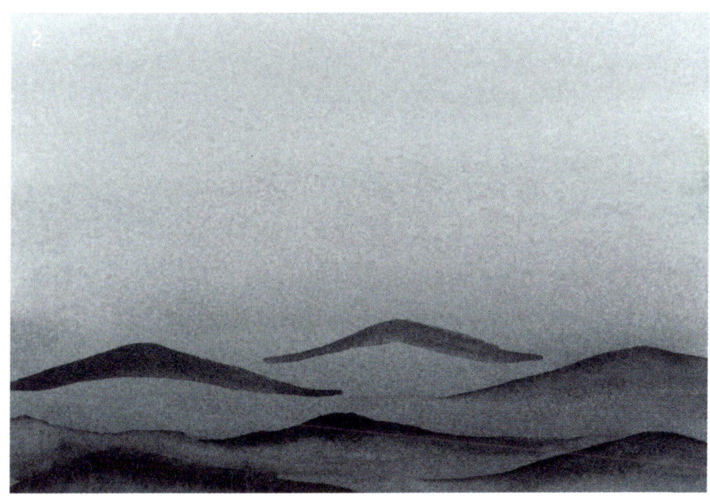

Step 2: Using your size 6 brush, pick up a dark wash of Payne's Grey and create a slightly flattened-out peak at the bottom of the page to resemble a wave. Wash and dry off your brush and blend out the bottom of the stroke. The peak of the wave should be the darkest. Working on one wave at a time, continue to paint more waves around the same size and darkness toward the bottom of the page.

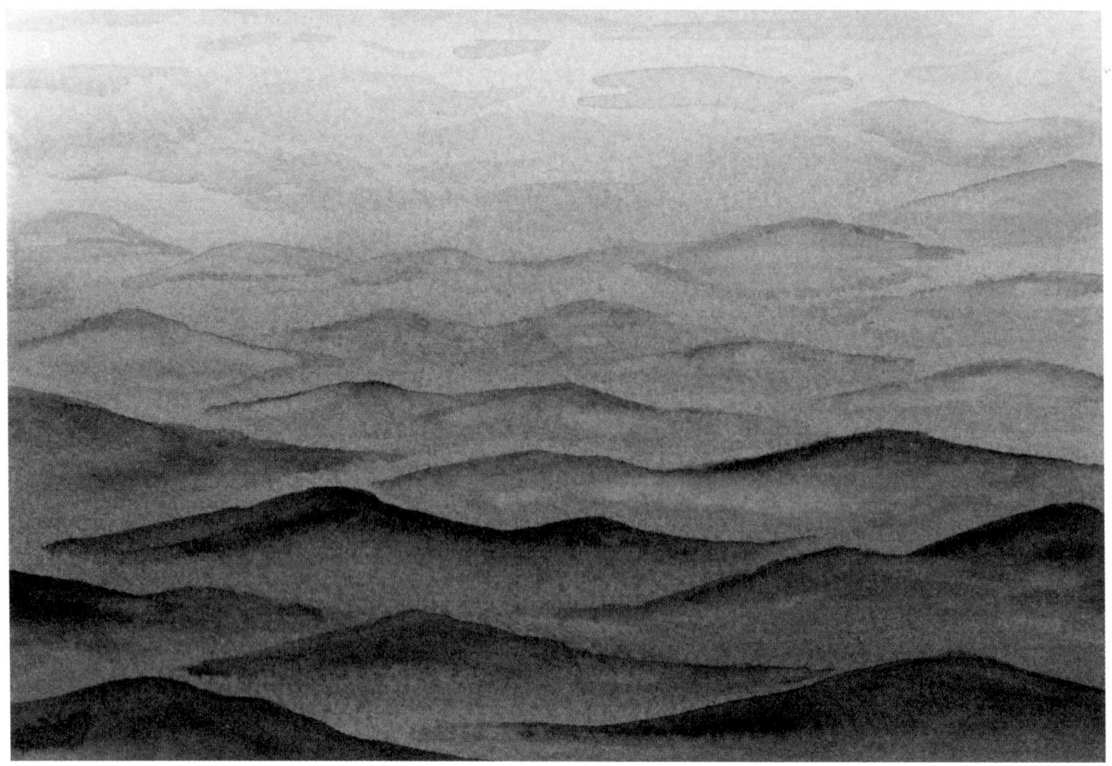

Step 3: Using the same technique, move up the paper and make more waves. The waves should grow smaller and lighter in colour as you move up the page. Let fully dry.

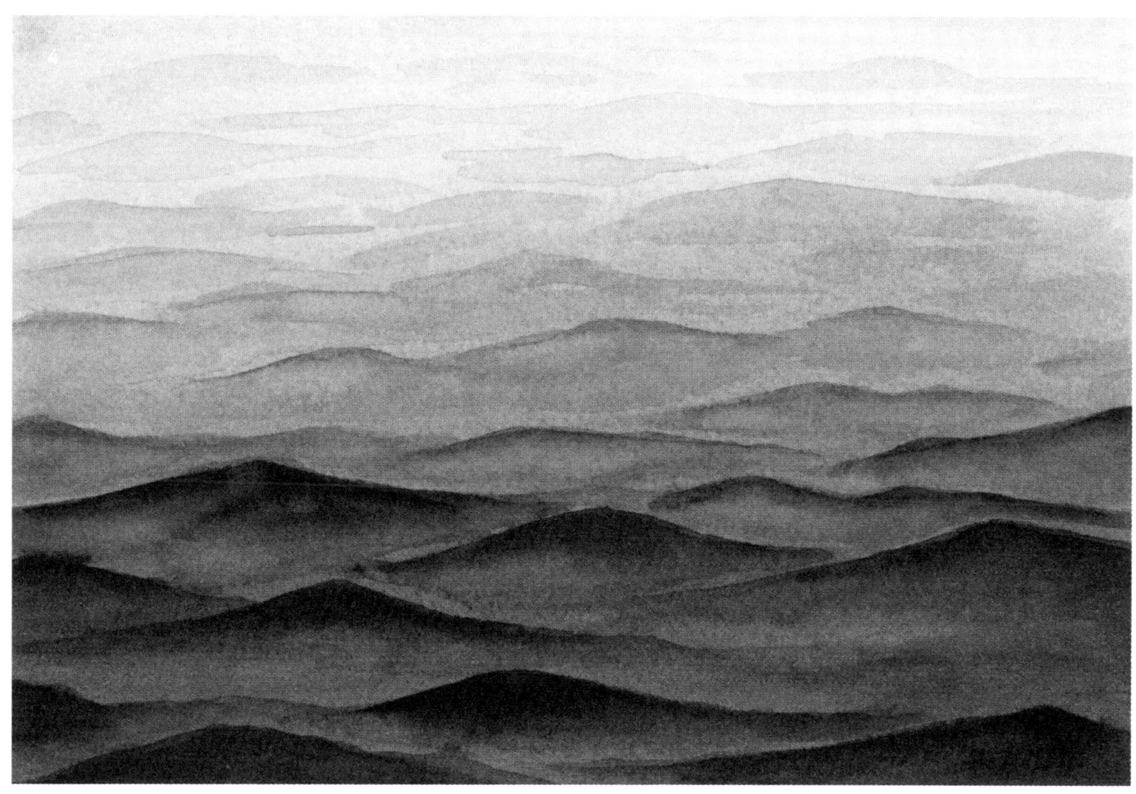

Step 4: To create a bit more depth, go back over any waves you feel could use a bit more darkness or shadow. This will help intensify deep waves.

chapter 8

FOOD

project one: watermelon

Techniques Used:

- Wet-on-wet
- Wet-on-dry
- Colour bleed
- Blending

Materials Needed:

- Watercolour paper
- Round brush sizes 6 and 12
- Five paint colours (modify colours with what you have)
- Clean jar of water
- Paper towel

Paint Colours:

- Winsor Red
- Permanent Rose
- Sap Green
- Perylene Green
- Black

Colour Mixing Recipes:

- Winsor Red and Permanent Rose

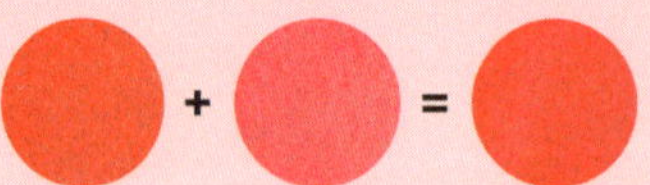

Step 1: With your size 12 brush, paint a wash of clean water over the full watermelon slice, except for the bottom skin. Then, pick up a mix of Winsor Red and Permanent Rose and tap it at the top of the watermelon slice, gradually moving it down to the base. Try to leave the base a bit lighter in colour, even a bit white.

Step 2: While still wet, take a small amount of Sap Green on your size 6 brush and paint along the base of the watermelon. This should cause the green to slightly bleed into the white and red. Leave to dry.

Step 3: Once fully dry, take your red and pink mixture and paint along the side of the watermelon. Gradually lighten the black paint as it blends into the green. Next, take your dark green and paint the skin of the watermelon. Lastly, using the tip of your size 6 brush, use black to create some watermelon seeds. See Part III (starting on page 142) for tracing pages for this project.

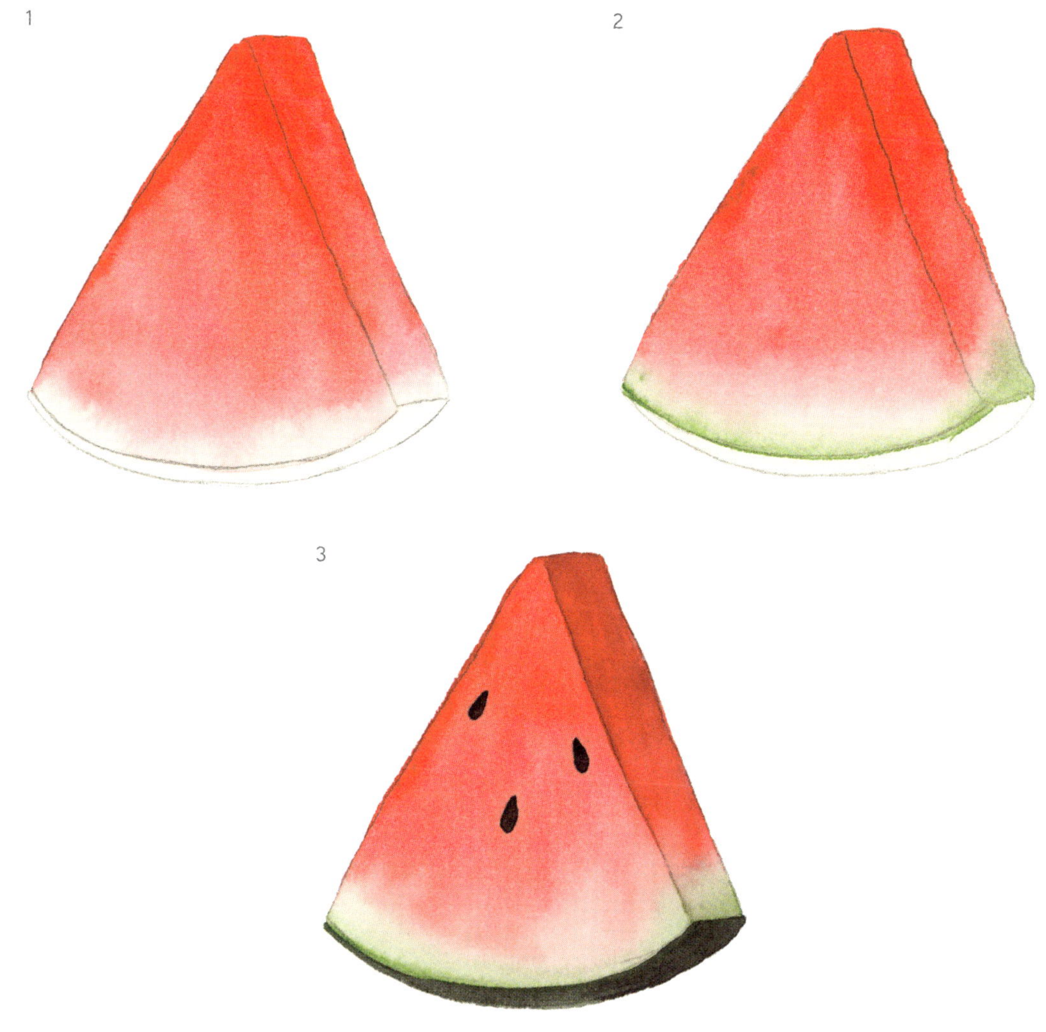

project two: avocado

Techniques Used:

- Wet-on-wet
- Wet-on-dry
- Colour bleed

Materials Needed:

- Watercolour paper
- Round brush size 6
- Four paint colours (modify colours with what you have)
- Clean jar of water
- Paper towel

Paint Colours:

- Cadmium Yellow
- Sap Green
- Perylene Green
- Burnt Umber

Colour Mixing Recipes:

- Cadmium Yellow and Sap Green

Step 1: Start by taking your mixture of Cadmium Yellow and a small amount of Sap Green and paint a wash all over the avocado, leaving the centre seed white.

Step 2: While still wet, tap a small amount of Cadmium Yellow to the centre of the avocado. Then, take some Sap Green and paint around the edge of the avocado, allowing it to bleed into the middle.

Step 3: While still wet, take your Perylene Green and paint around the outer skin of the avocado, allowing the darker green to slightly bleed into the Sap Green. Try and use less water and more pigment for the dark green to create a more concentrated bleed.

Step 4: Lastly, take a light wash of Burnt Umber and paint in the seed. Tap a darker value of Burnt Umber around one side of the seed to create a shadow. On the other half of the avocado, take a light wash of Sap Green and a small amount of Burnt Umber and fill in a crescent of the circle. Once the seed is completely dry, you can add some detailed lines around the shadow with your Burnt Umber. See Part III (starting on page 142) for tracing pages for this project.

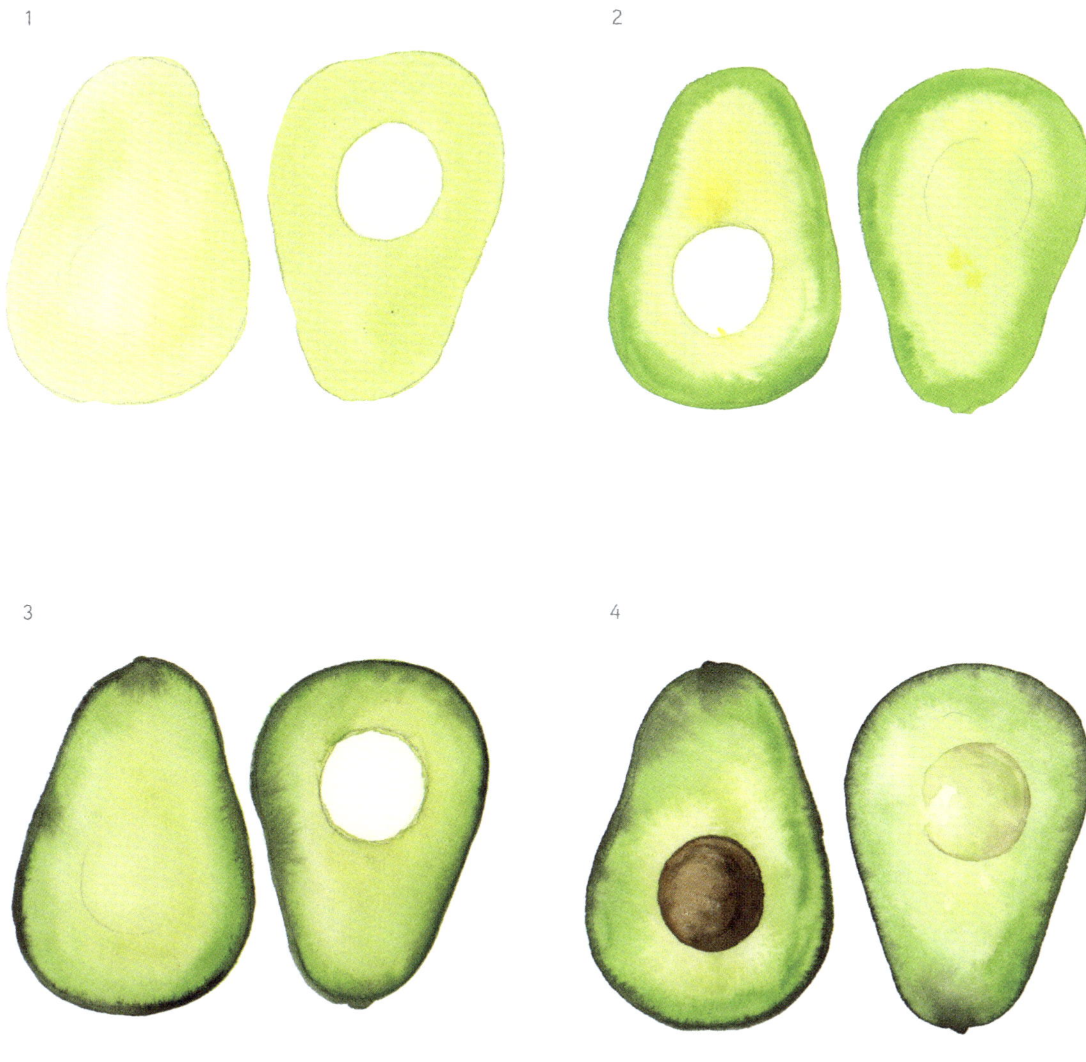

project three: donut

Techniques Used:

- Wet-on-wet
- Wet-on-dry
- Blending

Materials Needed:

- Watercolour paper
- Round brush sizes 6 and 2
- Six paint colours
- White ink (I used Dr. Ph Martin's Bleedproof White ink. Other great options are a white gel pen or white gouache)
- Clean jar of water
- Paper towel

Paint Colours:

- Permanent Rose
- Burnt Umber
- Yellow Ochre
- Phthalo Turquoise
- Cadmium Yellow
- Hooker's Green Dark

Colour Mixing Recipes:

- Permanent Rose and Hooker's Green Dark
- Yellow Ochre and Burnt Umber

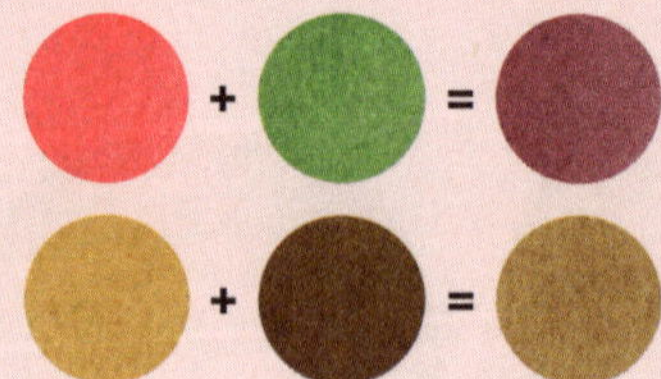

Step 1: Using your size 6 brush, start by painting a very light wash of Permanent Rose all over the icing of the donut. While still wet, take a slightly darker value of Permanent Rose and paint around the edges. If the colour bleeds too much, dab your brush on paper towel and blend it out a bit. Again, while still wet, add the shadow colour mix of Permanent Rose and a bit of Hooker's Green Dark at the bottom outline of the icing and the top inner part of the icing. Let it fully dry.

Step 2: Taking your mix of Yellow Ochre and Burnt Umber, paint the light wash all over the base of the donut. Take a slightly darker value of the colour mix and paint around the edges. Again, if the colour seems to bleed too much, clean it up a bit by dabbing your brush on your paper towel and blending it out. Let fully dry.

Step 3: With your size 2 brush, take some turquoise, pink, and yellow and create fun sprinkles on top of the icing. Next take a light wash of Burnt Umber and Yellow Ochre and dab some detail textures on the base of the donut.

Step 4: To add some fine detail to your donut, take some white ink and create little highlights on each sprinkle with your size 2 brush. Continue to use your white ink to add some highlights to the icing drips and on parts of the base of the donut. Lastly, take your icing shadow colour mix and add some small shadows on the underside of each sprinkle.

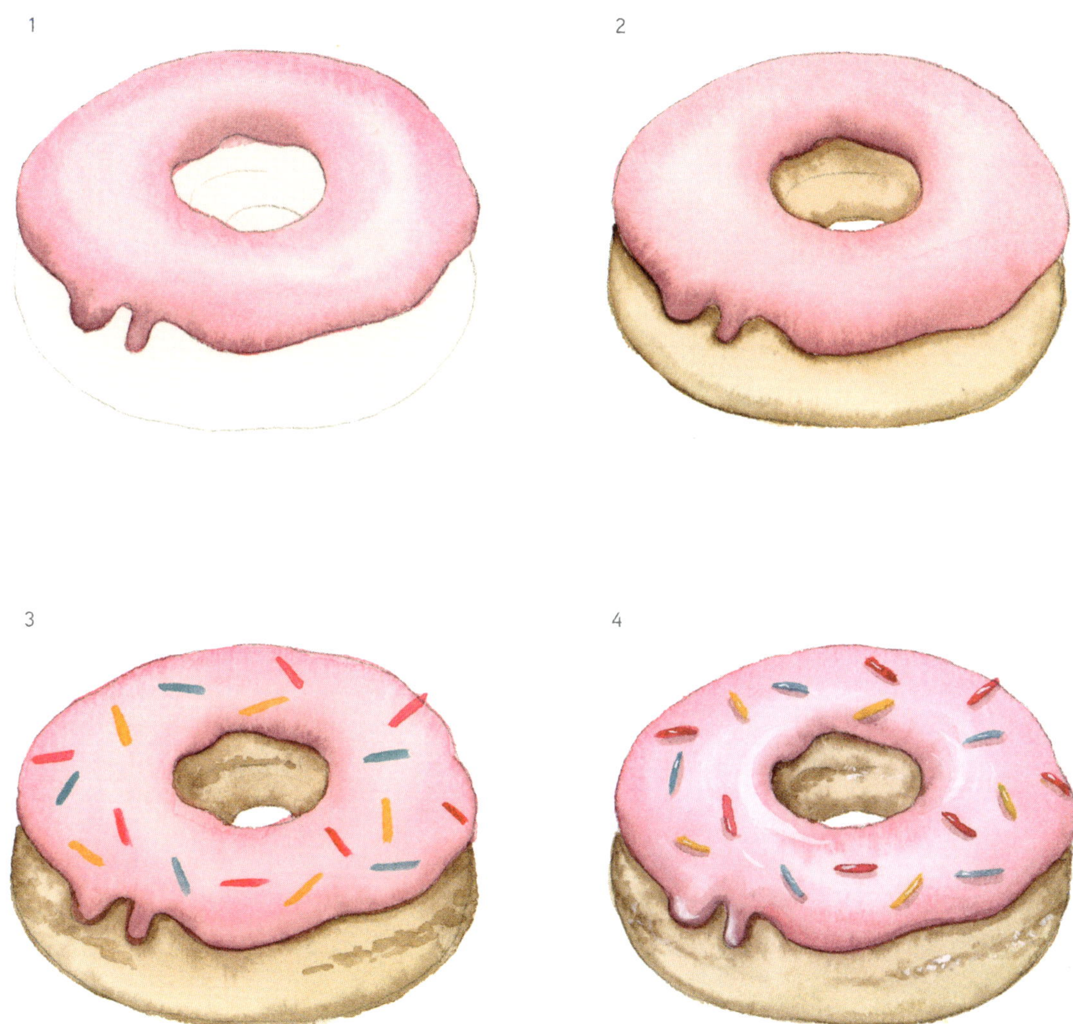

project four: cupcake

Techniques Used:

- Wet-on-wet
- Wet-on-dry
- Blending

Materials Needed:

- Watercolour paper
- Round brush size 6
- Four paint colours (modify colours with what you have)
- White ink (I used Dr. Ph Martin's Bleedproof White ink. Other great options are a white gel pen or white gouache)
- Clean jar of water
- Paper towel

Paint Colours:

- Permanent Rose
- Burnt Umber
- Phthalo Turquoise
- Hooker's Green

Colour Mixing Recipes:

- Permanent Rose and Hooker's Green

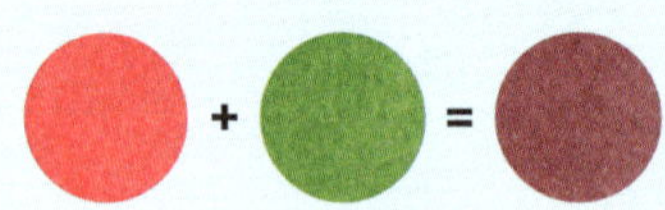

Step 1: Using your size 6 brush, paint a light wash of Permanent Rose all over the icing on the cupcake. Then paint a light wash of turquoise all over the cup. Tap a small amount of a darker value of turquoise to the right side of the cup to create a bit of a shadow. Let fully dry.

Step 2: Using a light wash of Burnt Umber, paint the cake part of the cupcake. While still wet, add a slightly darker value of Burnt Umber around the edges of the cake, leaving the centre light wash to act as a highlight.

Step 3: Using a slightly darker value of turquoise, paint lines down the cup. Gradually make them slightly darker on the right side of the cup.

Step 4: Using your icing shadow mix colour, paint a line along the top of each icing swirl, working on one swirl at a time. This should create some shadow and depth on the icing.

Step 5: Lastly, using your size 2 brush and a dark value of Permanent Rose paint, create some sprinkles on top of your icing. Once dry, use your shadow icing colour to create small shadows underneath each sprinkle. See Part III (starting on page 142) for tracing pages for this project.

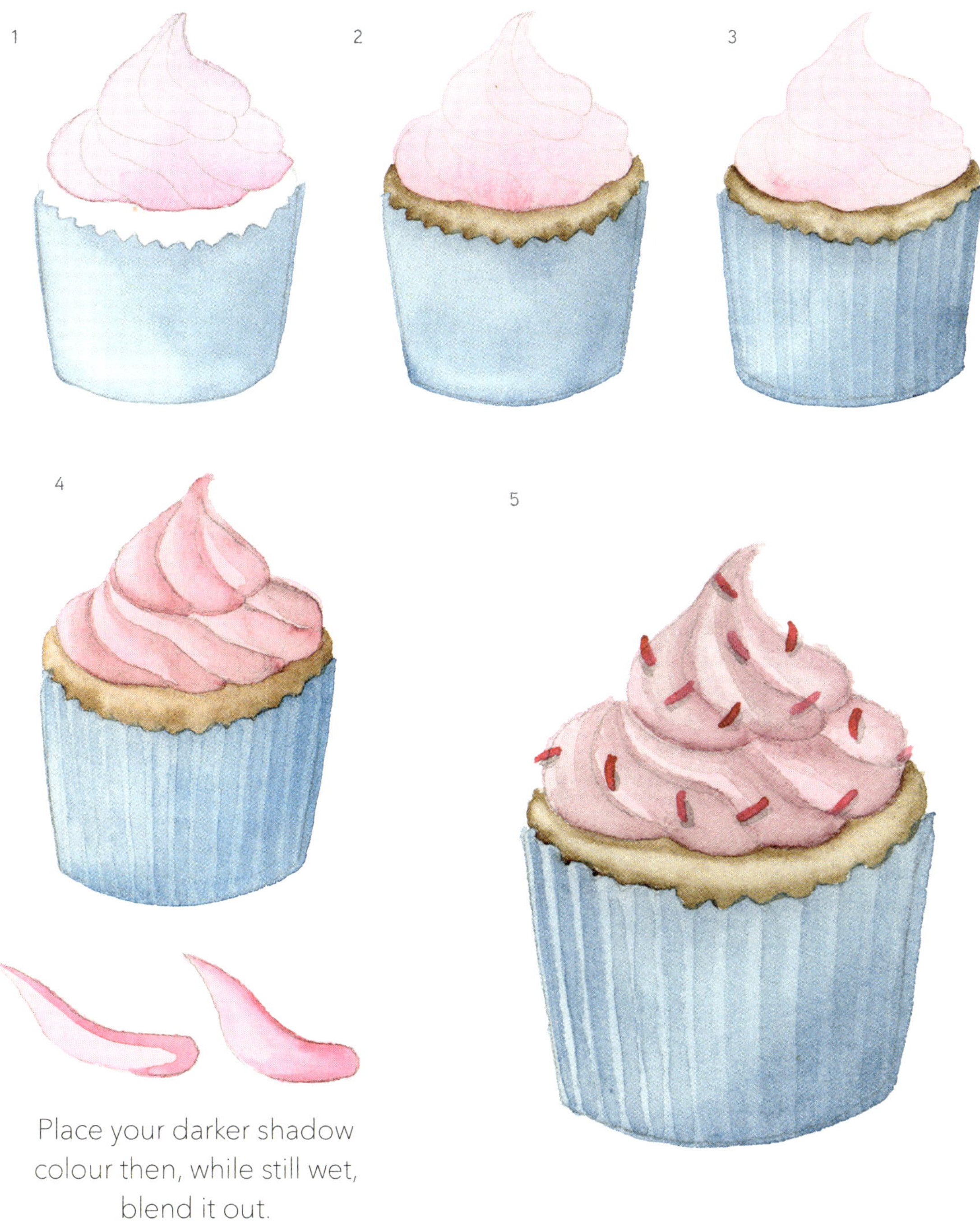

Place your darker shadow colour then, while still wet, blend it out.

chapter 9

ANIMALS

project one: robin

Techniques Used:

- Wet-on-wet
- Wet-on-dry

Materials Needed:

- Watercolour paper
- Round brush size 6
- Four paint colours (modify colours with what you have)
- White ink (I used Dr. Ph Martin's Bleedproof White ink. Other great options are a white gel pen or white gouache)
- Clean jar of water
- Paper towel

Paint Colours:

- Cadmium Yellow
- Winsor Red
- Burnt Umber
- Black

Colour Mixing Recipes:

- Cadmium Yellow and Winsor Red

- Burnt Umber and Black

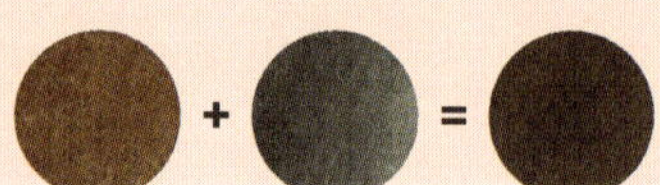

Step 1: Using your size 12 brush, lay down some clean water over the body of the bird. Leave the beak, eyes, feet, and back tail dry. Using the wet-on-wet technique, take some of your orange mixture and dab along the breast and the face of the robin. Next, take some of your dark brown mixture and dab along the top of the head, back, and wing of the robin. Lastly, take a light wash of black and dab toward the bottom of the robin. Let dry fully.

Step 2: Using our dark brown mixture, paint the feet of the robin. Next, take a light wash of the brown mixture and paint the back tail. While still wet, add some darker pigment to where the tail meets the bird, to create a bit of a shadow. Let fully dry.

Step 3: Let's add some detail. Using your size 6 brush, create some feather-like strokes using the tip of your brush and light pressure. On the orange section of the robin, take a darker wash of orange and create some feather strokes. Then take some of our dark brown mixture and paint some feather strokes over the back and wings. Next, add a slightly darker wash of grey and create some feather strokes on the bottom. Use your small size 2 brush to paint the eye and the beak with some black. Lastly, add some white ink feather strokes on the robin and dot the eye. See Part III (starting on page 126) for tracing pages for this project.

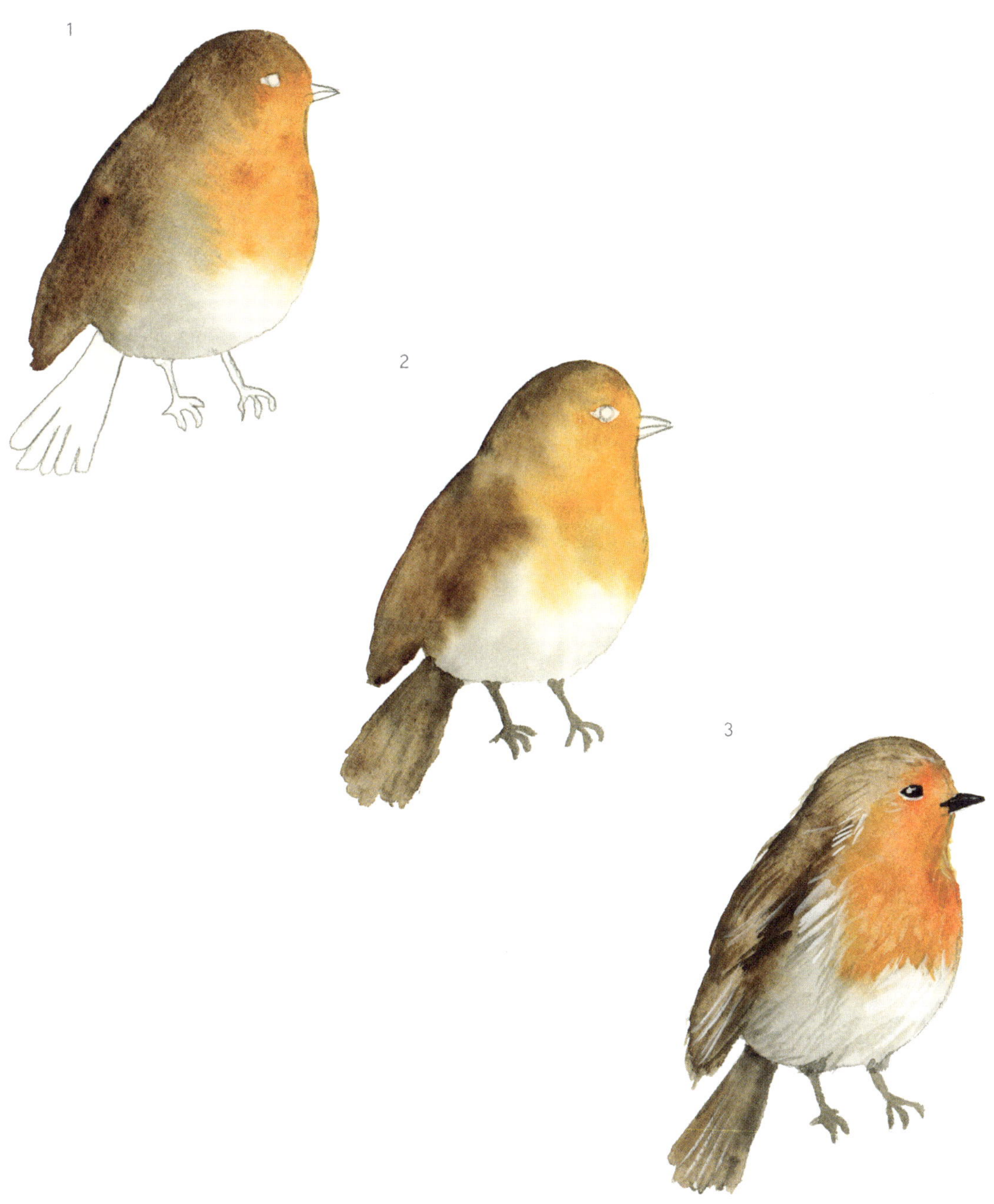

project two: rabbit

Techniques Used:

- Wet-on-wet
- Wet-on-dry
- Dry brush

Materials Needed:

- Watercolour paper
- Round brush size 6
- Three paint colours (modify colours with what you have)
- White ink (I used Dr. Ph Martin's Bleedproof White ink. Other great options are a white gel pen or white gouache)
- Clean jar of water
- Paper towel

Paint Colours:

- Black
- Permanent Rose
- Cadmium Yellow

Colour Mixing Recipes:

- Light Wash of Black
- Permanent Rose, and Cadmium Yellow

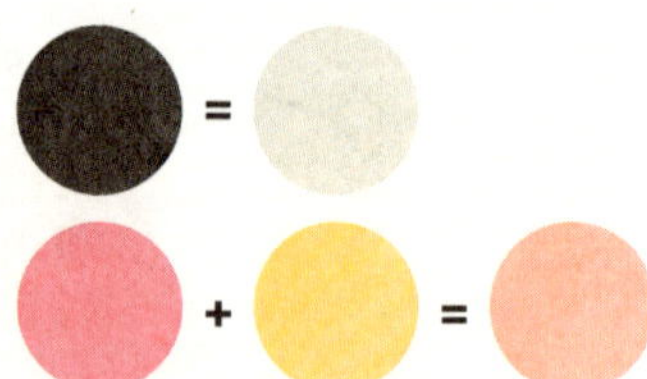

Step 1: Using your size 6 brush, start by painting a very light wash of grey all over the rabbit, leaving out the inner ear and eye.

Step 2: Using the wet-on-wet technique, take a slightly darker wash of the grey and tap some colour around the head and ears, the hind leg and body, and the creases in the feet. Let fully dry.

Step 3: Once dry, create some light fur strokes around the outline of the rabbit, using a light wash of grey and light pressure. You can even use the dry brush technique by drying off your brush, making sure there are no water droplets in the bristles, separating the bristles on your brush, and gently dabbing into dry-ish paint. Then use the separated bristles to create fur strokes on the rabbit. This will not damage your brush. Just be sure to swish it around in water once you're finished, and reshape your bristles to a point.

Step 4: Lastly, add some detail. Take a light wash of your pink and yellow mixture and paint the inner ear and the triangle of the nose. Then use your size 2 brush to paint the eyes of the rabbit black, as well as the nose and mouth. Lastly, take some white ink and create some more fur strokes, as well as a highlighted dot in the eye. See Part III (starting on page 142) for tracing pages for this project.

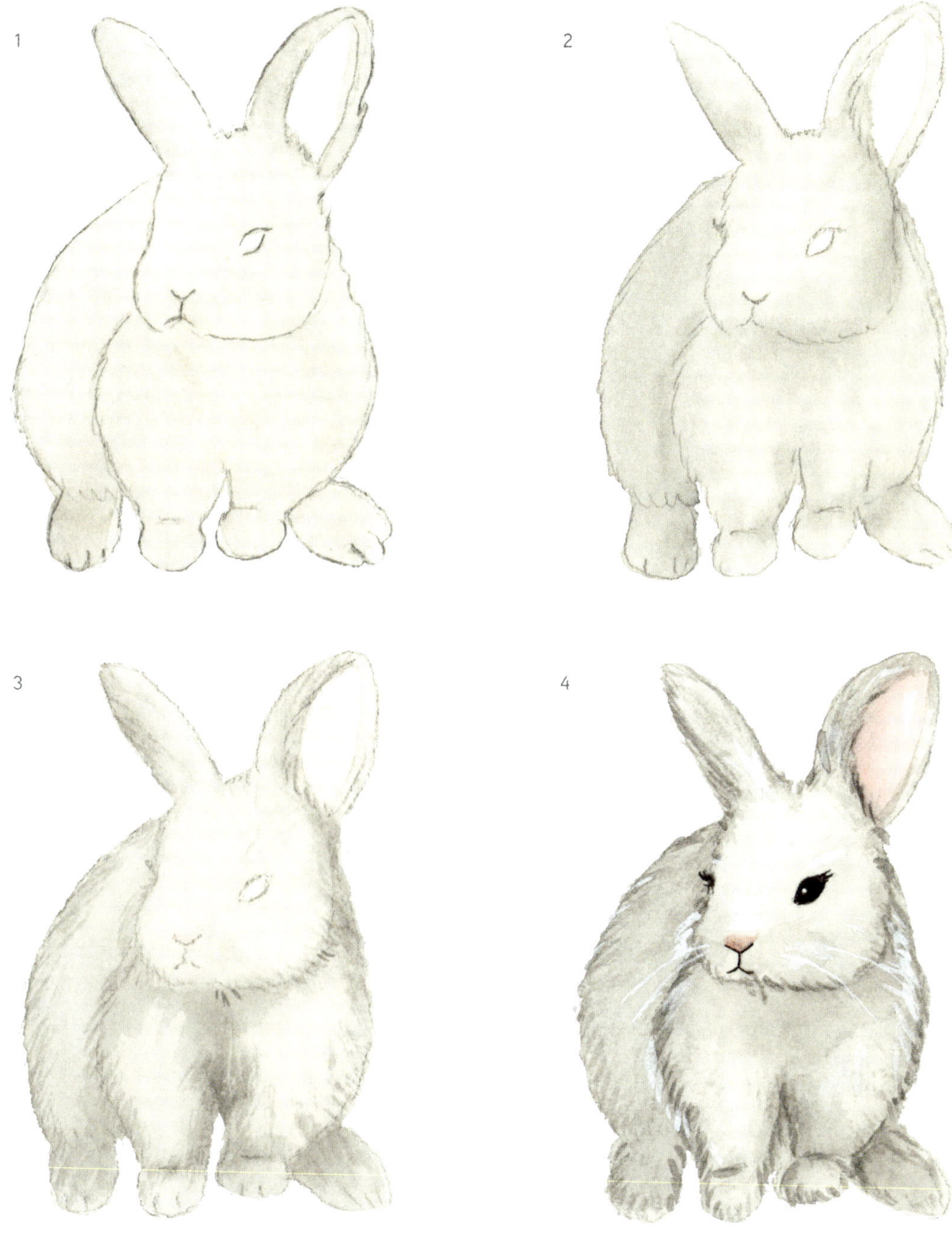

project three: lion

Techniques Used:

- Wet-on-wet
- Wet-on-dry

Materials Needed:

- Watercolour paper
- Round brush sizes 12, 6, and 2
- Five paint colours (modify colours with what you have)
- White ink (I used Dr. Ph Martin's Bleed-proof White ink. Other great options are a white gel pen or white gouache)
- Clean jar of water
- Paper towel

Paint Colours:

- Yellow Ochre
- Burnt Umber
- Black
- Cadmium Yellow
- Winsor Red

Colour Mixing Recipes:

- Burnt Umber and Black

- Cadmium Yellow and Winsor Red

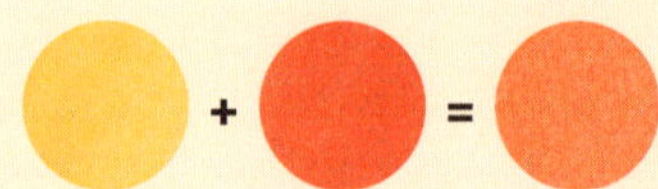

Step 1: Using your size 12 brush, paint a medium wash of Yellow Ochre all over the lion, leaving out the eyes, nose, and bottom jaw. Leave painting wet.

Step 2: Next, using the wet-on-wet technique, add some dark brown strokes around the face of the lion and on the lion's mane. Add some more curved strokes, using the orange mixture and Burnt Umber, to the mane as well. Lastly, tap some more Yellow Ochre to the face to darken it a little. Let fully dry. This is an awkward stage of the painting, as it may look a bit weird. Once more detail is added, it will come together.

Step 3: Once fully dry, take your size 6 brush and the dark brown mixture and add some thin curved strokes around the face and the mane of the lion. Also, with your dark brown, sharpen up the shape of the ears. Next, use some Burnt Umber to create more strokes on the mane, some small dots on top of the mouth, and some detail lines on the face.

Step 4: Using your size 2 brush, use the orange mixture to paint in the circles of the eyes. Let dry. Then use some black to outline the nose and mouth area as well as the eyes. Lastly, take some white ink and add a detailed outline to the bottom of the eyes, and add some whiskers. See Part III (starting on page 142) for tracing pages for this project.

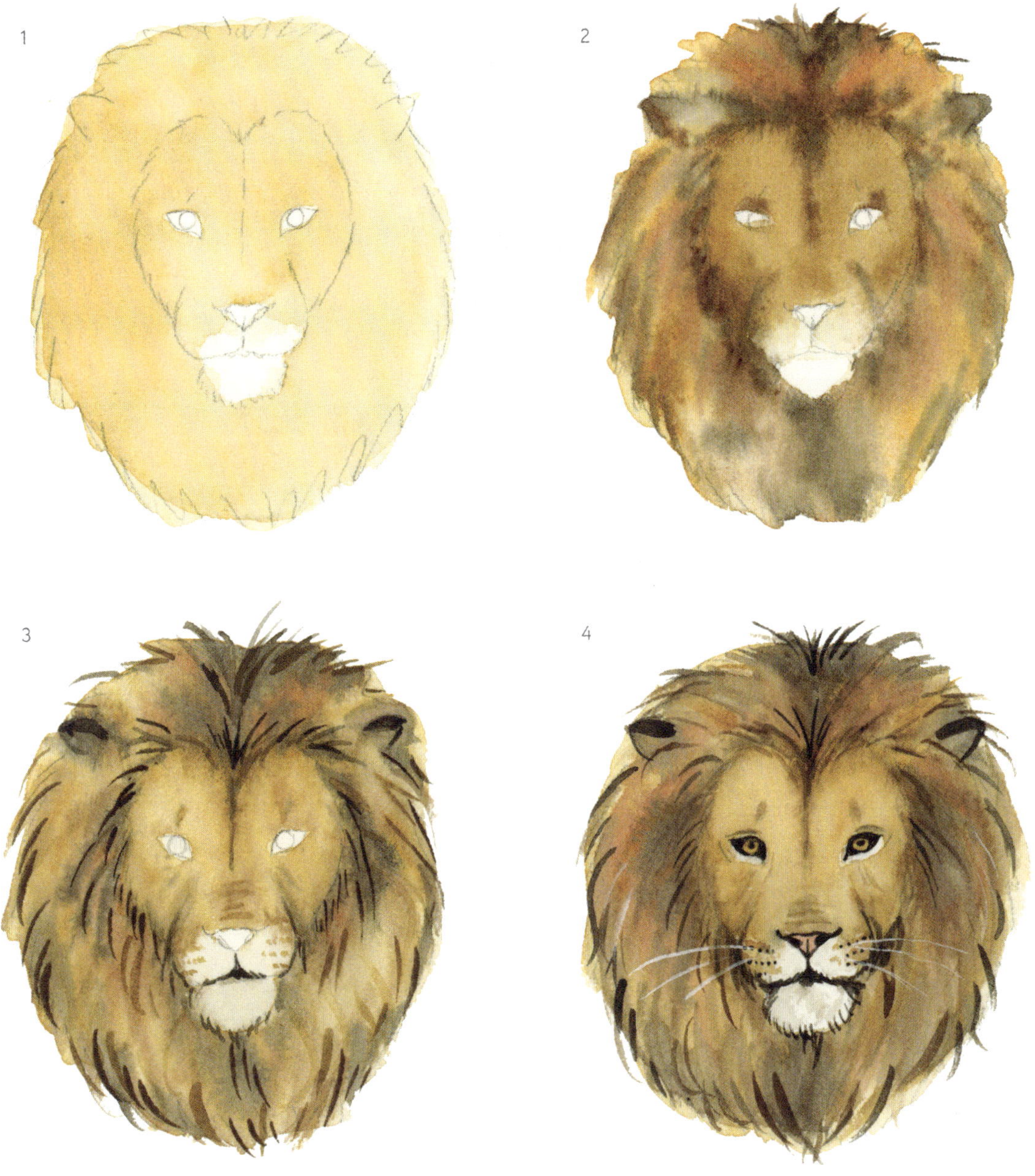

chapter 6:
botanical painting projects

tulip

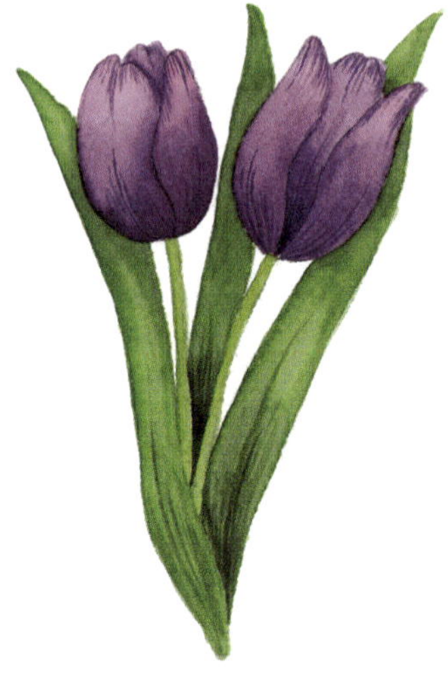

1. 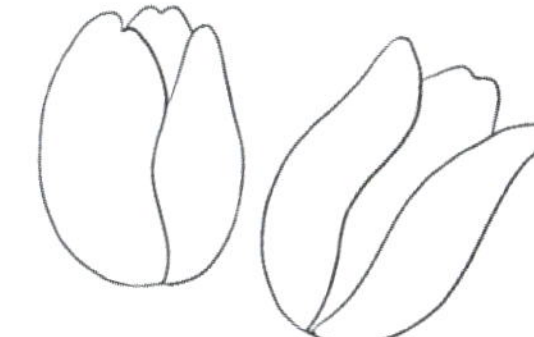

2. 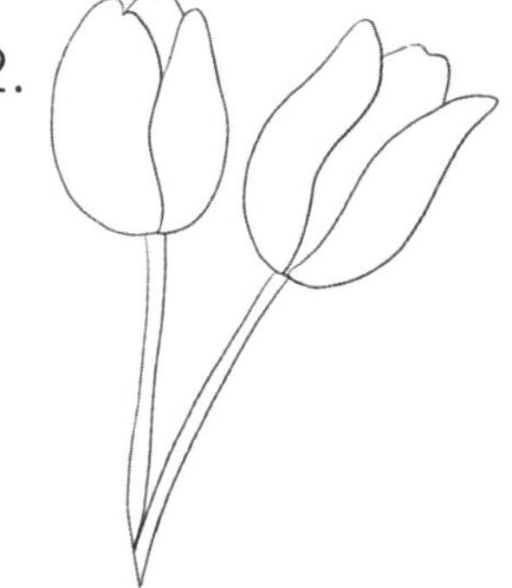

3. 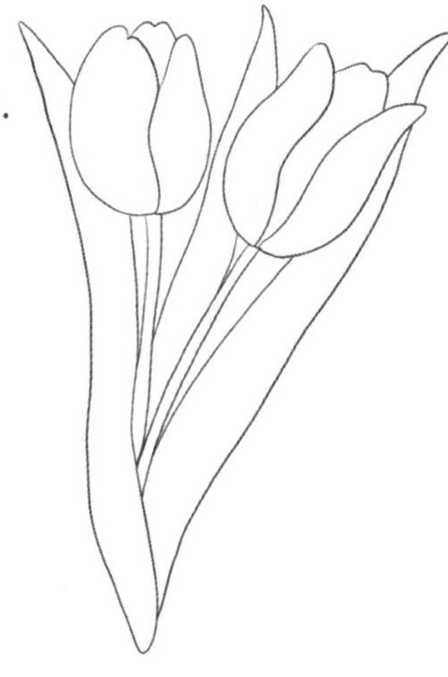

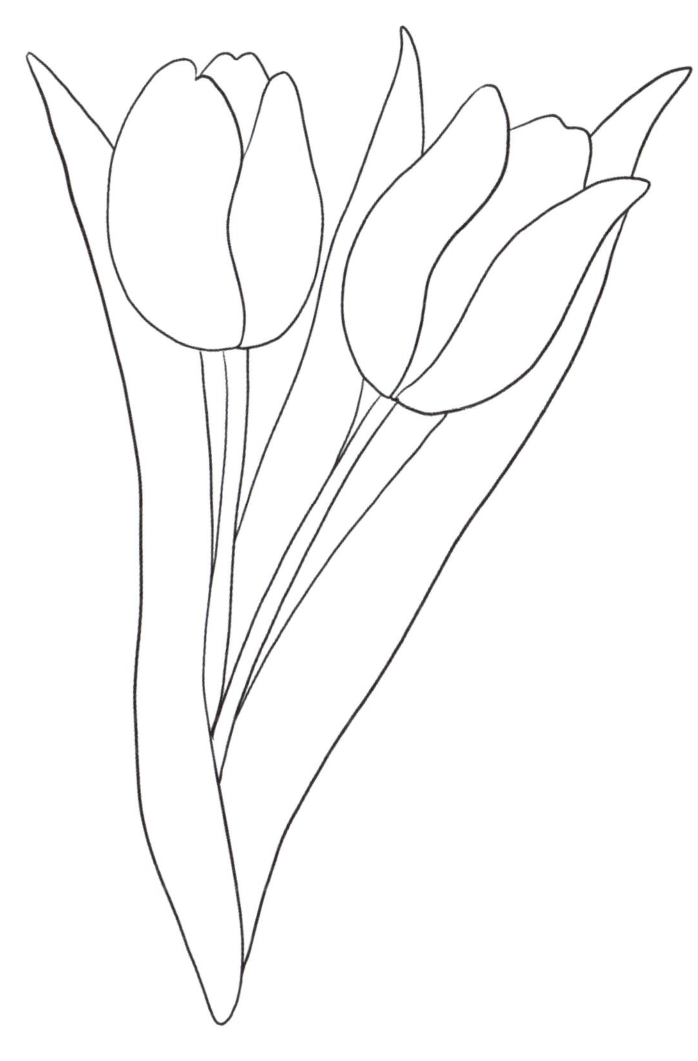

chapter 6:
botanical painting projects

cosmo

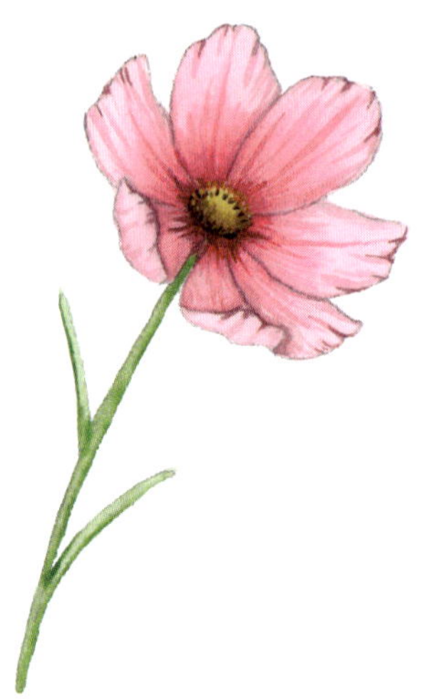

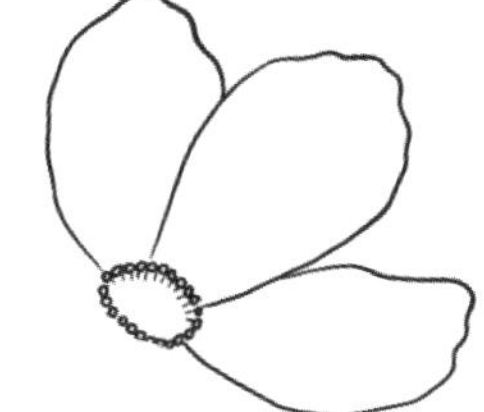

1.

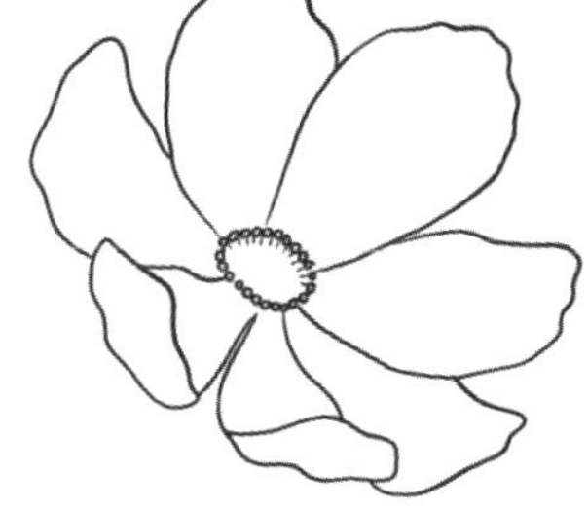

2.

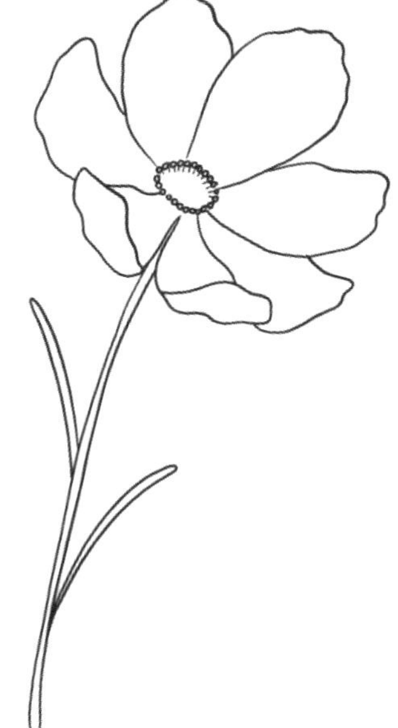

3.

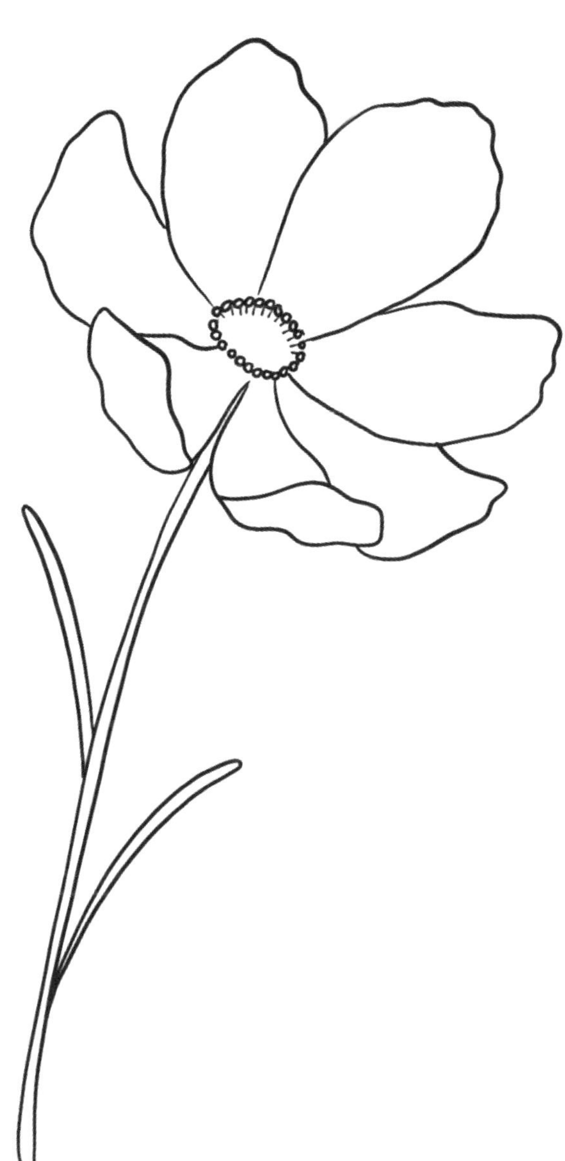

chapter 6:
botanical painting projects

eucalyptus

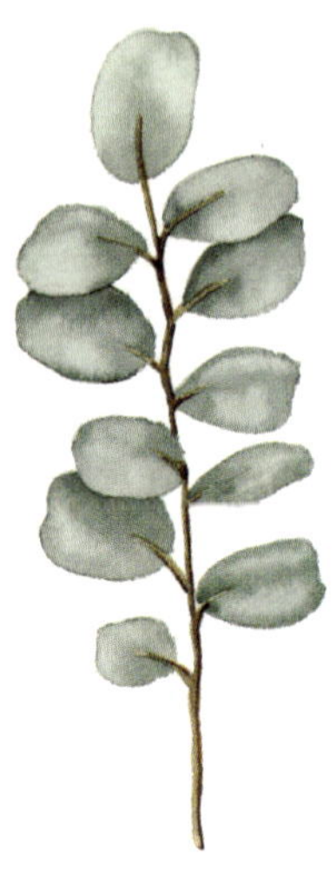

 1.

 2.

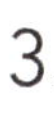 3.

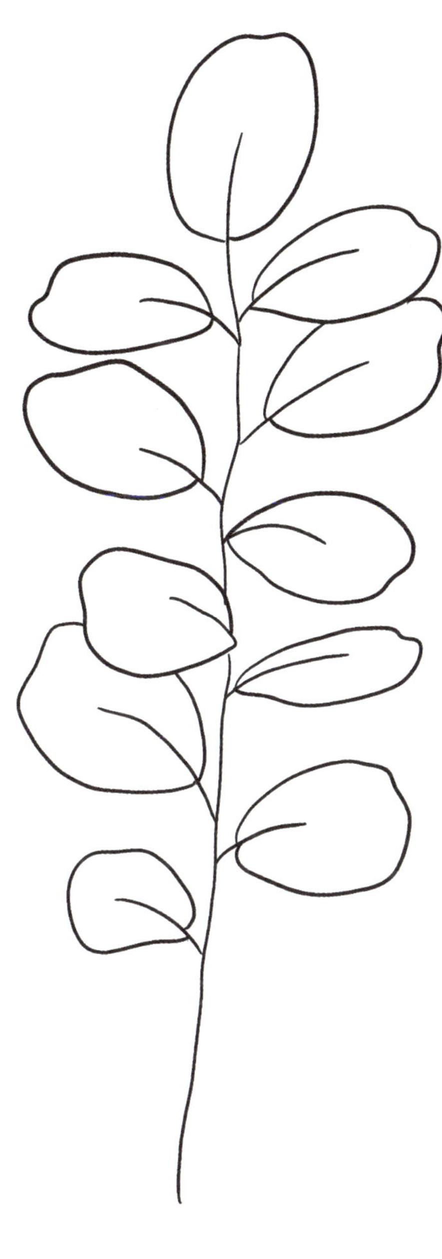

chapter 6:
botanical painting projects

cactus

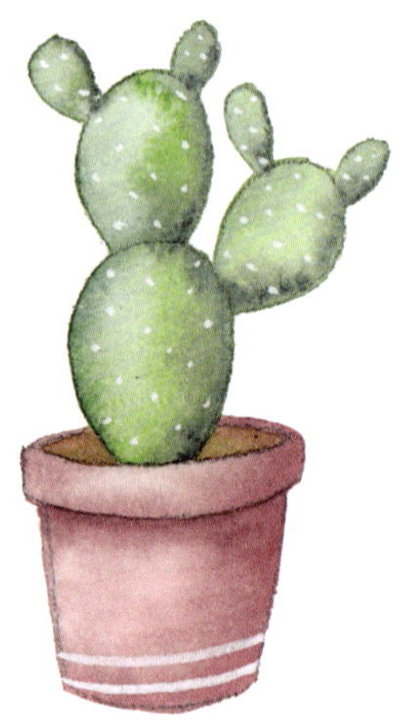

1.

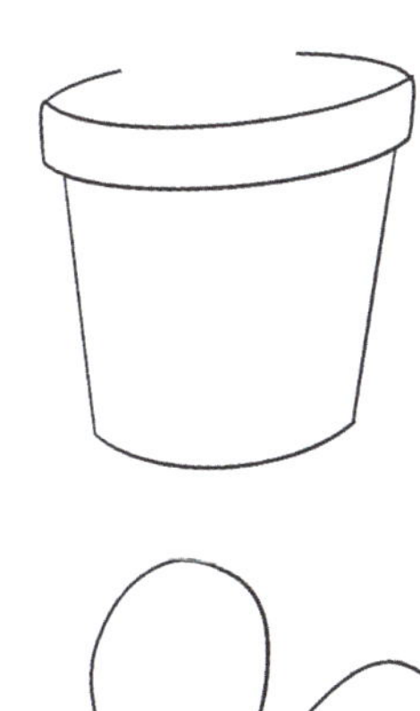

2.

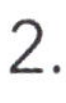

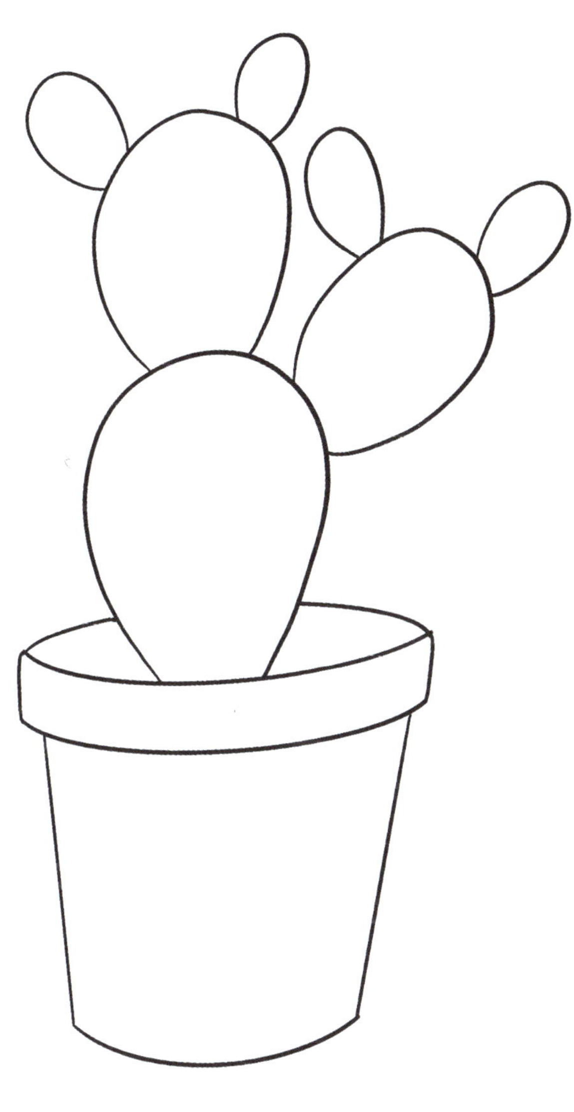

3.

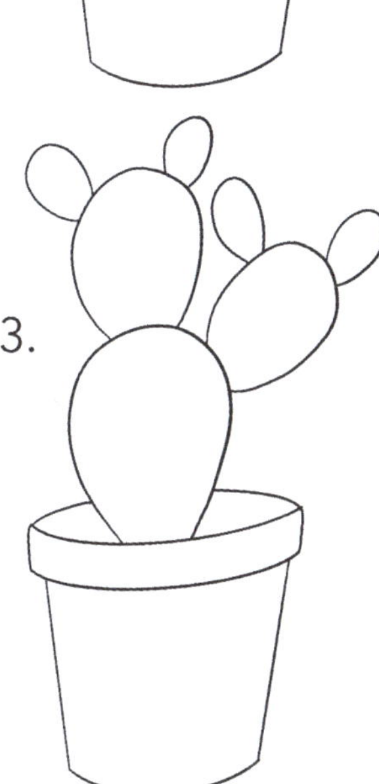

chapter 6:
botanical painting projects

monstera plant

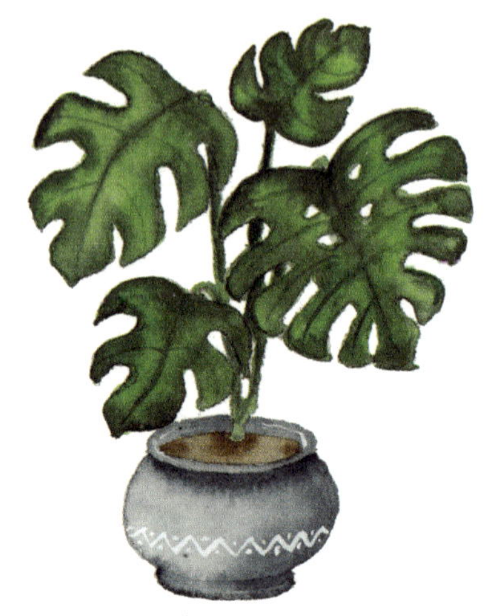

1.

2.

3.

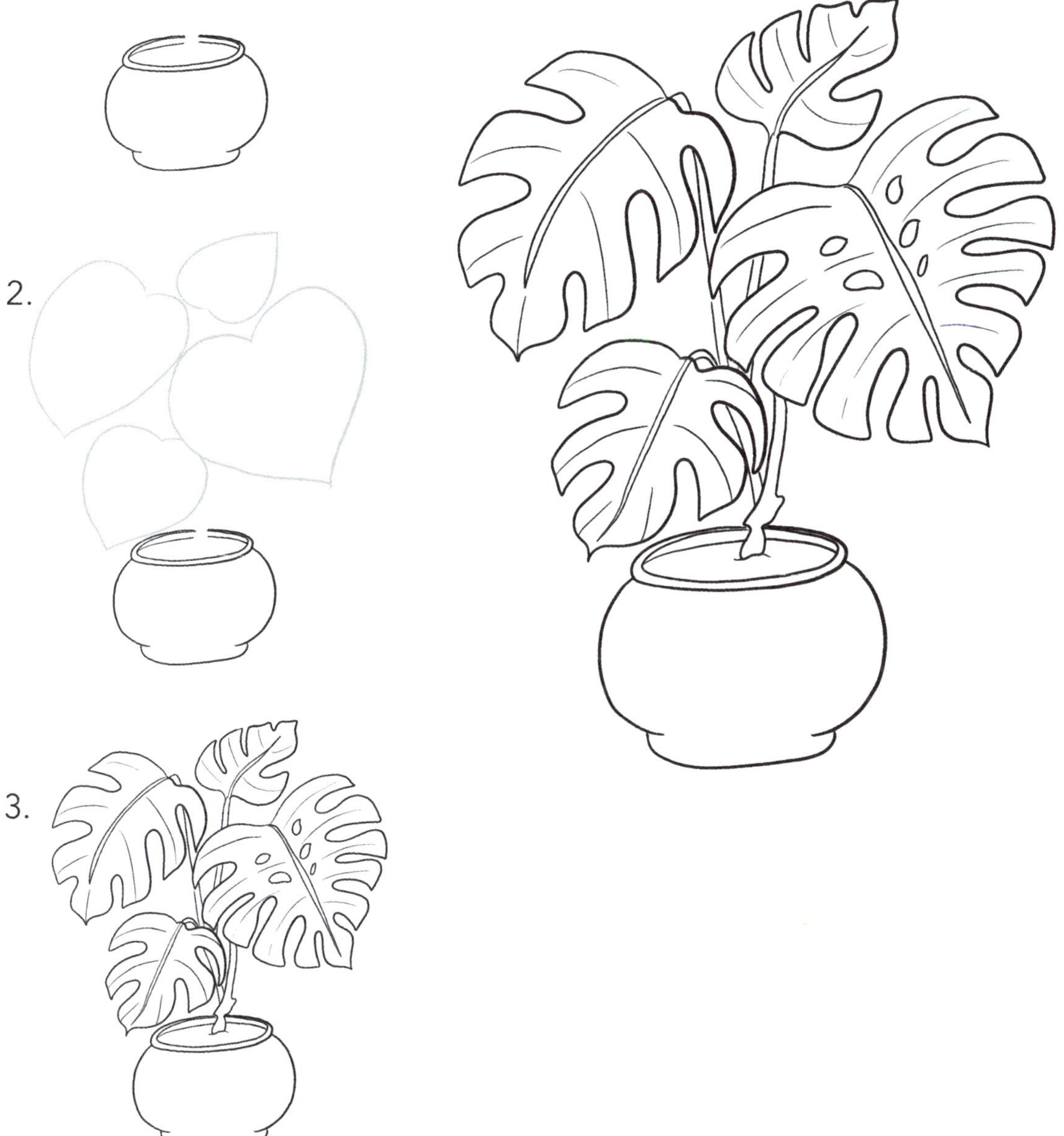

chapter 6: botanical painting projects

snake plant

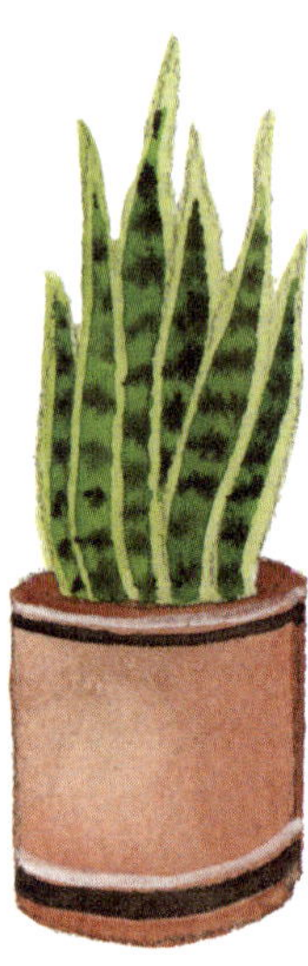

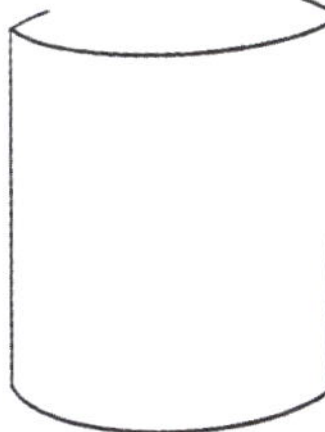
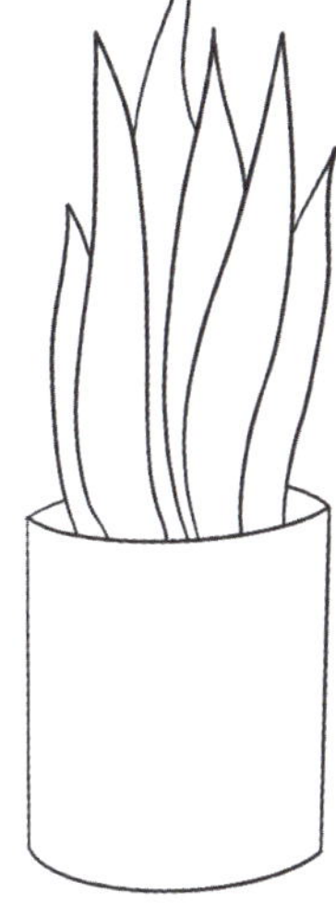
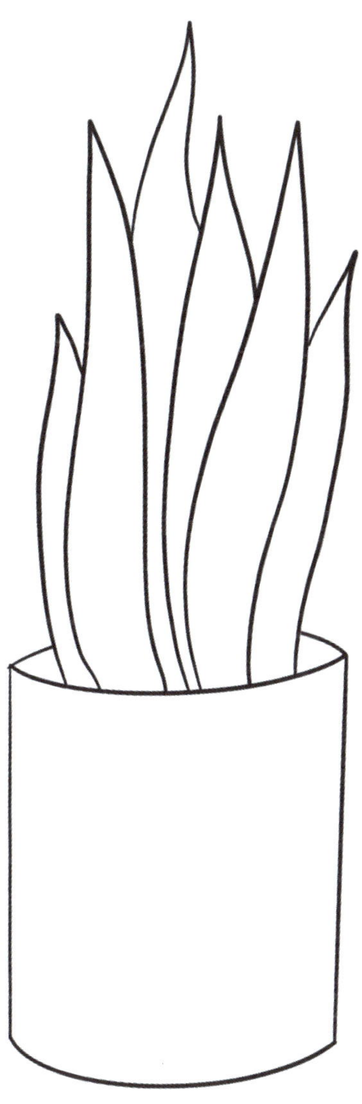

1.
2.
3.

chapter 8:
food

watermelon

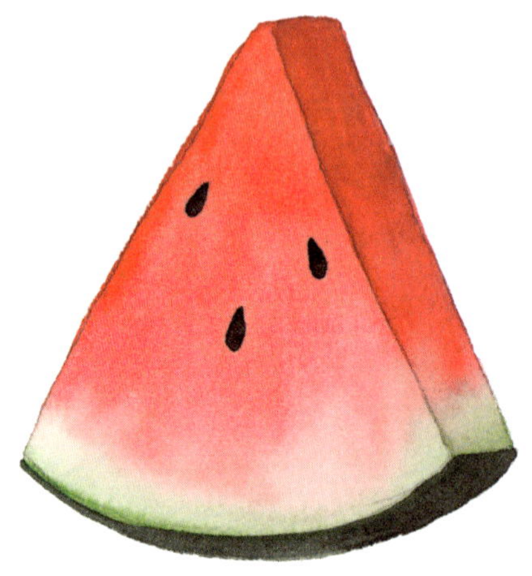

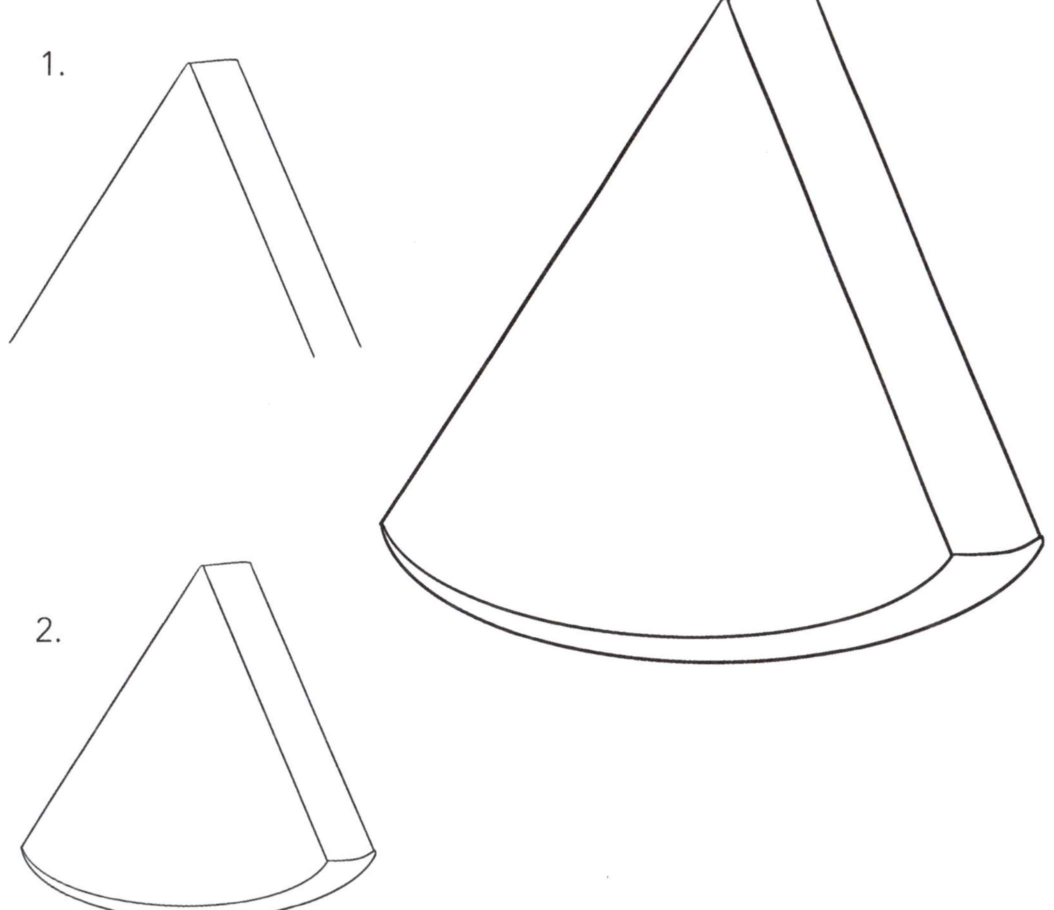

1.
2.

chapter 8:
food

avocado

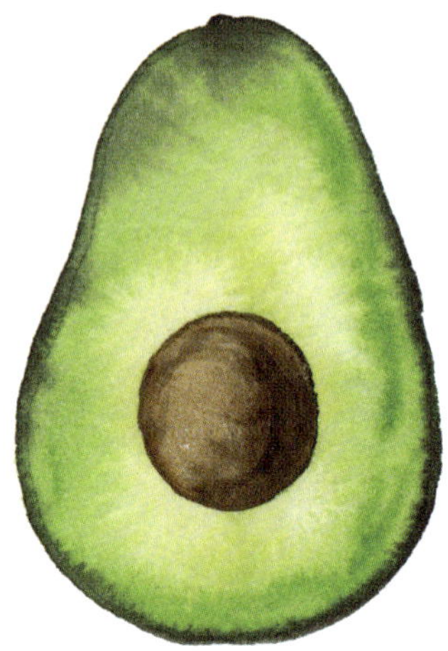

1.

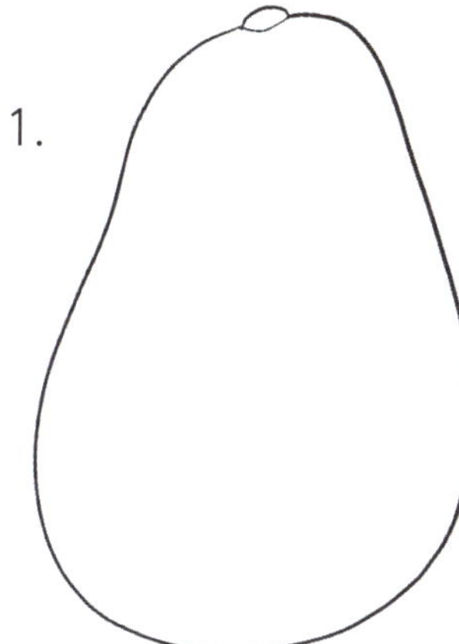

2.

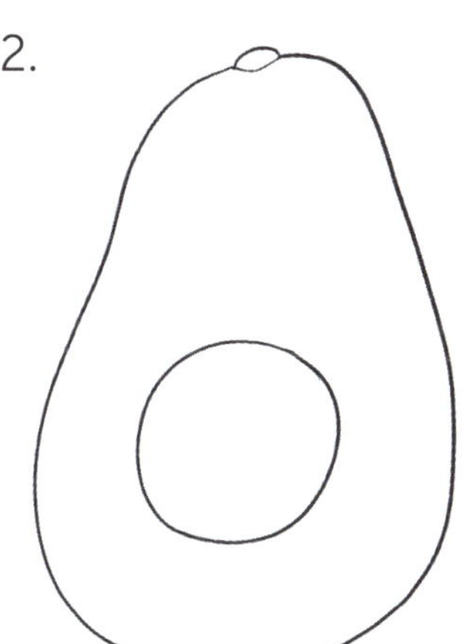

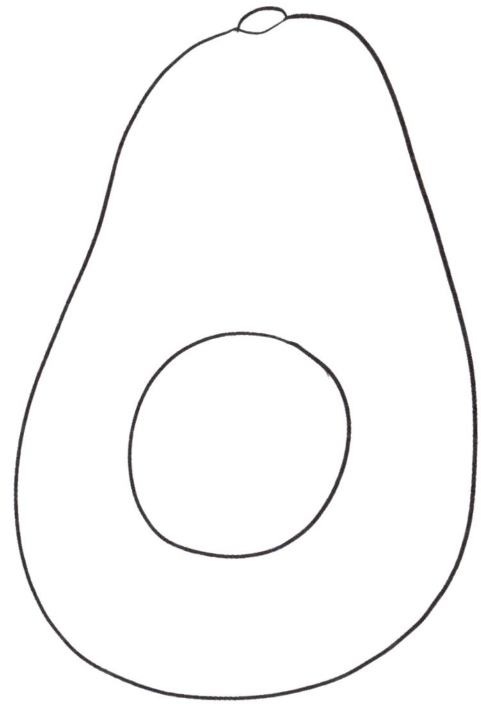

chapter 8:
food

donut

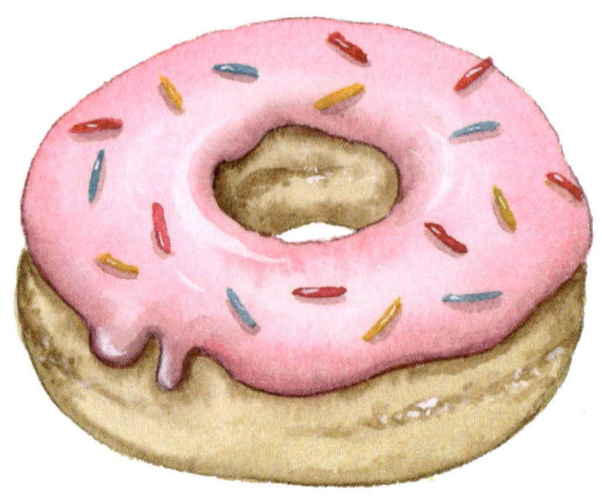

1. 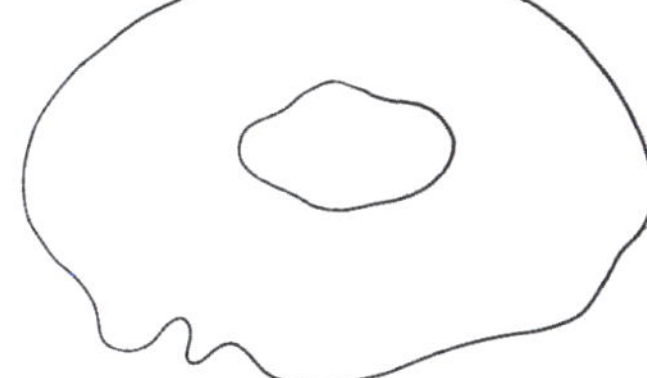

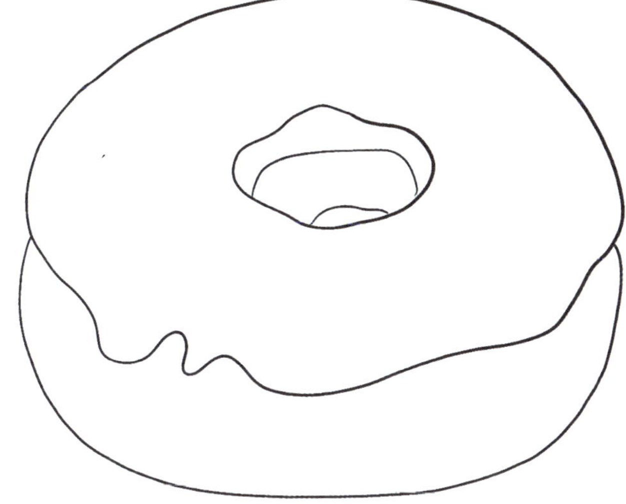

2. 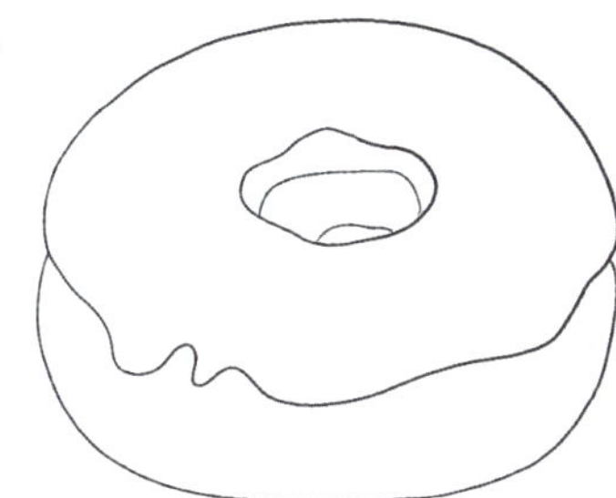

3.

chapter 8:
food

cupcake

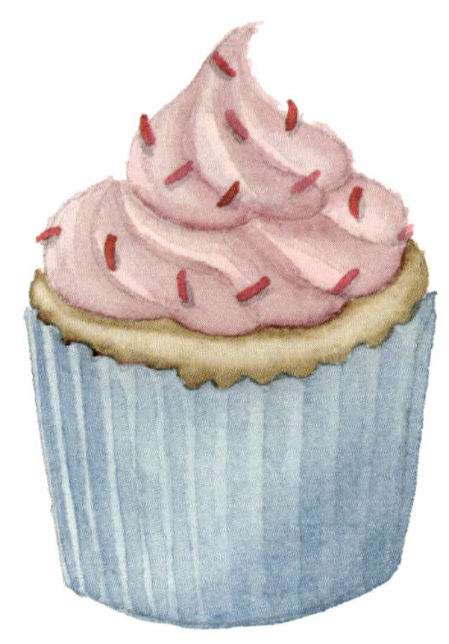

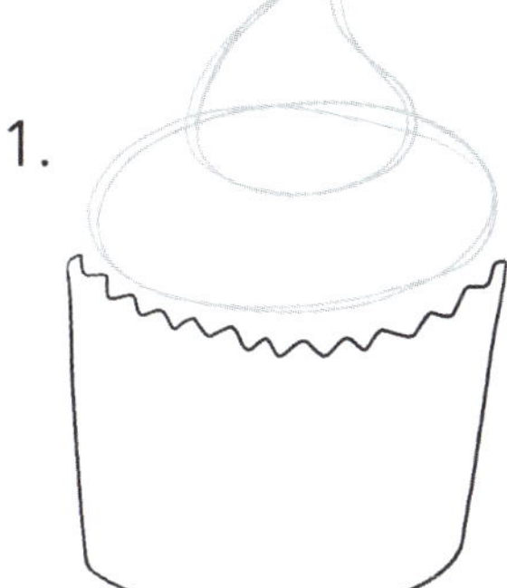

1.

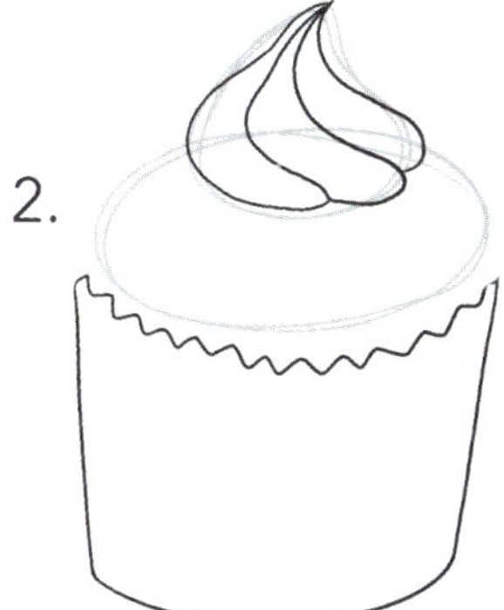

2.

3.

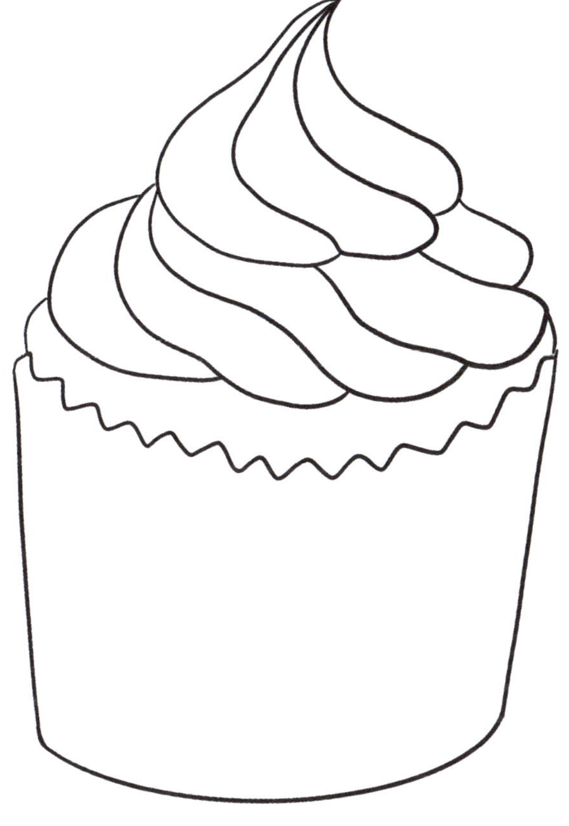

chapter 9:
animals

robin

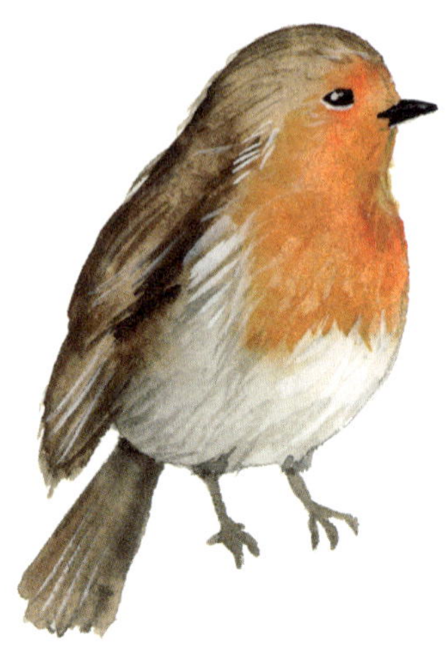

1.

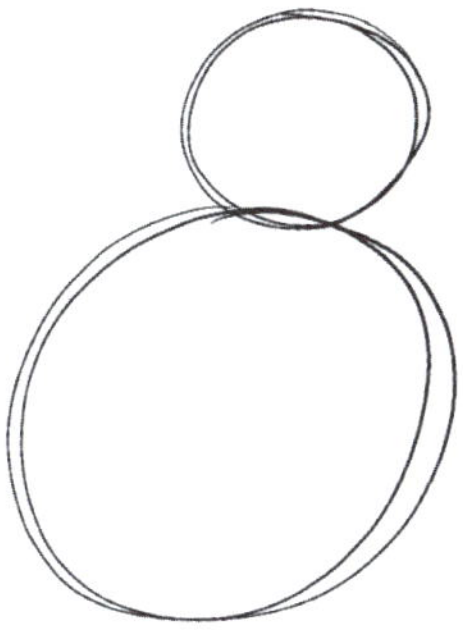

2.

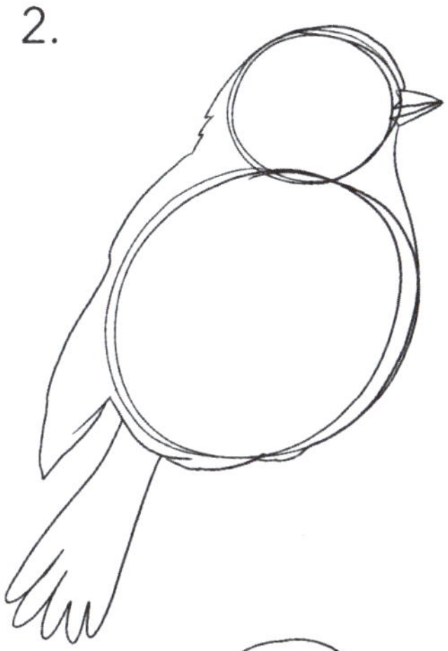

3.

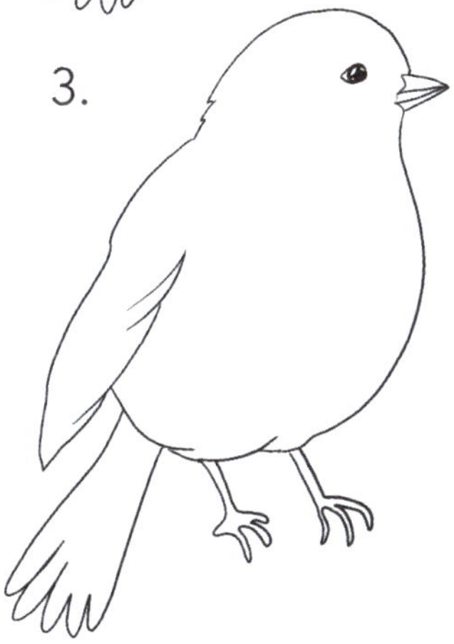

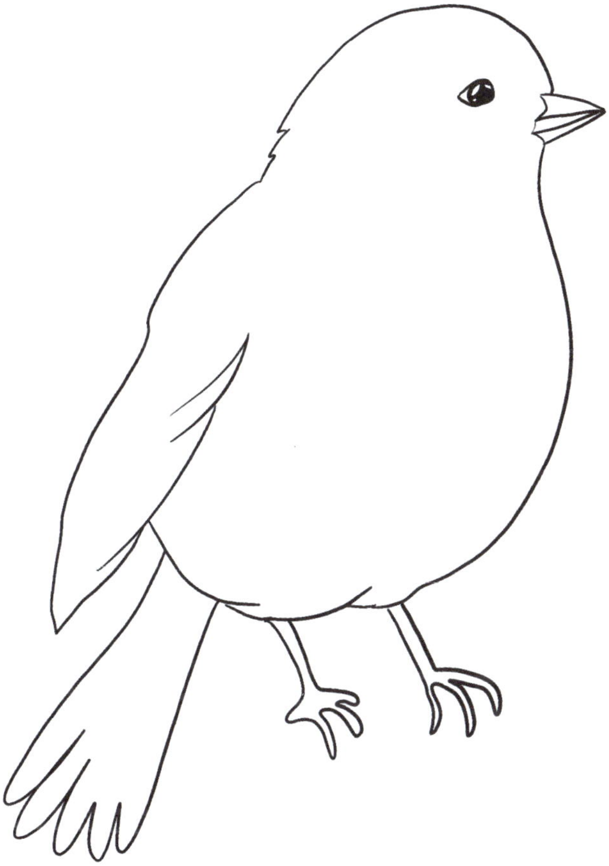

chapter 9:
animals

rabbit

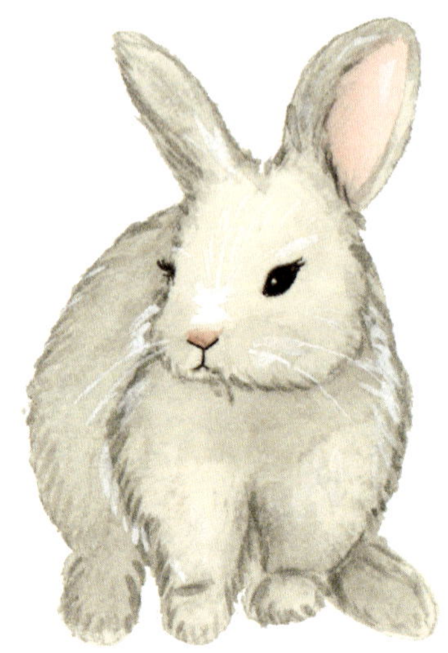

1.

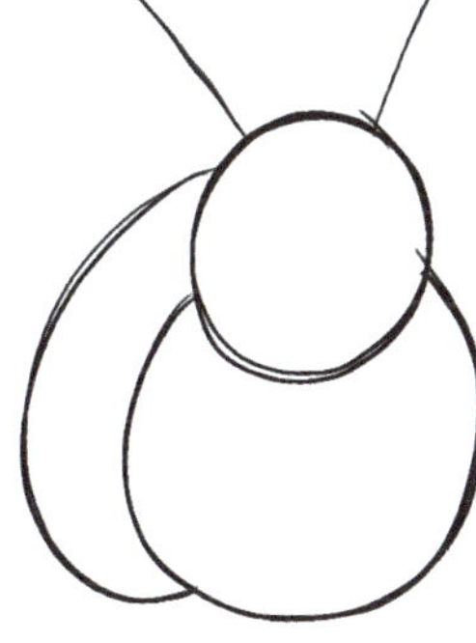

2.

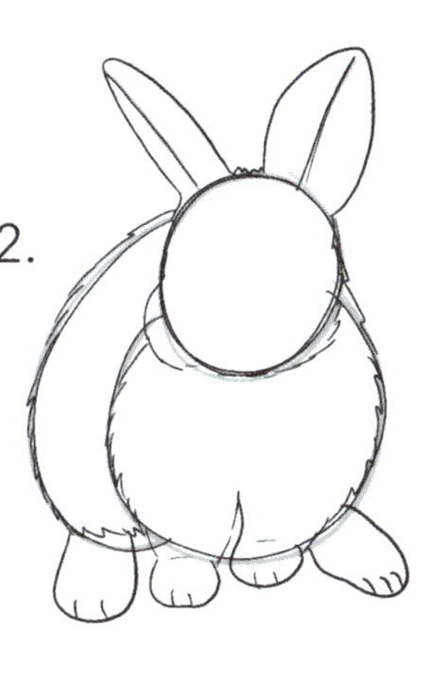

3.

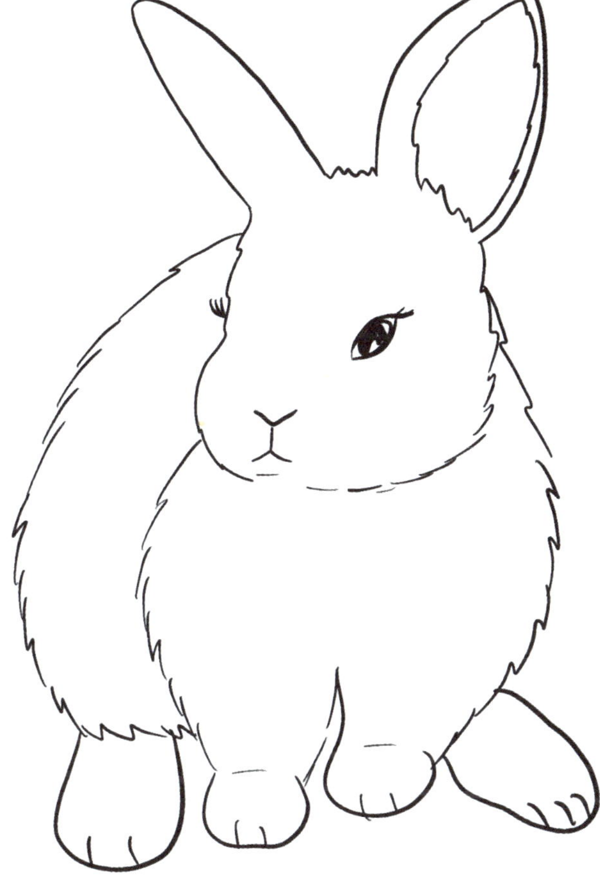

chapter 9:
animals

lion

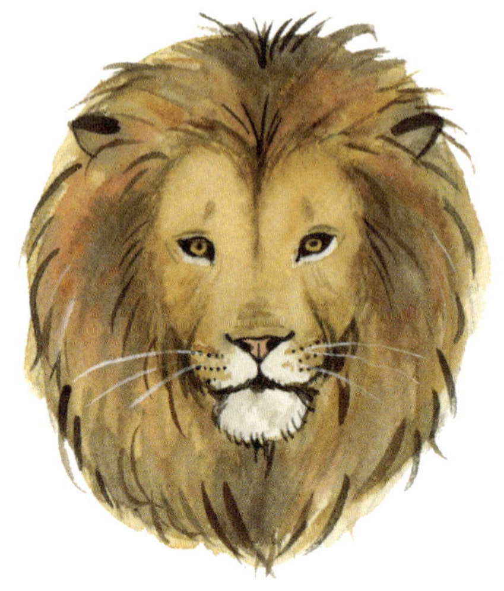

1. 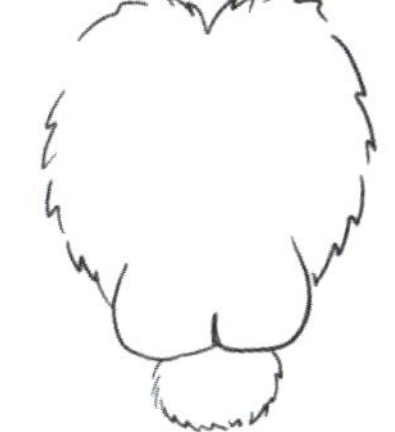

2. 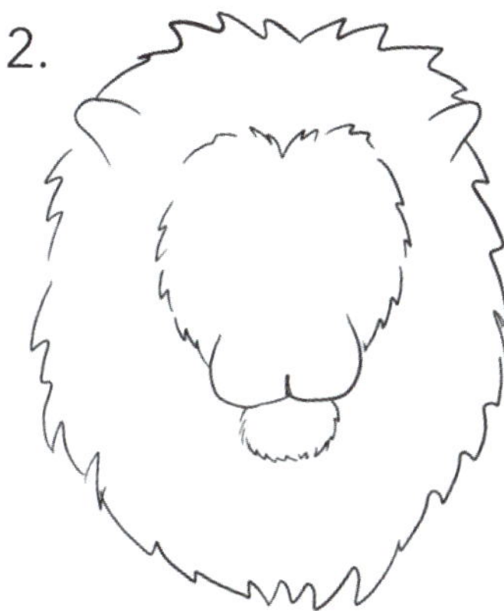

3. 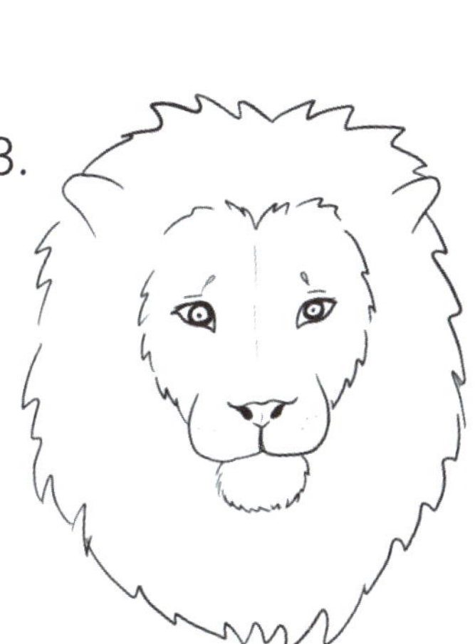

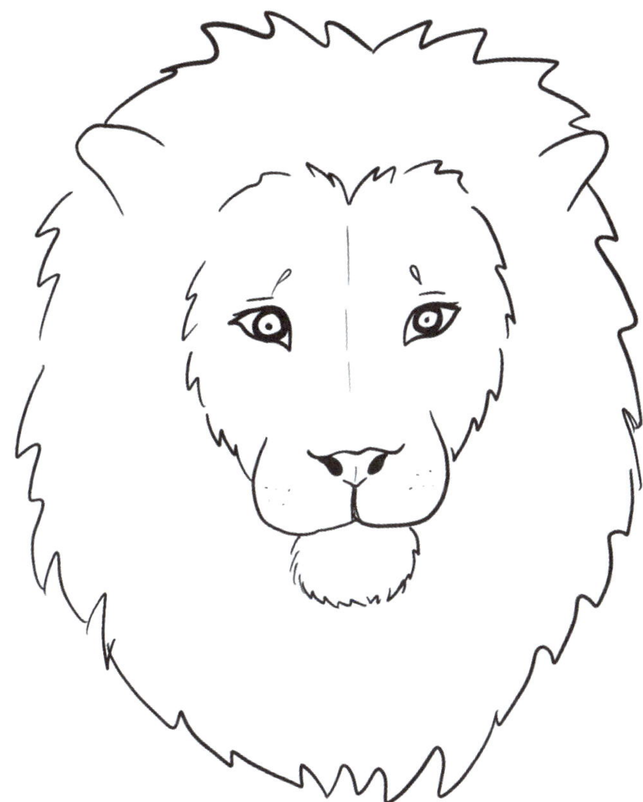

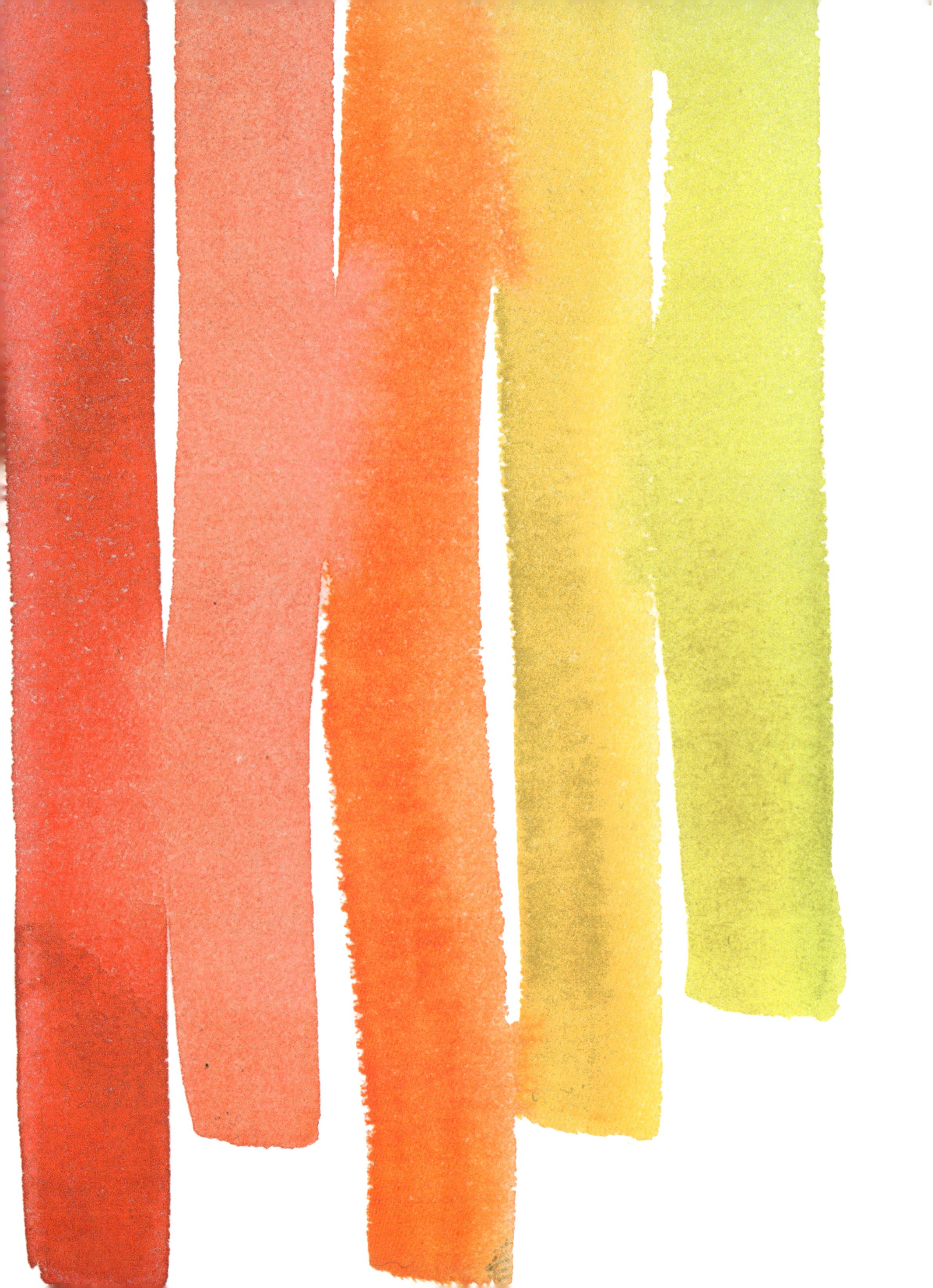

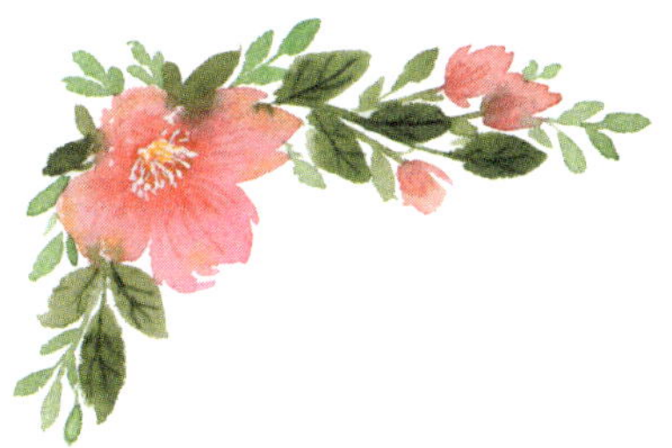

Final Thoughts

Now that you have finished this book and have been introduced to the basics of watercolour, what do you do now?

I get a lot of questions about how to find inspiration and how to discover your own painting style. This can definitely be a struggle for beginners, I know it was for me! I spent years trying to find my own style and trying to figure out who I was as an artist. But that's it, it took years. Years of practice, years of learning, years of playing around and discovering new techniques. It won't come to you right away, but take the time to practice and see what speaks to you as an artist, and it will come.

Watercolour painting isn't something you just become an expert in overnight. It takes a lot of time and practice and a lot of love. If this is something that you love to do, keep going and keep learning. I know that every time I pick up a paint brush, I learn something new.

As for where to find inspiration, I have a couple of tips. My main inspiration comes from the outdoors. I love walking around my neighbourhood and admiring others' gardens. In the winter I love to see how the snow falls on different objects outside. I always find the fresh air gives me that little push to create that I need. Another way I get inspired is to just lay down paint to paper with no intention to create something. You can try mixing new colour combinations, or even just creating colour swatches of your paints. It can be very therapeutic and inspiring to just play around with colour. Whatever works for you, just remember to release all pressure of being "perfect." The outcome of the painting isn't always what matters; it's the journey that we took to get there.

You've got this!

About the Author

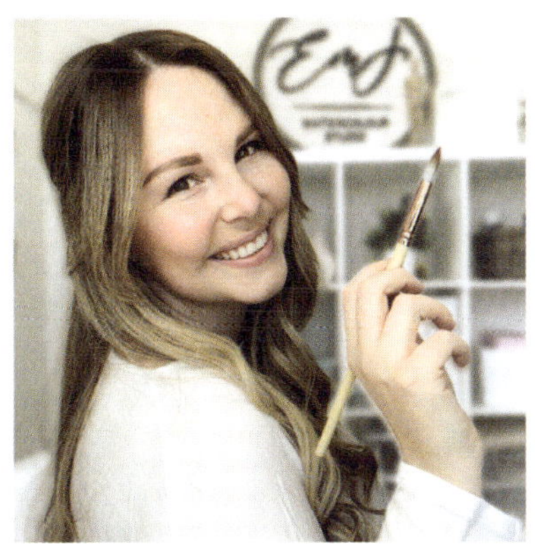

Emma Lefebvre has been dabbling in art since she began doodling in her binder at grade school. She attended an arts high school for three years, where her love for visual arts started to dwindle. Then came a time where she lost her love for it. It wasn't until she began struggling with depression and anxiety that the only thing that seemed to get her out of the house was the idea of walking through an art store. She came home one day with a cheap set of watercolours and started to paint.

It wasn't long until Emma found an amazing art community on Instagram that was equal parts inspiring and encouraging. Shortly after, she decided to use her background in teaching to spread the therapeutic effects of watercolour. What started as a quick YouTube video turned into a successful YouTube channel of creativity, calm, and inspiration. You can follow Emma's watercolour adventures on YouTube's *EmJ Watercolour Studio* channel.

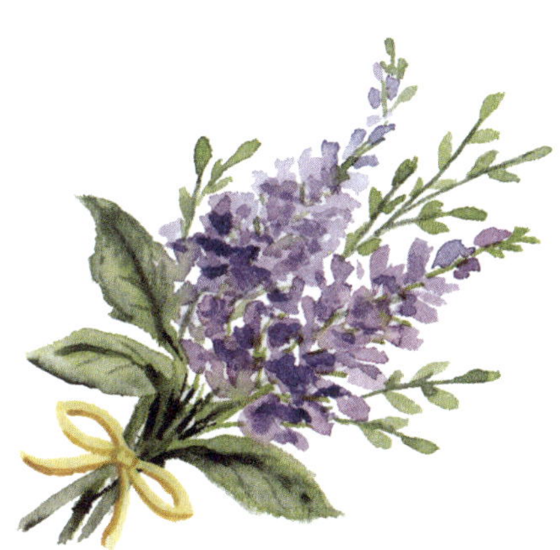

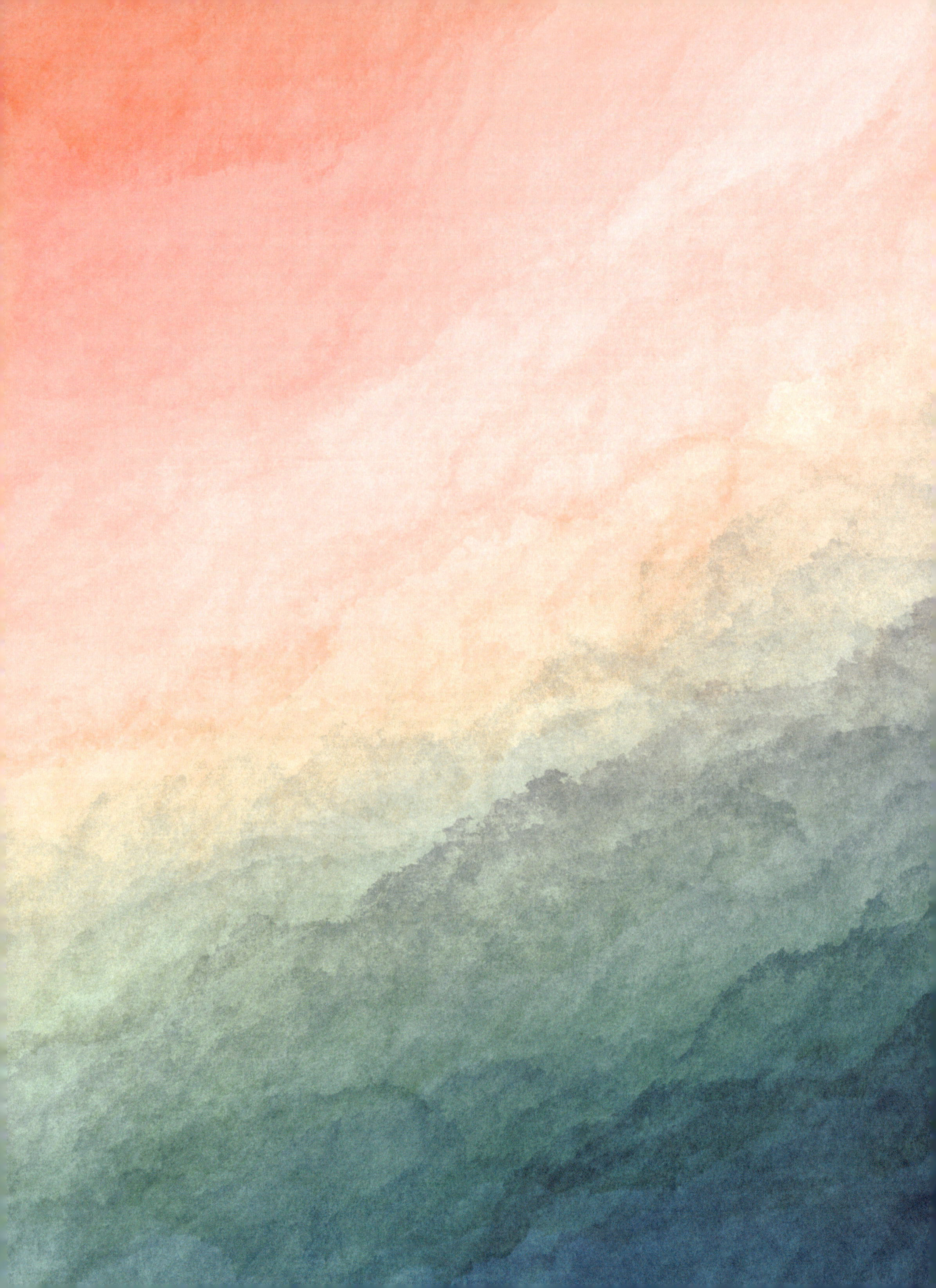

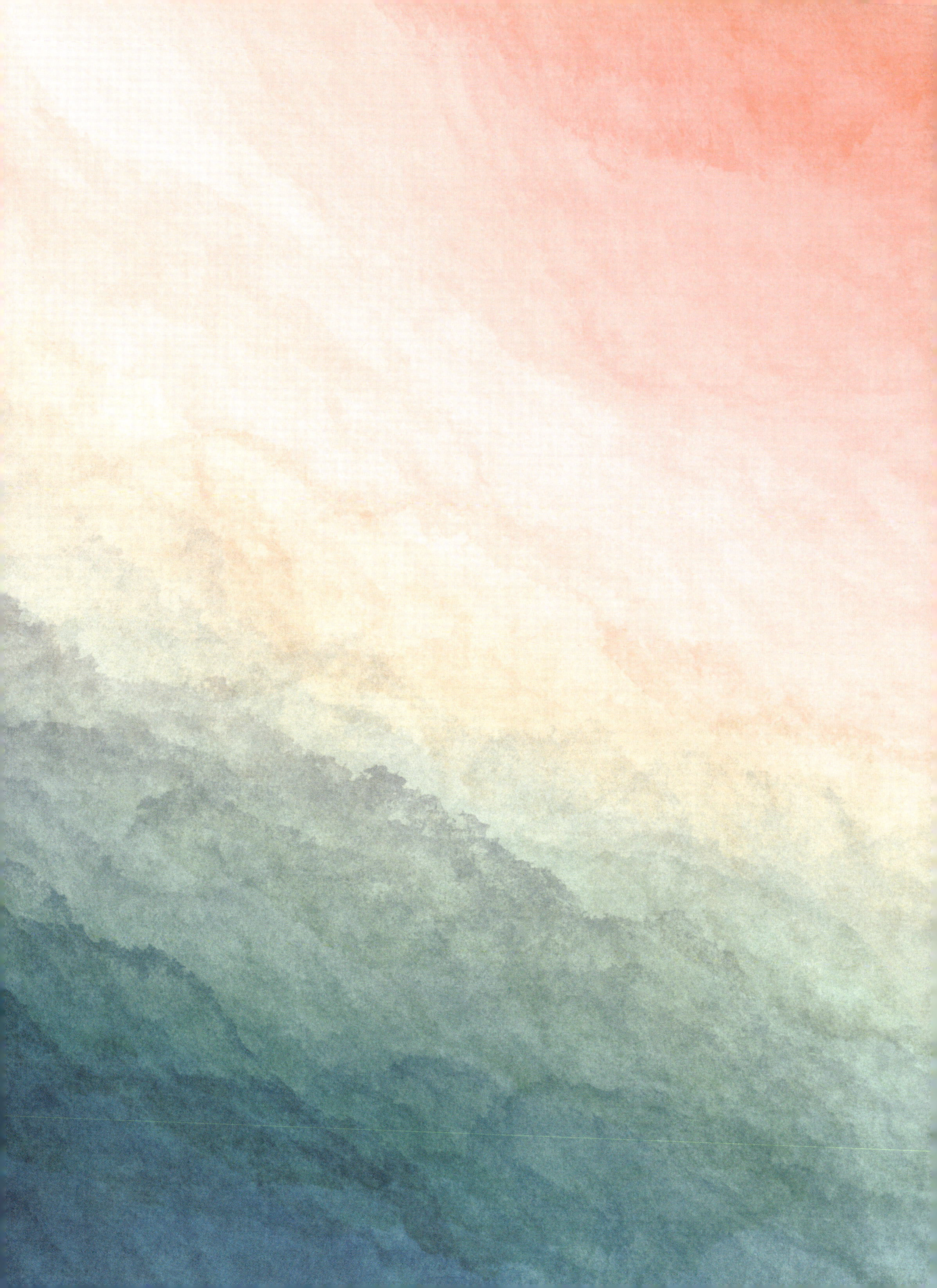

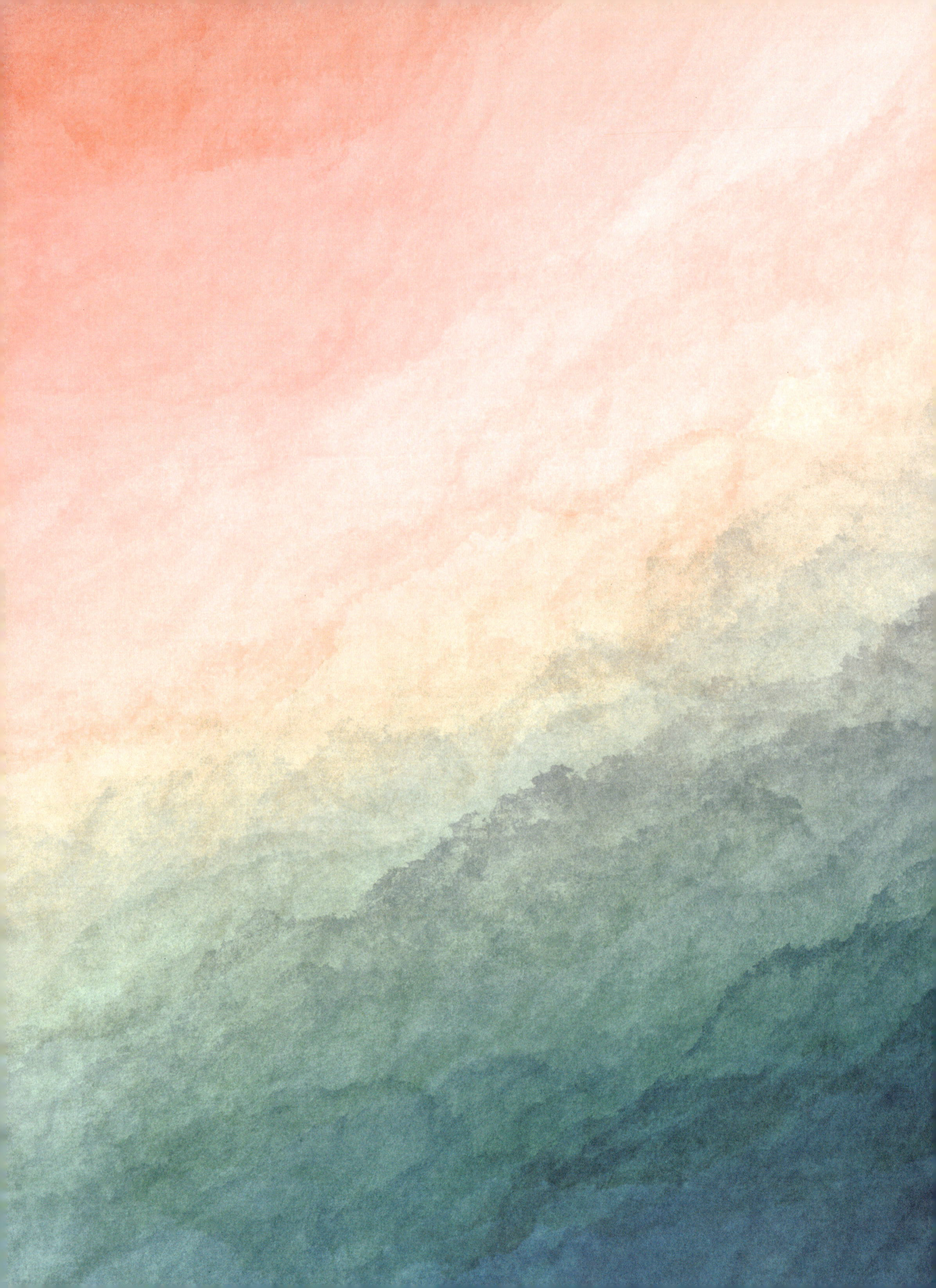